Habeas for the Twenty-First Century

Habeas for the Twenty-First Century

Uses, Abuses, and the Future of the Great Writ

NANCY J. KING AND
JOSEPH L. HOFFMANN

THE UNIVERSITY OF CHICAGO PRESS   CHICAGO AND LONDON

NANCY J. KING is the Lee S. and Charles A. Speir Professor of Law at Vanderbilt Law School.
JOSEPH L. HOFFMANN is the Harry Pratter Professor of Law at Indiana University Maurer School of Law.

The University of Chicago Press, Chicago 60637
The University of Chicago Press, Ltd., London
© 2011 by The University of Chicago
All rights reserved. Published 2011.
Printed in the United States of America
20 19 18 17 16 15 14 13 12 11   1 2 3 4 5

ISBN-13: 978-0-226-43697-5 (cloth)
ISBN-10: 0-226-43697-7 (cloth)

Library of Congress Cataloging-in-Publication Data

King, Nancy J., 1958–
    Habeas for the twenty-first century : uses, abuses, and the future of the great writ /
Nancy J. King and Joseph L. Hoffmann.
        p.   cm.
    Includes bibliographical references and index.
    ISBN-13: 978-0-226-43697-5 (cloth : alk. paper)
    ISBN-10: 0-226-43697-7 (cloth : alk. paper)   1. Habeas corpus—United States.
2. Detention of persons—United States.   I. Hoffmann, Joseph L., 1957–   II. Title.
    KF9011.K56   2011
    345.73'056—dc22

                                                        2010039371

Contents

Introduction

Habeas corpus, the "Great Writ," is a legal procedure almost contemporaneous in its earliest English origins with the development of the rule of law itself. For centuries, habeas has been used by American judges, and British judges before them, to inquire into the legal basis for a person's imprisonment and—if necessary—to provide a swift and effective remedy to those illegally confined. As such, the writ has come to occupy a treasured spot among the pantheon of the protectors of liberty.

Despite its ancient lineage, however, habeas corpus today remains as vital and controversial as ever. In June 2008, the U.S. Supreme Court decided the landmark case of *Boumediene v. Bush*, holding that noncitizens incarcerated at Guantanamo Bay, Cuba, as "enemy combatants" in the post–September 11 "war on terror" are constitutionally entitled to file habeas corpus petitions in federal court challenging their confinement. And in May 2010, the Court formally granted review in *Skinner v. Switzer* for the purpose of deciding whether habeas corpus is the proper method by which a death row inmate can seek to obtain access to DNA evidence that might prove his innocence. These cases, and many others, demonstrate the continued centrality of habeas corpus to the resolution of some of the key legal disputes of our time.

This is a book about the present condition of habeas corpus in the United States, and also about its future. We wrote this book to explain how and why habeas became what it is today, to identify the core purposes and major themes of the modern version of the writ, and to offer reform proposals that can help ensure the ongoing vitality of habeas as an effective and efficient legal remedy. Our goal is to inform and enlighten, but also to participate in a meaningful dialogue about habeas law and policy. We hope, in other words, that this book will make a difference.

We believe that a book like this one is sorely needed and long overdue. Habeas has, once again, risen to the forefront of the public's attention as a result of recent prominent cases like *Boumediene*. Much has been written about habeas corpus in recent years, in both popular and scholarly contexts. But we think our approach to the subject is virtually unique within the literature for three distinct and important reasons.

First, our book is uniquely comprehensive in its scope. Habeas scholarship tends to focus on one or another of the specific uses to which the writ is commonly put. For example, scholars of criminal procedure generally write about habeas as a part of the overall criminal justice system. They rarely see the relevance of habeas as it applies, for example, to immigration cases. Immigration scholars, in turn, frequently debate the proper role of habeas within the world of immigration law but do not often discuss its use in criminal cases. And those who study the federal courts, or federalism in general, typically engage in yet another completely separate scholarly conversation about habeas.

We believe that the best way to explain the role of habeas corpus in today's world, and to anticipate and plan for its future, is to study the writ in each of the most important realms within which it serves. Only by so doing can we identify the major themes that cut across the various applications of habeas. The most important of these major themes is that habeas is a remedy aimed at restoring the balance of governmental powers whenever that balance has been distorted or disrupted. This occurs most often as a result of a significant political or social crisis. In troubled times, habeas provides the judiciary with the power to step in and stop the more overtly political branches of the federal government, or the states, from overreaching and thereby infringing upon individual liberty. Habeas must always remain flexible, to enable meaningful judicial responses to unanticipated challenges, but must also be exercised with prudence, lest its misuse lead to a loss of respect for the writ and ill-advised limitations on its scope.

Second, the book is empirical in its orientation. Our analysis of habeas corpus is based on the latest data about habeas filings in the federal district courts. These data were compiled by Professor King and researchers from the National Center for State Courts as part of a major new study. Indeed, the decision to write the book originated with conversations between the authors about Professor King's study and its implications. The study, described in detail in chapter 4, provides the most complete picture of habeas litigation in federal district courts since the 1996 amendments to the habeas statute. The study reveals how the single most prevalent use of habeas today—as the means for federal courts to review the constitutionality of state criminal judgments—consumes valuable resources but provides little or no benefits. This harsh empirical reality drove our analysis of habeas in the specific context of state criminal justice, which in turn led to our overall thesis and policy recommendations about habeas in general.

Third, the book is both practical in its approach and self-consciously balanced in its ideological perspective. We are interested in habeas corpus not simply as a theoretical subject of study but because we believe that such theoretical study can be relevant to the future of habeas. Like many (if not most) legal academics, we are applied scholars. This book is about theory in practice, rather than theory for its own sake. In particular, we believe that our new way of framing the core purposes of habeas, as viewed across the entirety of the writ's broad doctrinal scope, can lead to better prescriptions for legislative and judicial habeas reforms that will make the writ both more efficient and more effective.

We have been guided throughout by a desire that any proposals we might make about the future of habeas should have a reasonable chance to be adopted and implemented. As such, our proposed reforms offer something of real value to those on both sides of the often pitched battles over how to deal with serious problems like terrorism, crime, and immigration. Our goal is to persuade those who stress the need for security and social stability as well as those who champion individual rights. We are respectful of the views of those who favor federal intervention to solve society's deepest ills as well as those who support state autonomy. In short, we intend this book to occupy a kind of ideological middle ground. Given our personal histories of working closely with judges, legislators, prosecutors, and defense attorneys alike on many hotly contested criminal justice issues, the middle ground is where we both tend to reside anyway.

More important, we suspect that a carefully balanced approach is the only way to effectively address the current deficiencies in the scope and application of the writ. Habeas *is* controversial, because the subjects with which it usually deals—terrorism, immigration, presidential power, criminal justice, prisons, the death penalty—are controversial. Given the stakes, sharp normative disagreements about matters of habeas history, law, and policy are probably inevitable, and reasonable minds will differ about what habeas has been in the past and what it should be in the future. We hope that our book addresses these topics in a fair and even-handed manner.

Finally, we must add a few words about habeas history. This book is thoroughly grounded in a modern understanding of the history of habeas corpus. But this is not a history book. We are not legal historians, nor have we engaged in the kind of original historical research necessary to resolve contested aspects of habeas history. We are consumers of habeas history, not producers.

Fortunately for us, and for all others who study habeas, we can turn for help to the pathbreaking work of leading scholars who have recently published cutting-edge habeas histories. The state-of-the-art historical account of habeas in England and early America is the new book by Paul D. Halliday, *Habeas Corpus: From England to Empire* (Cambridge, MA: Belknap Press of Harvard University Press, 2010). We have relied heavily on Professor Halliday's book as well as on works by Eric Freedman and Dallin Oaks, among others. We believe that the work of these leading habeas historians strongly supports the major themes of our book.

At the same time, however, our practical focus requires us to take our historical accounts of habeas corpus primarily from one preeminent source: the Supreme Court of the United States. Whenever historical accounts or interpretations of habeas history differ, we have relied most heavily on the accounts and interpretations that appear in majority opinions of the Court. In so doing, we do not mean to suggest that the Court is infallible. We recognize that the Court's view of habeas history might be (indeed, often is) disputed by habeas historians and that the Court might even be flat-out wrong. But we decline to tilt at that particular windmill. In pragmatic terms, because the Court largely controls the ultimate interpretation of both the habeas corpus statutes and the United States Constitution, its view of habeas history—and not that of the historians—matters most. For this reason, we have adopted the Court's prevailing consensus about habeas history as the starting point for our theoretical and normative analyses.

We have written this book for a wide range of potential readers, including scholars and nonscholars alike. In so doing, we have necessarily introduced some subjects with a level of background explanation that would not be needed by experts in habeas or criminal justice. At the same time, we have undoubtedly covered other subjects in such a detailed and theoretical manner that the book will test the patience of those who are not as knowledgeable about these areas. Our hope is that, overall, we have struck an appropriate balance between these two extremes.

Given the possibility, however, that no such balance can actually be achieved, we suggest that those who are already familiar with habeas history, law, and policy might wish to focus their attention primarily on chapters 1, 2, 4, 5, and 8. In these chapters, we introduce our most important empirical and theoretical claims about habeas, and we present our most significant proposals for habeas reform. Chapter 1 outlines our general approach to defining the major themes of habeas; chapter 2 presents our analysis of habeas review of detentions for reasons other than criminal conviction (including the terrorism and immigration cases); chapter 4 describes in detail the results of Professor King's recent empirical study of habeas filings in the federal district courts; chapter 5 contains our proposals for the future of habeas review of state criminal cases; and chapter 8 discusses what we believe to be the most appropriate role for habeas in the context of capital litigation.

We would like to thank many individuals and institutions for their kind support as we worked on this book. We are grateful to the Vanderbilt Law School and the Indiana University Maurer School of Law for providing us with the time and resources to write the book. We thank Craig Bradley, Jerry Israel, Mike Newton, Ed Rubin, Ryan Scott, Suzanna Sherry, Chris Slobogin, Steve Vladeck, and the participants in the Harvard Law School's 2008 Criminal Justice Forum for their comments, suggestions, and advice. Of course, all mistakes that remain in the book are attributable solely to us.

Among all those who helped us along the way, two people—Dean Lauren Robel of the Maurer School of Law and Jean Ledwith King—deserve special mention for reading over our entire manuscript and providing us with incredibly helpful assistance. And we would also like to pay special recognition, and give special thanks, to Professor Bill Stuntz of Harvard Law School, who over his career has consistently helped to shape the way we think about almost everything in criminal law and criminal procedure and who has always been a dear and cherished friend as well. Last, but certainly not least, our most heartfelt appreciation goes out to our respective spouses, Timothy Babb and Mary Hoffmann, for putting up with us as we spent many late nights, weekends, and vacations working on this book. Without their love and encouragement, the book would never have happened.

CHAPTER ONE

An Introduction to the Writ of Habeas Corpus

In October 2001, Lakhdar Boumediene, a thirty-five-year-old Algerian, was arrested by local authorities in Sarajevo, Bosnia, and charged with plotting with five other Algerians to bomb the local U.S. and British embassies. Boumediene, who was living in Sarajevo with his wife and two young daughters while working for the Red Crescent, the Muslim equivalent of the Red Cross, protested that he was completely innocent, but to no avail. Although a Bosnian court ruled in his favor and the bombing charges were promptly dismissed, in January 2002 Boumediene was transferred to U.S. custody and flown in shackles to Guantanamo Bay, Cuba, where he was imprisoned as an "enemy combatant." Thus began a seven-and-a-half-year nightmare.[1]

While at Guantanamo Bay, Boumediene was interrogated repeatedly about his alleged ties with al-Qaeda terrorists, including—according to his account—a sixteen-day period during which he was questioned both night and day.[2] Boumediene denied knowing anything about terrorism, but his past—including a passing acquaintance with another Algerian in Bosnia who was linked to al-Qaeda, as well as some time spent in Pakistan, during which, he said, he worked at a school for Afghan orphans—raised suspicions. For his first two years in captivity, Boumediene tried to answer the questions asked of him by his U.S. captors, but eventually he decided that his words were falling on deaf ears and he became uncooperative. Although his wife continually wrote him letters, the letters were never delivered to him. In December 2006, in a last-ditch effort to assert his innocence, Boumediene went on a hunger strike; as a consequence, he was force-fed through a nasal tube twice each day for more than two years.

Meanwhile, in late 2004, volunteer lawyers acting on Boumediene's behalf filed a petition for a writ of habeas corpus, asking a federal district court in Washington, D.C., to inquire into the legality of his detention. The U.S. government responded that as a noncitizen held outside the sovereign territory of the United States, Boumediene had no legal right to seek habeas corpus. Initially, the lower federal courts ruled against Boumediene; he lost in January 2005 in the federal district court and again in 2007 in the U.S. Court of Appeals for the D.C. Circuit.[3]

On June 12, 2008, however, the U.S. Supreme Court held, in a landmark 5–4 decision, that Boumediene and others like him at Guantanamo Bay enjoyed a constitutional right to petition for a writ of habeas corpus.[4] Pursuant to that decision, on November 20, 2008, U.S. District Judge Richard Leon, appointed to the court by President George W. Bush, ruled in Boumediene's favor, granting the petition. In his opinion Judge Leon noted that the U.S. government's allegations against Boumediene—which by that time no longer even included the Sarajevo bomb plot but instead consisted entirely of vague accusations that Boumediene planned to go to Afghanistan to wage jihad—were all based on a single, uncorroborated source. Judge Leon concluded that Boumediene's detention could not legally be justified on "so thin a reed" and ordered his release from custody.[5]

After several months of diplomatic negotiations France agreed to accept Lakhdar Boumediene. He was flown, still in shackles, to Paris, where he spent ten days in a hospital due to the aftereffects of his hunger strike. On May 15, 2009, Boumediene, now age forty-three, was finally freed and reunited with his wife and daughters. They celebrated with a pizza at a small Paris restaurant. Boumediene later told the *Washington Post*, "When we were at the restaurant, I told my wife that for the first time I felt like a man again, tasting things, picking things up in my fingers, eating lunch with my wife and my two daughters."[6] In an ABC News interview he added, "I cried, just cried. Because I don't know my daughters. The younger, when I moved from Bosnia to Gitmo, she had 18 months, only 18 months. Now 9 years. Now she's big."[7]

*   *   *

What freed Boumediene was the writ of habeas corpus, one of the most important and cherished procedural innovations in the shared legal histories of England and the United States. The roots of the Great Writ date back many centuries. In England, habeas originated as a means to protect the jurisdiction of the royal courts over royal subjects, but gradually it became a vital weapon in the ongoing struggle to impose the rule of law upon those who confined others in the king's name.[8] In early America, the Framers believed habeas to be the ultimate weapon in defense of individual liberty and therefore chose to protect it from suspension during peacetime by including a provision to that effect in Article I of the United States Constitution.[9] After the Civil War, habeas helped the federal government guarantee the ultimate supremacy of federal law and federal Reconstruction policies.[10] Almost one hundred years later, during the civil rights era, habeas again assumed this role as a key means by which the federal courts could enforce unpopular federal laws against recalcitrant and on occasion obstructionist state officials.[11] Today, in far-ranging controversies involving alleged terrorists, suspected illegal aliens, and convicted criminals, habeas continues to check the abuse of government power.

But what, exactly, is the writ of habeas corpus? In what ways has it changed over the centuries to serve the most urgent needs of society? And how should courts today use the immense powers that habeas corpus affords? These fundamental questions—questions that go to the very heart of our system of government—are the subject of this book.

Recognizing that scholarship about habeas is almost as extensive as its history, our aim in this volume is to provide a compact, accessible, yet comprehensive analysis of habeas corpus in all of its diverse applications, an analysis that is grounded in history yet based on the latest empirical research and that includes specific, normative recommendations for habeas reform. We believe that there are important lessons about habeas that can be learned only through such a broad and comprehensive approach to the subject—lessons that are all too easily overlooked when, as usually happens, the study of habeas is compartmentalized by focusing on the writ's use in one or another particular context.

In this introductory chapter we begin with a brief explanation of the habeas remedy, as it originated and evolved in the English common law, and its subsequent development in the United States. This introduction serves as a foundation for the chapters that follow. We end the chapter with an outline of our distinctive approach to habeas reform, an approach based on the core principles of flexibility and prudence that have shaped and defined habeas throughout its history. If habeas is to continue to fulfill its vital role of protecting individual liberty in times of serious conflict, these same core principles must guide our reform efforts today.

The Habeas Remedy and Its English Common Law Origins

The Great Writ of habeas corpus is first and foremost a legal procedure. Habeas creates no substantive legal rights; instead it provides a remedy in court for the violation of legal rights or neglect of a legal duty. To put it another way, habeas is a procedural mechanism for the judicial enforcement of rights and duties that are granted, imposed, or recognized elsewhere in the law.

Habeas corpus, moreover, is not a single procedural remedy. It is rather a type of remedy that over the centuries has taken many different forms.[12] What all of the different forms of the writ had in common is that each involved a court order to bring a prisoner to the court for some judicial purpose. The Latin phrase *habeas corpus* means literally that "*you*," that is, the person with custody over the prisoner, must "have the body" of the prisoner produced in court at the place and time ordered by a judge.[13]

The most well-known and most historically significant form of habeas corpus—and the one that is the sole subject of this book—is the version called habeas corpus *ad subjiciendum* (literally, "you have the body, to submit to").[14] This is a writ issued by a court to require the production of the body of a prisoner for the purpose of inquiring into the legal basis for the prisoner's custody. This particular form of habeas corpus was described by the great British scholar Sir William Blackstone as "the most celebrated writ in the English law."[15] It is the one that mattered most to the English parliament of the seventeenth century, to the Framers of the United States Constitution during the eighteenth century, and to anyone else, before or since, who has believed in the basic principle that government must at all times remain subject to the law, as that law is interpreted and applied by judges.

A petition for a writ of habeas corpus *ad subjiciendum* technically initiates a civil case against the person with custody of the prisoner, usually a prison warden or superior government official. The petition can be filed either by the prisoner, or (as may be necessary in cases in which the prisoner is held incommunicado) by a third person entitled to act on the prisoner's behalf. Historically, upon receipt of a properly filed habeas

petition, the judge would issue the writ and require the physical production of the prisoner in order to conduct an inquiry into the legality of the
custody.[16] Today, as a general matter, the judge issues an order requiring
the person with custody of the prisoner to show why the writ should not
issue.[17] The judge may take testimony from witnesses and receive other
kinds of factual evidence relevant to the determination of the habeas petition. If there is a valid legal basis for the custody, then the petition will
be denied. If, on the other hand, the custody of the prisoner is judged to
be unlawful, then the writ will issue, either unconditionally (requiring
his immediate release) or conditionally (meaning that release will be required if certain conditions are not met within a prescribed amount of
time).

The nature of the habeas remedy is relatively straightforward. The
source of judicial authority to issue the writ, however, is more complicated, an unusual hybrid of common law, constitutional law, and statute. The writ originated in the English common law, law that was created not by the legislature but by judges deciding individual cases. The
common law approach, a hallmark of the Anglo-American legal system,
permits legal rules to be defined, and redefined, by judges to fit new circumstances and values as they change over time, thus ensuring that the
law will always be reasonably responsive to the needs of contemporary
society.[18] Habeas corpus was employed by judges in England possibly
as early as the fourteenth century and was well developed by the seventeenth century.[19] Originally it was a manifestation of the royal prerogative, used to compel compliance with the dictates of the King's Bench,
to secure the presence of those accused of a felony so that they could be
arraigned and tried, and to settle jurisdictional disputes between that
court and various rival courts.[20] The judges of the King's Bench gradually adapted the writ to serve as a limitation on the detention power of
those who confined others in the king's name.

A statutory form of the writ eventually emerged as well, extended by
Parliament in 1641 to authorize judges to release those imprisoned arbitrarily for treason or felony by an order of the Crown, by the Privy Council, or by the successors to the Star Chamber.[21] And the famous Habeas
Corpus Act of 1679 enacted procedures to make the statutory form of
habeas a more effective remedy. Included were provisions that tripled
the number of judges who could issue the writ by extending habeas powers to the Exchequer and Common Pleas courts, that codified judicial
authority to issue the writ between court sessions, and that prevented

the transfer of prisoners to distant places by those seeking to thwart the effectiveness of the writ.[22] But these statutory reforms would never have succeeded as a meaningful check on those exercising royal power if they had not ratified the increasing independence with which judges already had begun to wield their common law habeas powers.

From the writ's earliest use through Parliament's repeated suspensions starting in the late eighteenth century, the writ of habeas corpus proved a flexible and potent tool for English judges to use in addressing political and social crises as they arose throughout the British empire. As Professor Paul Halliday writes in his groundbreaking history of the writ in England, "during periods of instability or war, the writ met new forms of constraint generated by fear" and was "at its most effective when judges used it to address new problems."[23]

The common law of habeas extended to the American colonies, whose leaders enshrined in statutes the judicial power to use the writ to free those unlawfully detained. Habeas subsequently became part of the law of the newly independent American states.[24] Even today, state court review of unlawful detention through the writ of habeas corpus remains widely available in its historical form, although state legislatures have supplemented the habeas remedy with statutes authorizing judicial review of criminal judgments for those serving criminal sentences, often termed "state postconviction review."[25]

In the United States today, however, the most prominent version of habeas corpus is not the review available in state courts but the writ available in federal courts, under federal law. This book deals exclusively with the federal version of the writ, and it is this version to which we shall refer as, simply, habeas corpus. If a habeas petition is filed in a federal court, requesting an inquiry into the legality of the prisoner's detention and seeking the issuance of the writ by a federal judge, it is within the scope of our consideration. As a foundation for understanding how federal habeas applies in different contexts today, and to set the stage for the chapters that follow, we offer next a brief account of the genesis and evolution of federal habeas.

The Habeas Authority of the Federal Courts

As we have seen, judicial use of the writ of habeas corpus long predated both the U.S. Constitution and the statutes that first created the lower

federal courts. Because the Framers seem to have assumed, even before the Constitution was ratified, that habeas would exist in the new
United States of America, the common law history of habeas has long
been viewed as important to modern-day interpretations and applications of the writ. As Chief Justice John Marshall declared in 1807,
"[F]or the meaning of the term habeas corpus, resort may unquestion-
ably be had to the common law. . . ."[26]

Habeas corpus arose from the common law and eventually was codified by Congress, but it is also has a constitutional dimension. The Framers believed that habeas corpus was as important a check on the powers of the new and potentially dangerous federal government as any of
the other limits enshrined in Article I of the Constitution. They referred
to habeas with reverent admiration, similar to the way they viewed the
other two venerated components of our legal system: the criminal jury
and the Constitution itself. The Framers viewed habeas as a crucial—
perhaps even the most crucial—protection for individual liberty against
a potentially tyrannical new federal government. Among the threats to
freedom that habeas could help to prevent, according to the Federalist,
were "arbitrary imprisonments" by the executive, identified as "the fa-
vorite and most formidable instruments of tyranny,"[27] and "[a]rbitrary
impeachments, arbitrary methods of prosecuting pretended offenses,
and arbitrary punishments upon arbitrary convictions," described as
"great engines of judicial despotism."[28]

Yet the Framers did not provide in the Constitution for habeas corpus jurisdiction in the federal courts; instead, they allowed for its suspension only under very limited circumstances. The Suspension Clause
of Article I, Section 9, provides, "The privilege of the writ of habeas corpus shall not be suspended, unless when in cases of rebellion or invasion
the public safety shall require it."[29] The clause reflects the Framers' con-
demnation of the parliamentary suspensions of habeas review for those
detained in America for treason beginning in 1777.[30] It also suggests that
the Framers believed that habeas jurisdiction in the federal courts would
arise automatically upon ratification of the Constitution, either because
habeas was an inherent power of the federal judiciary or because habeas
jurisdiction surely would be enacted into federal statutory law by Congress immediately after ratification.[31]

Almost contemporaneously with the ratification of the Constitution, habeas corpus indeed became a creature of federal statute. Congress conferred habeas jurisdiction upon the newly created lower federal

courts, as well as upon individual justices of the U.S. Supreme Court, in Section 14 of the original Judiciary Act of 1789:

> That all the before-mentioned courts of the United States, shall have power to issue writs of *scire facias, habeas corpus*, and all other writs not specially provided for by statute, which may be necessary for the exercise of their respective jurisdictions, and agreeable to the principles and usages of law. And that either of the justices of the supreme court, as well as judges of the district courts, shall have power to grant writs of *habeas corpus* for the purpose of an inquiry into the cause of commitment.—*Provided*, That writs of *habeas corpus* shall in no case extend to prisoners in gaol, unless where they are in custody, under or by colour of the authority of the United States, or are committed for trial before some court of the same, or are necessary to be brought into court to testify.[32]

From 1789 forward, the scope and meaning of habeas corpus in the federal courts—although originally derived from the English common law writ and protected by the Suspension Clause of the Constitution—has also depended upon statutory language and congressional intent. In turn, the scope and meaning of the Suspension Clause have been grounded in understandings of habeas derived from both the common law and the Judiciary Act. The Supreme Court has held that, whatever else the Suspension Clause may do, the clause certainly protects the scope of the writ as it existed in 1789.[33]

Habeas corpus stands almost uniquely at the confluence of the common law (from whence it originated), federal statutory law (which, in 1789, implemented it for the federal courts), and constitutional law (which provides that it cannot be suspended in peacetime). The role that habeas plays in contemporary America continues to be defined initially by Congress through various habeas statutes, but its scope and application are controlled ultimately by the Supreme Court through interpretation of those statutes as well as of the Suspension Clause.

The prevailing view of the early history of habeas in America, as recounted by the Supreme Court, is that the original scope of the federal judicial power to issue the writ of habeas corpus under the 1789 act was rather limited. Habeas relief was not extended to persons serving sentences after being convicted of a crime.[34] Furthermore, the writ was available under the 1789 act only to those held under federal authority; it did not extend to persons held in state custody. State prisoners were restricted to their remedies, if any, under state law.[35] This did not change until 1833, when, in response to the passage of South Carolina's Nullification Ordinance, Congress granted access to the writ to persons imprisoned by the states while acting under federal authority.[36] In 1842, when Great Britain protested New York's detention of a Canadian soldier, the writ was extended to foreign nationals imprisoned by the states while acting under the authority of their foreign governments.[37]

The biggest change in the scope of habeas corpus occurred immediately following the Civil War. The war represented the vindication of federal authority against opposition by the states of the Confederacy and resulted in a series of significant shifts in the balance of federalism. Among them was the Fourteenth Amendment to the Constitution, articulating a new concept of federal citizenship and for the first time authorizing the federal government to protect individuals against violation of their newly minted federal rights by their own state governments.[38] Accompanying the promulgation of the Civil War amendments was the Habeas Corpus Act of 1867, expanding the general benefits of the writ and, for the first time, clearly extending those benefits to all persons held in state custody.[39]

The 1867 act was specifically designed to address the political and social crisis of Reconstruction. It empowered the lower federal courts to protect federal officials and the newly freed slaves from abusive imprisonment by the defeated Confederate states. Because such abuses sometimes occurred within the state criminal justice systems, the act extended habeas to reach even imprisonments pursuant to criminal convictions. For many years thereafter, however, as we will discuss later, habeas review was available only when such judgments of conviction were either facially invalid or considered to be beyond the jurisdiction of the courts that issued them.[40]

For more than eighty years after the 1867 act, the use of habeas corpus by the federal courts ebbed and flowed with the changing needs of the times, even though the statutory language remained the same. For example, habeas was pressed into service as a remedy for accused polygamists prosecuted by the federal government in the Utah Territories in the 1880s, by alleged former Communists targeted for deportation during the Red Scare in the 1920s, by federal criminal defendants convicted without counsel in the 1930s, and by Americans of Japanese descent held in relocation centers during World War II.[41]

In 1948, as part of a general revision of the federal codes and in recognition of some of the judicially wrought changes in the scope of habeas corpus, habeas was split into three distinct statutes: 28 U.S.C. § 2241, the descendant of the general habeas corpus provisions contained in the original Judiciary Act of 1789; 28 U.S.C. § 2254, the descendant of the Habeas Corpus Act of 1867 for state prisoners; and 28 U.S.C. § 2255, a new and more efficient statutory substitute for habeas corpus for federal prisoners who sought to challenge the legality of their federal criminal convictions and sentences.[42] These three statutes, although subsequently amended, remain in effect today. Under Section 2241, habeas is available as a remedy for all those who are not challenging a criminal judgment, including those imprisoned in violation of federal law without any conviction at all. Section 2254 provides habeas review for those serving a sentence for a state crime, and Section 2255 is available to those serving a sentence for a federal crime.

In the 1950s and 1960s, habeas review of state criminal cases under Section 2254 played an important role in a second major crisis of federalism. The Supreme Court, under the leadership of Chief Justice Earl Warren and Justice William J. Brennan, responded to recurring and serious injustices inflicted upon state criminal defendants—especially minorities and the poor—by interpreting the Due Process Clause of the Fourteenth Amendment to require the states to provide defendants with various new federal rights.[43] At the time, most states lacked modern postconviction judicial review processes that would enable these rights to be vindicated in state court. In addition, some state officials were hostile to the Court's imposition of these rights, and some state judges were reluctant to enforce them. The Court expanded the scope of habeas review under Section 2254 to allow the lower federal courts to assist with the challenging task of overcoming these structural and attitudinal barriers. The Warren Court's expansion of habeas helped push the states to reform their judicial review processes and encouraged state judges to accept responsibility for enforcing these new federal rights.[44]

Today, the crisis of federalism that prompted the Warren Court to expand habeas review under Section 2254 no longer rages. Habeas reversals of state criminal convictions have become extremely rare—with one notable exception. The exception is in capital cases, where federal habeas courts regularly intervene to set aside death sentences. Capital cases are special not only because the stakes are so high but also because the federal constitutional standards that apply in these cases continue to be strikingly unstable and highly controversial. As long as this remains so, habeas is likely to play a significant role in protecting the constitutional rights of death row inmates.[45]

In this book, we will examine all of these disparate applications of habeas corpus. A comprehensive analysis of habeas, informed by new empirical research, will expose the common themes and core principles that can lead to a better understanding of the role of habeas corpus across its many discrete applications.

The Role of Federal Habeas: A Functional Guide to Reform

This chapter began with the story of Lakhdar Boumediene, a man whose freedom was secured by the Great Writ of habeas corpus. The story's ending represents a triumph of individual liberty and the rule of law. But the true significance of Boumediene's story lies deeper. Habeas is not simply about providing incarcerated individuals like Boumediene with a remedy, as important as that role may be. Even more importantly, as Boumediene's case illustrates, habeas provides the judiciary with the authority to rein in the executive, the legislature, or the states whenever they threaten individual liberty by disregarding federal law. To put it another way, habeas provides a remedy for individuals, but it is a remedy that, at its core, serves to address fundamental problems with institutions of government.

The Great Writ, we argue, is most valuable as a response to the periodic political or social upheavals that have disrupted the "'delicate balance of governance' that is itself the surest safeguard of liberty."[46] In the words of Justice Brennan, one of the writ's most passionate defenders, "It is no accident that habeas corpus has time and again played a central role in national crises, wherein the claims of order and of liberty clash most acutely, not only in England in the seventeenth century, but also in America from our very beginnings, and today."[47]

In particular, resort to the writ has allowed the federal judiciary to vindicate the federal law that protects individual liberty when, in response to political or social crises, that law is disregarded by the political branches of the federal government or by state governments. Habeas corpus, in other words, is essential to rectify periodic imbalances in the federal separation of powers or between the federal government and the states. The first of these circumstances, usually in the guise of overreaching by the executive, has been a basis for habeas jurisdiction since its inception. The second—serious instability in the balance of federalism resulting in the states' disregard of federal law—became recognized as a legitimate ground for habeas after the Civil War.

To serve this vital institutional role effectively, habeas law requires an unusual degree of flexibility so that it can be adapted to unforeseen (and unforeseeable) changes in circumstances. The contours of the writ must remain reasonably vague so that judges will be capable of responding appropriately to future events, unknowable to either the Court or Congress. Habeas, in the hands of a vigilant judiciary, is uniquely well suited to resist new and unanticipated abuses of the power of imprisonment. This may be the underlying reason for what Chief Justice William H. Rehnquist once described as "this Court's historic willingness to overturn or modify its earlier views of the scope of the writ, even where the statutory language authorizing judicial action has remained unchanged."[48]

The case of Lakhdar Boumediene amply demonstrates why the Great Writ has, for centuries, been viewed with such respect and admiration. But there is another side to the story of habeas—a side that once led Supreme Court Justice Robert Jackson to predict the "progressive trivialization of the writ until floods of stale, frivolous and repetitious petitions inundate the docket of the lower courts and swell our own."[49] New empirical evidence, presented in this book, demonstrates that Justice Jackson was absolutely right. As he accurately foresaw more than a half-century ago, habeas cases have, "as a class, become peculiarly undeserving."[50]

The problem is that for every Lakhdar Boumediene, there are thousands of other habeas corpus petitioners like Ronald Graham. Graham, a repeat offender, had been released from a Kansas prison under supervision, after serving ten years of a term of fifteen years to life that he received after being convicted in 1987 for the third in a series of serious drug crimes.[51] While on release, he was again arrested, charged with new drug crimes, and returned to prison to serve out the rest of his previous life sentence. After first agreeing to plead "no contest" to one of the new charges, Graham then changed his mind and dismissed his lawyer. In 2000, he was convicted after a bench trial on the new drug charges and sentenced to another twelve-and-a-half years, to run consecutively with the life sentence.

Six years later, after the Kansas courts had four times considered and rejected various challenges to Graham's new conviction and sentence (on direct appeal and in two separate state postconviction proceedings), he filed two federal habeas corpus petitions under Section 2254. In one he challenged his 2000 conviction, and in the other he tried to challenge his 1986 conviction, even though he had already filed three unsuccessful federal habeas petitions challenging that same conviction before. The Tenth Circuit denied him permission to file yet another habeas challenge to the 1986 conviction but remanded the petition involving the 2000 conviction to the district court for further action.

Graham's habeas petition had no chance from the start. One of his claims, for example, was that the trial court should not have admitted evidence about two of his prior drug convictions. The trial court, however, had a very good reason for doing so. During the trial, Graham tried to argue that the pair of shorts and jacket in which the drugs were found, inside his car, did not actually belong to him. Unfortunately for him, Graham had told exactly the same story—without success—in both of his two prior drug cases; hence, admitting evidence about those prior cases was not error.[52]

Eventually, the district court and the Tenth Circuit agreed that none of Graham's claims had any legal merit at all, but it took a twenty-one-page written memorandum opinion in the district court to say so, as well as a separate opinion denying Graham permission to file an appeal and a nine-page opinion from the Tenth Circuit, which found that the claims were not even "debatable." At every opportunity, Graham sought review of each state and federal court decision in the U.S. Supreme Court, but the Court denied certiorari each time, the last time in October of 2007.[53]

The prolonged legal saga of Ronald Graham is not newsworthy, remarkable, or historic, as Boumediene's was. But to those who are familiar with habeas litigation today, it is typical. The mundane, repetitive, and ultimately futile federal habeas proceedings in Graham's case exemplify what gives habeas a bad name. Even before filing the petition challenging his 2000 conviction, Graham had over a period of six years obtained judicial review of that conviction six separate times, including twice by the Kansas Supreme Court and twice by the U.S. Supreme Court, and was already serving a life sentence for another crime that itself withstood four separate fruitless habeas petitions. Nevertheless, he was able, by filing a habeas petition and paying a five-dollar filing fee, to command at least the passing attention of no fewer than thirteen federal judges: one in the district court, three in the Tenth Circuit, and nine on the U.S. Supreme Court. Counting the preliminary, merits, appellate, and certiorari stages of habeas litigation, his federal petition was reviewed on six separate occasions before finally being put to rest. Two of the judges felt the need to write lengthy opinions before denying Graham's claims. All of this, despite the fact that each and every one of the judges who reviewed Graham's petition agreed that his claims were without any merit.

The case of Ronald Graham shows how habeas corpus can turn into a massive waste of time, energy, and societal resources. And when this happens, it threatens to undermine the foundations of habeas itself. Habeas is a powerful source of judicial authority, but it can be a fragile source as well. Without restraint in its application, the writ's "extraordinary prestige"[54] can be squandered through overuse. Imprudent use of habeas corpus, especially after the particular political or social crisis that gave rise to its expansion has passed, poses two related dangers. The first is that politicians and the general public—and even some federal judges—may begin to question the need for, or the extent of, such habeas litigation. When this happens, habeas becomes increasingly susceptible to attack through legislative or judicial restrictions that may deprive the writ of the flexibility that has been its primary strength for over two centuries. The second danger, exemplified by the *Graham* case, is that the overextension of habeas review can impose a substantial strain on limited public resources—resources that can often be put to much better use.

For these reasons, the courts, and especially the U.S. Supreme Court, should be careful to exercise the extraordinary authority provided to the federal judiciary by habeas corpus only when such authority is truly needed. As an exceptional and equitable remedy, habeas should be pressed into service only when there is no other procedure that can reasonably ensure meaningful judicial review of the legality of a challenged detention. Once an adequate substitute for habeas is developed that reasonably meets the need for judicial review to enforce federal law, then habeas should recede, to be preserved for future situations when it might once again be needed.

As we will explain later, the Supreme Court should interpret the habeas statutes freely, and the Suspension Clause aggressively, in order to preserve its judicial prerogative to control the appropriate scope of the writ. This is necessary in order to ensure flexibility in the application of habeas. But in addition to doing so, the Court, and the lower federal courts as well, should also become much more willing than they have been in the recent past to decline the exercise of habeas jurisdiction in certain situations. As Justice Lewis Powell once wrote, "There has been a halo about the 'Great Writ' that no one would wish to dim. Yet one must wonder whether the stretching of its use far beyond any justifiable purpose will not in the end weaken rather than strengthen the writ's vitality."[55] If the federal courts do not exercise their extraordinary habeas jurisdiction prudently, they may someday find themselves precluded or deterred, by either legislation or stare decisis, from invoking that jurisdiction when it becomes truly necessary.[56]

*   *   *

In this book, we discuss five contemporary applications of habeas corpus review. Chapter 2 addresses the review of detentions without conviction of any crime, including detention by military or immigration authorities. Chapter 3 examines the development of habeas review of state convictions and sentences in noncapital cases under 28 U.S.C. § 2254, with chapter 4 detailing new empirical findings and chapter 5 containing our proposals for reform in this context. Chapter 6 discusses the review of noncapital convictions and sentences for federal crimes, implemented today under 28 U.S.C. § 2255, the modern statutory substitute for traditional habeas. Habeas review of state and federal death sentences is addressed in chapters 7 and 8. The review of administrative decisions made by prison and parole authorities that affect the timing of release from custody is the subject of chapter 9.

In each of these disparate contexts, we consider whether or not the current scope and application of habeas review is consistent with its preeminent role in protecting individual liberty in times of crisis. In the end, we conclude that in some of these contexts, the federal courts should continue, and even expand, their relatively liberal use of habeas corpus. When no other meaningful judicial remedies are available to protect fundamental freedom from governmental oppression that violates federal law, the need for habeas corpus is most acute. Executive detentions without any criminal conviction, such as the imprisonment of Lakhdar Boumediene, present such a situation.

In other contexts, we argue that the use of habeas corpus should become much more restrained. For example, the federalism crisis that originally gave rise to a special need for broad federal habeas review of state criminal judgments has now largely passed, and state criminal justice has been transformed in important ways that render federal habeas courts essentially incapable of providing meaningful additional protection for individual liberty in such cases. A recent empirical study, conducted by one of the coauthors together with researchers from the National Center for State Courts, illustrates how pointless habeas litigation in state non-capital criminal cases has become, an enormous use of resources producing almost no benefit.[57] As a result, in this context, federal and state judges, legislators, and officials, as well as the public, increasingly see habeas as a burdensome waste of time, energy, and money. We suggest that Congress, with the Court's concurrence, should amend the habeas statute to restrict the scope of habeas review of state noncapital criminal cases and should reallocate the resources currently wasted on habeas litigation to more effective reforms of ongoing problems in state criminal justice, including improvements to state defense representation services.

By contrast, capital cases—both state and federal—present a very different situation. The same empirical study shows that habeas continues to play an important role in the enforcement of federal constitutional rules that are unique to the death penalty. These rules are still evolving and still engender resistance from state courts. For these reasons, we do not propose to limit habeas review of capital cases; instead, we suggest some ways to make such review more efficient and effective.

Finally, in the particular context of litigation about early release decisions by corrections officials, we contend that Congress should step in to enact a new "adequate substitute" for habeas. Whenever repeated challenges to particular types of detention recur with sufficient frequency, and whenever petitions raising those recurring issues become relatively routine, Congress should shift those challenges away from habeas to alternative statutory procedures. Such alternatives can provide a better forum for judicial review under rules and procedures that are specifically tailored to the needs and circumstances of the particular situation.

In the end, all of these recommendations are shaped by the dual themes of flexibility and prudence in the exercise of habeas jurisdiction, themes that emerge from a comprehensive examination of the history and contemporary reality of habeas in all of its many applications. Flexibility is needed to allow the judiciary to use habeas effectively in response to serious political or social crises that are not yet foreseen. Prudence will best preserve that effectiveness for times when it is truly needed.

There is a striking contrast between the reverential terms used to describe habeas corpus by the Framers and by the Supreme Court in *Bou-*

mediene and the disparaging way that habeas is all too often described by federal judges and state officials who must deal with the thousands of habeas petitions filed each year by convicted prisoners like Ronald Graham. Rather than a "vital instrument for the protection of individual liberty,"[58] habeas today is viewed by many as a prime source of vexatious, time-consuming, often abusive, and ultimately meritless litigation. We hope to provide a fresh perspective, as well as sound proposals for reform that will help to dispel this negative perception and preserve for the future the Great Writ's extraordinary value.

CHAPTER TWO

Habeas and Detention without Conviction

The target of most habeas corpus petitions today is the criminal process. Day in and day out, prisoners file petitions alleging that their convictions and sentences are invalid because of constitutional violations by police, prosecutors, defense attorneys, juries, and judges. This may be the most well-known use of habeas, but it is not its most important nor its oldest function. Instead, the "core" of the habeas corpus remedy is the review of detention without conviction.[1] In this chapter, we will explain why this has historically been so and why the Supreme Court should continue to be exceptionally vigilant about preserving habeas review for those who have not been found guilty of a crime but are confined nonetheless.

In times of crisis or fear, a formal criminal prosecution can be risky for a government seeking to control or to deter those who are viewed as posing serious threats to security. A public trial before an impartial jury, with the right to defense counsel, cross-examination of witnesses, and a "beyond reasonable doubt" burden of proof, is not the quickest or easiest route to detention. Nor is criminal prosecution a viable strategy when the available proof of criminal conduct is thin, inadmissible, or classified and therefore dangerous to disclose. And prosecution is out of the question when one threatens future harm but has committed no crime in the past. Detention without conviction is the obvious alternative.

The Framers of our Constitution were well aware of the problem of imprisonment without conviction, a problem that arose regularly both before and during the late eighteenth century. The Framers recognized that the power to confine a person "by secretly hurrying him to jail, where his sufferings are unknown or forgotten" is a particularly "dangerous engine of arbitrary government."[2]

Today imprisonment without conviction has taken new forms. It is often authorized by statute and has acquired its own new labels: "regulatory detention" or sometimes "preventive detention." Those terms reflect the notion that the purpose of confinement under one of these statutes is not punishment for past criminal conduct but the achievement of some other regulatory aim, such as preserving public safety by incapacitating those who pose a future risk of harm. Military imprisonment of enemies who would engage in combat against us is one example. So is civil commitment of those considered dangerous because of mental impairment or infectious disease. Even detention that was originally designed to achieve purposes other than safety—such as the detention of aliens until they can be deported or removed—has been used periodically to incapacitate those considered dangerous. Because detention can disable those who may do harm more quickly and quietly than the cumbersome criminal process, it has always been an enticing option for a government in desperate times.

When the Constitution was written, it was this threat—not the threat of incarceration after an unjust conviction—to which the habeas remedy was primarily addressed. The common law writ of habeas corpus, which the Framers enshrined in the Suspension Clause, had been developed precisely to protect against unlawful detention without conviction. Section 14 of the Judiciary Act of 1789 also was interpreted to provide a remedy for those who were not serving criminal sentences after conviction.[3] As the Supreme Court has recognized, "At its historical core, the writ of habeas corpus has served as a means of reviewing the legality of Executive detention, and it is in that context that its protections have been strongest."[4]

Along with this historical basis there are two functional reasons for placing detention without conviction at the center of habeas corpus policy. The first is the recognition that because of reduced judicial oversight, detention without conviction poses a risk of injustice for the individual detainee that is especially acute. Procedures required by the Bill of Rights help to protect those accused of a crime against mistaken and unsupported accusations. Bypassing these requirements increases the risk of confinement on false allegations or without lawful basis. The process leading to detention without conviction is invariably less careful and may involve no judge at all. And there are typically fewer opportunities for judicial scrutiny of imprisonment after the fact.

This lack of judicial scrutiny is most acute for those incarcerated without conviction by federal authorities. For state detainees, federal habeas review is usually the second bite from the judicial review apple, because state detainees have already had access to the state law version of habeas review in the state courts. For a prisoner confined by federal authorities, however, a federal habeas corpus petition may be the only way he can bring a challenge to his confinement to the attention of any judge. Habeas in this context has long served as a crucial stopgap, providing a means to obtain judicial review of individual decisions under new detention schemes until Congress creates a specific mechanism for judicial review that is tailored to the specific situation. Habeas is a relatively blunt instrument, ill suited as a permanent device for correcting error in the routine operation of an ongoing regulatory detention scheme, such as pretrial detention or civil commitment. But habeas has proven effective as a temporary solution until alternative routes to judicial review become available as well as a powerful catalyst prompting lawmakers to create those alternative review procedures.

There is a second, and even more important, justification for the priority status that habeas review of detention without conviction has received over the years. Habeas not only helps to protect the rights of individual detainees, it also serves a key structural function, helping to preserve the ongoing stability of this nation's democratic form of government. Without habeas, Congress could authorize the executive branch to summarily confine classes of people not only bypassing the procedures required by the Constitution in criminal cases but also avoiding all review by the judicial branch. If the executive's arbitrary power over individual liberty were to stand unchecked either by a distrustful legislature or by an independent judiciary, the federal government could become the very kind of oppressive regime that the Founders fought a war to escape. In short, without judicial review of executive detention, the potential for abuse of federal power by its chief executive—the risk of tyranny—is at its apex.

Enter the Suspension Clause. This clause in Article I of the Constitution prevents Congress from giving the president or his agents unfettered power to incarcerate those whom they claim pose a threat to public safety. The Framers recognized, when they drafted limits on congres-

sional power in Article I, that the perceived necessity for swift and secret action in times of crisis could lead Congress to agree with the president that the participation of the judiciary in detention decisions poses
a risk to public safety. The clause preserves at least some level of judicial review of detention decisions precisely in those situations in which
Congress attempts to eliminate such review, except in the most dire of
emergencies—cases of "rebellion or invasion."[5] Congress and the executive might agree to lock up those persons most despised or feared, but
the Suspension Clause ensures that such persons cannot be held captive
without some review by the independent judiciary. In this sense, the writ
of habeas corpus is, in the Court's words, "an indispensable mechanism
for monitoring the separation of powers."[6]

Recognizing this integral relationship between instability in the governmental balance of powers brought on by political or social crisis and
the necessity for habeas corpus review, the Framers acknowledged that
"pendular swings to and away from individual liberty were endemic to
undivided, controlled power." They knew that in England, denial or suspension of the writ "occurred in times of political unrest, to the anguish
of the imprisoned and the outrage of those in sympathy with them." They
designed the Suspension Clause precisely "to protect against these cy-
clical abuses."[7] It is this institutional justification for habeas review, not
its ability to correct individual injustices, that warranted placing habeas
among the other structural constraints on federal power in the Constitution itself. And it is this justification for habeas review that must, in the
future, continue to guide habeas policy.

In sum, the Court's repeated recognition that "the need for habeas
corpus is more urgent" whenever a person is detained without conviction
has two rationales, both of which we develop in this chapter.[8] First, detention without conviction lacks the procedural safeguards that in criminal cases help to protect against errors in the decision to confine, including the participation of an impartial judge and jury. Habeas is a crucial
safety net that is available to such a prisoner when other alternatives for
judicial review have yet to take shape. Second, and more importantly, by
helping to ensure that federal power remains divided between the political branches and the independent judiciary, habeas serves as a vital
structural protection for democracy and the rule of law during times of
unrest. A quick tour of the use of the writ during several challenging
periods in American history will illustrate how the federal courts have
used habeas corpus to accomplish these two functions.

Habeas as Stopgap to Protect Individual Liberty

We begin with the role of the writ in two contexts: the detention of those accused of a crime and awaiting trial and the civil commitment of those considered a danger to themselves or others because of a mental disorder. In these situations, habeas has regulated continued confinement after an initial judicial order of incarceration, until some alternative means of judicial oversight—such as the right to appellate review—was made available for that purpose.

Judicial Review for Court-Ordered Detention: Pretrial Detainees

One of the easiest ways to imprison a person without conviction is simply to charge him with a crime and put off his trial indefinitely. This is, of course, unconstitutional. The government can hold an alleged criminal for only so long without trial. Eventually, an accused has the right to a jury's verdict on the government's charge. The Bill of Rights addressed this problem with a quintet of provisions: the Fourth Amendment limited the government's initial authority to arrest a suspect; the Grand Jury Clause of the Fifth Amendment ensured charges would be reviewed by a grand jury; the Speedy Trial Clause of the Sixth Amendment prohibited lengthy delays awaiting trial; the Bail Clause of the Eighth Amendment regulated the terms under which pretrial release could be denied; and the Due Process Clause of the Fifth Amendment protected liberty against arbitrary deprivation generally. But for many years after the Framing, pretrial detention orders could not be appealed (nor could final convictions).[9] So how were limits on pretrial detention to be enforced?

Habeas corpus initially provided the answer. When the federal government was in its infancy, the Supreme Court reviewed and granted four habeas petitions filed by prisoners awaiting trial on charges of treason. One case involved John A. Burford, a shopkeeper who had been thrown in jail in 1806 upon a warrant issued by eleven justices of the peace who had agreed that Burford "is not of good name and fame, nor of honest conversation, but an evil doer and disturber of the peace of the United States, so that murder, homicide, strifes, discords, and other grievances and damages, amongst the citizens of the United States, concerning their bodies and property, are likely to arise thereby. . . ." The warrant ordered that Burford remain locked up unless and until he could find a group of supporters who were willing to put up collateral worth $4,000 (the equivalent of about $80,000 today) and to guarantee that he would be on good behavior for the rest of his life. The Supreme Court, led by Chief Justice John Marshall, was appalled. "That warrant states no offence. It does not allege that he was convicted of any crime." Finding Burford could not be held unless the warrant stated "some good cause certain, supported by oath," the Court granted the writ.[10]

Habeas was also the remedy invoked by the Supreme Court in 1795 to order the release on bail of a leader of the Whiskey Rebellion in Pennsylvania who had been charged with treason.[11] And in 1807, in the politically charged case *Ex parte Bollman*, Chief Justice Marshall again found the basis for pretrial detention lacking. He therefore ordered the release of two men awaiting trial on treason charges in connection with Aaron Burr's conspiracy, finding that there was not sufficient evidence to support the charges.[12]

After more than a century of inactivity during which lower courts assumed the primary responsibility of policing pretrial detention,[13] the Court in the 1950s again exercised its habeas power to regulate abuses in pretrial detention of those accused of plotting against the government. This time the perceived threat to the nation's security was communism. Loretta Stack and eleven communist leaders were accused of conspiring to overthrow the United States government. Charged under the now notorious Smith Act, Stack's bail and that of each of her cohorts was set at $50,000 (the equivalent of more than $400,000 today). When her motion to reduce bail was denied, she filed a petition for habeas corpus and then appealed the trial judge's denial of that petition all the way to the Supreme Court. For good measure, Stack also filed an original habeas petition with the Court itself.

The Court in *Stack v. Boyle* issued a short but stinging decision.[14] The opinion could have been limited to the concluding paragraphs, in which the Court held that the constitutionality of orders limiting pretrial release may be raised on appeal before trial and that such an "interlocutory appeal" must be pursued before habeas relief can be considered.[15] But the Court apparently decided that a more forceful rebuke to the prosecution and the lower courts was needed to guard against future abuses of pretrial detention:

> The Government asks the courts to depart from the norm by assuming, without the introduction of evidence, that each petitioner is a pawn in a conspir-

acy and will, in obedience to a superior, flee the jurisdiction. To infer from the fact of indictment alone a need for bail in an unusually high amount is an arbitrary act. Such conduct would inject into our own system of government the very principles of totalitarianism which Congress was seeking to guard against in passing the statute under which petitioners have been indicted.[16]

The Court upheld the dismissal of Stack's habeas petition but remanded the case to the lower courts so that she could file a new motion to reduce bail, which the Court indicated should be granted, with an interlocutory appeal available to ensure the correct outcome.

The *Stack* case and the pretrial detention challenges that followed in its wake illustrate a basic pattern that we trace throughout this book. Whenever habeas provides the only means for judicial review of a challenged detention, the Court tends to use it aggressively, particularly in politically turbulent times. Once substitute mechanisms for judicial review become available, and the conditions precipitating the heightened risk of unlawful detention subside, the Court becomes more restrained in its use of habeas. In the nineteenth century, when orders denying pretrial release were not reviewable by writ of error or appeal, habeas supplied the Court in *Bollman* with the means to ensure that those held for trial on charges of treason were confined lawfully.[17] By 1950, the Court in *Stack* had more options. It was able to shift the oversight of orders regarding pretrial detention from habeas review to interlocutory appellate review, where those claims would receive swift attention. Ever since the decision in *Stack*, detainees have raised on interlocutory appeal the same constitutional challenges to pretrial detention that formerly would have been raised in habeas By 1966, Congress had crafted a statute specifically authorizing and regulating appellate review of decisions denying pretrial release.[18] Habeas, once the primary means of judicial review available for correcting unlawful pretrial detention, is no longer needed for that purpose.

Judicial Review for Court-Ordered Detention: Civil Commitment

The Constitution also limits the confinement of those who pose a danger to themselves or others because of mental illness. Federal habeas review has played a regulatory role here as well, allowing federal courts to shape and enforce the constitutional standards for involuntary civil commitment.

For much of this nation's history, with few exceptions, federal authorities did not confine the mentally ill; that was left to the states, subject to review by the state courts. By 1882, for example, Congress had provided for the commitment of those charged with federal offenses who become "insane" while in the custody of the United States, but it was not until 1949 that Congress authorized federal authorities to confine those charged with a crime but incompetent to stand trial.[19] For persons committed under the 1949 act, and for the small number of unfortunates sent to federal custody in St. Elizabeth's Hospital in Washington, D.C., the only mental institution run by the federal government, the writ of habeas corpus initially was the only method of securing a judge's oversight of their continued detention.

Case-by-case habeas review of these detention decisions followed the familiar pattern, eventually being displaced by alternative review mechanisms more suited to the particular task. Just as the federal judiciary's continued oversight of pretrial detention in habeas emphasized to Congress the need to develop a new statutory scheme that included adequate judicial review of decisions denying pretrial release, habeas oversight of civil commitments also helped to shape the statute that authorized judicial review of such cases.

As with pretrial detention, habeas review was first displaced, at least partially, by appellate review. By the 1950s, courts generally agreed that criminal defendants who were committed as incompetent had the right to appeal the initial commitment decision. Uncertainty remained, however, about how long a prisoner who was unlikely to regain competency could be confined. Reviewing one of these cases on appeal in 1956, the Supreme Court found that the 1949 act authorized continued detention but noted that "habeas corpus [is] always available when circumstances warrant."[20] Lower courts interpreted this ruling as establishing a constitutional limitation of "reasonableness" on the duration of confinement. They also readily accepted the Court's invitation to use habeas corpus to enforce this limitation. In order to ensure that confinement was constitutional, lower courts granted habeas relief in numerous cases over the next several years.[21] And in 1962, the Court itself granted the writ to free a petitioner held at St. Elizabeth's. The petitioner had not claimed to be insane at the time of the crime with which he had been charged, but the judge nevertheless found him not guilty by reason of insanity and sent him to be confined in St. Elizabeth's. The Court concluded that federal law did not authorize the involuntary commitment of one who had neither claimed insanity nor presented evidence to support an acquittal by reason of insanity and ordered the detainee released unless civil commitment proceedings were promptly commenced.[22]

When Congress finally adopted a new statute governing the confinement of the insane in 1984, it codified a new judicial procedure for testing continuing confinement, authorizing the same kind of judicial review that habeas had formerly provided.[23] In cases reviewing the confinement of the mentally ill, just as in cases reviewing pretrial detention, habeas served as the emergency means for obtaining needed judicial oversight until Congress established an adequate alternative.

The same pattern is repeating itself again today in litigation about a new type of regulatory detention: the civil commitment of sex offenders who have completed their prison terms. Fear of sex offenders—particularly those who prey on children—has prompted sweeping detention schemes. The latest wave of outrage has led nineteen states and Congress to enact new "sexual predator" statutes that authorize the indefinite civil confinement of convicted sex offenders who have completed their criminal sentences but who under statutory criteria are found to be at risk of reoffending. Confining these individuals under general civil commitment statutes would not be possible, because those statutes require proof of both a serious mental disorder and recent behavior indicating that the individual is dangerous to himself or to others. Treatment for the disorder while confined is required, as well as periodic review and release once the individual is no longer considered mentally ill or dangerous.[24] Sexual predators, on the other hand, can be locked away without these protections. As of 2007, nearly three thousand sex offenders had been committed under such laws.[25]

So far, the Court has used a combination of appellate and habeas jurisdiction to oversee the administration of confinement under these sexual predator statutes in the states.[26] The legality of detention under the federal statute, the Adam Walsh Act, enacted in 2006,[27] is being tested both on appeal and in habeas challenges in the lower courts.[28] Once again, habeas is serving as a vital remedy for those detained under a new regulatory detention scheme, and habeas will probably continue to play that role unless or until the Court finds that an adequate alternative for judicial review exists. As the petitioner argued more than two hundred years ago in *Ex parte Bollman*, the Supreme Court possesses the "power to protect the liberty of the citizen, by the writ of habeas corpus, against the enterprizes of inferior courts, which may be constituted for the purposes of oppression or revenge."[29]

Habeas as Structural Safeguard of Democracy: Immigration

In two other contexts—immigration and military detention—Congress has expressly limited the judiciary's power to review the executive's decision to detain. Habeas has proven especially important here, not only as a means for correcting illegal detention in individual cases but also as a structural check: habeas can force the executive and legislative branches to change their policies regarding the detention of large groups of individuals. Another basic pattern has been repeated again and again in both contexts. Congress and the executive serve up a new detention scheme designed to neutralize what they consider an imminent threat to security, only to have the federal courts knock it down by granting habeas relief. Repeated rounds of revision and rejection follow, until the judicial branch finally determines that the modified regulatory scheme passes constitutional muster.

Rounding up aliens for detention and deportation, particularly in dangerous times, has a long history in this country. Beginning with the Alien and Sedition Act of 1798, Congress has repeatedly empowered the executive to detain and remove or deport those entering or remaining in the country without proper documentation. For almost as long, the Court has used its habeas power to control this authority, ensuring that aliens are detained for reasons sanctioned by law. In fact, before 1952, the only judicial review available for these decisions was habeas corpus. Even today habeas remains, in some circumstances, the sole avenue by which immigration detainees can seek relief in court. A brief tour through our nation's most difficult periods illustrates how the Court has used habeas review to curb excesses of the political branches in confining noncitizens. Nowhere, other than perhaps in military detention, has the writ been more troublesome to executive policy than in immigration.

The Exclusion of Chinese

In the late nineteenth century, thousands of Chinese laborers came to the West Coast of the United States. The influx was considered an imminent danger to U.S. interests. One circuit judge stated that the Chinese "presence here in overwhelming numbers was felt by almost all thoughtful persons to . . . menace our interest, our safety, and even our civilization."[30] The result was later described by the Supreme Court: "As they grew in numbers each year the people of the coast saw, or believed they saw . . . great danger that at no distant day that portion of our country would be overrun by them, unless prompt action was taken to restrict their immigration. The people there accordingly petitioned earnestly for protective legislation."[31]

Congress responded to what became known as "the Yellow Peril" with the Chinese Exclusion Act of 1882, and thousands of Chinese were denied admittance and detained on their ships.[32] They sought relief through habeas corpus in the federal courts in California, arguing that they did not fall within the law's restrictions. By 1890 the federal courts had received over seven thousand habeas corpus petitions on behalf of Chinese immigrants.[33] The two overworked federal judges who heard this flood of petitions—Judge Ogden Hoffman, the only federal district judge for all of California between 1866 and 1886, and his colleague Circuit Judge Lorenzo Sawyer—considered each case individually, holding hearings night and day for months on end.[34] Many Chinese were released after the court held that they had proper documents and that their exclusion from the country was in violation of federal law. Congress fought back, amending the immigration statute in 1884.[35] Justice Stephen J. Field, visiting California on circuit, quickly interpreted the new act restrictively to bar habeas review of these cases, over the dissent of Judges Hoffman and Sawyer. Before the year was over, Field's decision had been reversed by the Supreme Court, and the habeas grants continued.[36]

The political platforms of Democrat Grover Cleveland, elected president in 1884, and Republican Benjamin Harrison, elected in 1888 each called for greater efforts to exclude the Chinese.[37] Congress agreed, amending the law again in 1888 to limit the reentry of Chinese laborers who had left the country and sought to return.[38] The 1888 act was challenged in habeas as a treaty violation but in 1889 was upheld by the Supreme Court.[39] In the meantime, between October 1, 1888, and December 1, 1890, more than 1,400 Chinese filed habeas corpus petitions. Less than half of these petitions were decided by the end of that period, and of those, 86 percent ended in an order releasing the petitioner. Until their deaths in 1891, Judges Hoffman and Sawyer persevered in evaluating each petition, even as the crush of cases took its toll on their health[40] and their decisions granting relief subjected them to sustained criticism and public outrage.[41]

Anarchists, Germans, and Communists

At the turn of the century, anarchists assassinated several heads of state, including William McKinley, President of the United States. His assassination in 1901 shocked the nation and prompted the Anarchists Exclusion Act of 1903, which authorized the exclusion of "anarchists" and "those opposed to government or law."[42] The threat posed by anarchists prompted in 1908 the establishment of the Federal Bureau of Investigation. The FBI today characterizes anarchists as "the first modern-day terrorists—banding together in small, isolated groups around the world; motivated by ideology; bent on bringing down the governments they hated."[43] In 1916 German saboteurs exploded two million tons of war materials packed into railroad cars in downtown Manhattan, leaving pockmarks from shrapnel on the Statue of Liberty.[44] The Bolshevik Revolution followed in 1917. Fearing a worldwide revolution, Congress amended the Anarchists Exclusion Act in 1918 to authorize the deportation of any alien, no matter how long a lawful resident, who was affiliated with or possessed material from subversive organizations.[45] By 1919 the Red Scare was in full swing. Dozens of bombings and bomb attempts took place. After a letter bomb reached the home of a former U.S. senator and blew off the hands of his maid, the attorney general of the United States (his own home destroyed by a bomb) commenced a roundup of three thousand suspected Communists, anarchists, and other political radicals, detaining them for deportation.[46]

During these dangerous times, the writ of habeas corpus remained available to those targeted as potential threats. The 1918 act purported to preclude judicial review of deportation orders, but the federal courts continued to review them anyway, using the writ.[47] For the most part, the habeas petitions that reached the Supreme Court were denied, but in 1939 the Court held that the government had overstepped the law and could not use the statute to rid the country of people who had once been Communists but were no longer.[48] After a lower court applying this decision rebuffed the attorney general's efforts to deport Harry Bridges, a well-known labor leader and head of the West Coast Longshoremen's Union, Congress amended the statute to clarify that former member-

ship was indeed sufficient ground for deportation. When Bridges was detained for deportation under the revised statute, he again sought habeas
relief. The Court granted it in 1945, concluding that the finding of "af-
filiation" was based on "too loose a meaning of the term."[49] In the next
year, habeas corpus petitions challenging deportation increased sixfold,
78 percent of them filed in the Southern District of New York.[50] Once
again, the Court used habeas to prevent the executive from disregarding
legal limits in its attempt to incapacitate those it considered enemies.

For the next several decades, the Court's habeas review of executive
action on immigration matters took a deferential turn. In 1948 the Court
narrowly refused to second-guess the decision to deport as "dangerous"
a German who had entered the country legally in the mid-1930s and who
had been arrested and held under the Alien Enemy Act since the day after Pearl Harbor in 1941. Justice Hugo Black's dissenting opinion characterized as "pure fiction" the Court's conclusion that the nation was "still
at war with Germany" in June of 1948.[51] In 1949, the Soviets successfully
tested their first atomic bomb, China fell to the Communists, Alger Hiss
was tried as a Soviet spy, and the second communist crisis descended
upon the federal government, prompting Congress to pass the Immigration and Nationality Act of 1952. The act expanded mandatory expul-
sion to aliens suspected of subversive activities "prejudicial to the public
interest" and precluded judicial review of discretionary decision making
except in habeas corpus.[52] In a 1953 deportation case, the Court warned
in dicta that its authority to review immigration detention in habeas was
undiminished.[53] Yet the Court did not exercise that review to constrain
the cold war Congress. It upheld the denial of release on bond, based on
hearsay evidence presented ex parte, to alien Communists awaiting deportation proceedings.[54] It also upheld the deportation of an Italian who
had belonged for a short time to the Communist Party as a young man
two decades earlier. The Court stated, "It would be easy for those of us
who do not have security responsibility to say that those who do are taking Communism too seriously and overestimating its danger. . . . We, in
our private opinions, need not concur in Congress' policies to hold its
enactments constitutional. Judicially we must tolerate what personally
we may regard as a legislative mistake."[55] In the 1960s and 1970s, the
primary target of the Court's habeas power shifted from the detention
of aliens by federal authorities to the detention of U.S. citizens by their
own state governments. It would take another national crisis—the ris-
ing threat of global terrorism beginning in the 1990s—before the Court

would once again use its habeas powers to interfere with executive authority in immigration detentions.

The Mariel Cubans Seek Habeas Relief

While the Supreme Court was focusing its habeas attention elsewhere, the lower courts filled in to respond to an unexpected emergency in immigration detention on a scale even larger than the one that faced federal judges in California in the late 1880s. Between April and September 1980, an assortment of boats carrying 125,000 people landed in Key West, Florida. The "Mariel Boatlift," or "Freedom Flotilla" as it came to be known, carried primarily Cuban refugees from Fidel Castro's regime. But also included were several thousand people who had been serving sentences in Cuba for minor and major crimes and who had been given a stark choice: serve an even longer sentence or get on a boat to the United States. About 10 percent of those who arrived were mentally ill or had been convicted of violent crimes.[56] The massive emigration was a "catastrophic event for the United States,"[57] and, as with other catastrophic events in the nation's history, habeas corpus played a key role.

Military processing centers were quickly created, and most of the refugees were released. But the Immigration and Naturalization Service (INS) did not free 1,800 of those whom it considered too dangerous to release. Cuba refused to take them back.[58] Most of these 1,800 detainees were moved to a federal prison in Atlanta. Like the Chinese detained off the West Coast a century earlier, the detainees turned to the federal courts for help and found a federal trial judge willing to take on the attorney general.

Faced with more than 1,500 habeas petitions seeking release, a remarkable spike in petitions that is visible in figure 2.1, Judge Marvin Shoob had U.S. magistrate judges flown in from around the circuit to assist in holding hearings.[59] Within a few months, Judge Shoob had ordered the government to free hundreds of the Cuban refugees who had been detained for lack of papers and had no criminal history. When the prison refused to release the first prisoner he had ordered freed, Judge Shoob personally called the warden's office. "I'm sending two federal marshals over to the penitentiary right now," he told the official who had defied his order. "They are going to arrest you. You will spend the weekend in the Fulton County jail. Then you will be brought before me on Monday." The prisoner was released.[60]

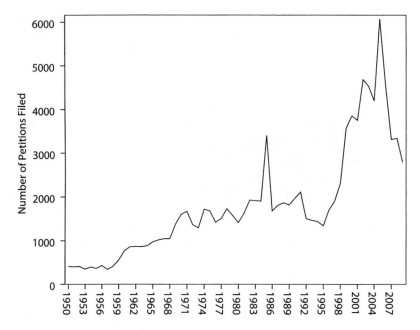

FIGURE 2.1. Federal 2241 Petitions Filed, 1950–2009

After Judge Shoob called the government's handling of the situation a "disgrace," an unnamed Justice Department official told the *Chicago Tribune* that Shoob was an "activist judge who is trying to run the nation's immigration policy from his chambers" and challenged him to visit the prisoners. Shoob declined the invitation, stating that he could not tell whether a Cuban was dangerous by looking at him in his cell.[61] President Carter, like so many presidents before him, was attempting to protect Americans by locking away, without a hearing, those his administration feared were dangerous. Judge Shoob, like so many federal judges before him, was getting in the way.

Over the next few years, Shoob, as well as other judges, would order the release of hundreds of additional detainees for whom the government could not demonstrate dangerousness. Shoob personally reviewed between two and three thousand habeas petitions, most of them handwritten and in Spanish, with the help of a roomful of translators. Some 2,500 detainees were released through a screening system that the INS set up under threat of one of his court orders.[62]

In 1983 Shoob ruled that the Cubans could not be imprisoned indefinitely, that they had a right to due process, and that the government had to prove the need to detain each and every one. This ruling was reversed by the Eleventh Circuit in 1984, and the Supreme Court declined review. Undaunted, Shoob in 1985 adopted a different theory, holding that detainees with no criminal history or mental illness had been invited to come to the United States by a statement made by President Carter and that this invitation created a liberty interest triggering a right to due process, including a hearing. The court of appeals disagreed.[63]

By 1987, 3,822 Cuban detainees remained in INS custody, concentrated in two overcrowded corrections facilities in Georgia and Louisiana. Many of them had been returned to custody after completing sentences for crimes they committed after being released earlier. (Not all of those crimes were serious. One detainee, for example, was sent back to prison for six years after he drove his own car without a license plate.) Some of the detainees had been in prison since 1980 and had not received a single hearing during that seven-year period. Hundreds of the detainees were mentally ill, and a 1986 congressional report warned that the conditions of detention were "brutal and inhumane."[64] In November 1987, the detainees rioted and took over their prisons. The negotiated resolution included individual reviews for each detainee. The INS streamlined its screening processes, and during the seven months after the uprising, two-thirds of the detainees were released.[65] Most of those who remained in prison would eventually be freed as a result of another habeas decision, but that decision did not occur until 2005. By then the Supreme Court was relying on the writ to rein in the response of the political branches to the next national crisis: al-Qaeda and the global war on terror.

Immigration Law and Terrorism in the Twentieth and Twenty-First Centuries

A new terrorism threat struck home in the 1993 attack on the World Trade Center, and habeas once again became the judiciary's primary means of checking efforts by the political branches to control terror through detention without conviction. On the immigration front, Congress in 1996 enacted both the Antiterrorism and Effective Death Penalty Act of 1996 and the Illegal Immigration Reform and Immigrant Responsibility Act (IIRIRA), which expanded the grounds for exclusion and deportation. These statutes removed the attorney general's discretion to waive deportation of aliens convicted of a crime and required that such aliens, along with certain categories of noncriminal immigrants, be detained without bond pending deportation and removal.[66] The number of aliens who were detained increased. For example, in 1999, over ten thousand people who had been legal permanent residents were detained and deported for convictions of crimes, as compared with only 4,200 in 1996. And the length of detentions increased as well. In 1999, only 851 immigration detainees had been held for more than three years; by 2001, however, that number had increased to several thousand.[67]

The number of habeas petitions filed in district courts increased with enforcement efforts, as did appeals of deportation orders. The government claimed that the 1996 statutes stripped the federal courts of jurisdiction to review through habeas certain deportation orders and discretionary immigration determinations, but many federal courts resisted that position and granted the petitions anyway.[68] The INS also adopted the practice of indefinitely detaining aliens who were unlikely to be removed but who represented a threat to the community or would likely flee if released. Detainees from countries that lacked repatriation agreements with the United States were especially hard hit because their home countries refused to allow them to return. With no other hope of release, detainees filed habeas petitions in the federal courts. The Supreme Court soon agreed to decide both controversies, reasserting the judiciary's power to review executive detention through the writ.

In *INS v. St. Cyr*, the Court rejected the argument that it lacked jurisdiction to review an agency decision that the petitioner—a lawful permanent resident who had pled guilty to a drug offense in state court—was ineligible for discretionary relief from deportation. The Court affirmed the lower court's decision that habeas remained available to challenge the INS interpretation of the law and that the writ should be granted. The Court reasoned that interpreting the 1996 act to have withdrawn habeas review without providing an "adequate substitute for its exercise" would present "a serious Suspension Clause issue." It emphasized that the writ of habeas corpus has long served as a means of reviewing the legality of executive detention. To avoid the constitutional question, the Court concluded that although Congress had barred "judicial review" generally, the statute did not express a clear legislative intent to prohibit habeas corpus review.[69]

The same year, in *Zadvydas v. Davis*, the Court also rebuffed the government's position on indefinite detention of those awaiting deportation.[70] Kestutis Zadvydas was born to Lithuanian parents in a refugee camp in Germany and therefore lacked citizenship anywhere. Zadvydas was ordered to be deported from the United States after serving his sentence for misdemeanor drug offenses and had been confined by immigration authorities for more than four years when he filed his habeas petition. His case was eventually joined with that of Kim Ho Ma. Ma was ordered deported after serving a short sentence for manslaughter, but Cambodia, a country he fled at age seven, refused to take him back. Both petitioners faced indefinite detention with no prospect of release; both received habeas relief from the Supreme Court.

Echoing the position of Judge Shoob more than two decades earlier, the Court held that indefinite detention of prisoners like Zadvydas and Ma raised "serious constitutional concerns." The Court concluded that the detainees were entitled to due process and that although it was presumptively reasonable to hold them pending deportation for up to six months, after that period expired the government must either release them or show a significant likelihood of removal in the reasonably foreseeable future. The Court noted that "[f]reedom from imprisonment—from government custody, detention, or other forms of restraint—lies at the heart of the liberty" that the Constitution protects. In the few months between the day that *Zadvydas* was handed down and September 11, 2001, about eight hundred long-term detainees were released.

Four years later, the Court interpreted the removal statute to require the same protection for aliens apprehended at a port of entry. This included the hundreds of remaining Cubans who had arrived in 1980 and who were still being held indefinitely in immigration detention. Of the approximately 1,750 Mariel detainees still in custody at the time of the Court's January 2005 decision,[71] all but twenty-six, each with mental and physical health conditions impeding release, were freed by the end of 2006.

The September 11, 2001, terrorist attacks prompted a reaction reminiscent of the panic and outrage that had followed the violent terrorist attacks a century before. Understandably, the government resorted to all available means to respond to the terrorist threat. Criminal prosecutions for terrorism crimes escalated tenfold, facilitated by sweeping offense definitions.[72] Predictably, the option of criminal prosecution was rejected for many suspected terrorists, and regulatory detention filled the gaps. Several forms of regulatory detention were put to use, including military detention, material witness warrants,[73] and, of course, immi-

gration orders. Just as predictably, the Supreme Court exercised its habeas jurisdiction to closely monitor these developments. The result has
been another high-stakes tug-of-war among the three branches of government, with Congress and the executive on one side and the Court on
the other.

Both Congress and the president moved quickly after the attack to
use immigration law to contain the terrorist threat. Within a few months,
immigration enforcement was completely restructured under the Homeland Security Act.[74] The USA Patriot Act authorized the detention of
persons posing a national security threat beyond the six-month removal
period established in *Zadvydas*.[75] At least 762 aliens identified through
terrorism investigations were detained on immigration charges.[76] Within
a year and a half, nearly three thousand people had been detained.[77] A
much larger number, many from Arab and Muslim countries, were swept
up "indiscriminately" and confined before and after a determination of
their immigration status.[78]

The number of immigration detentions soared. In 2003, the Court rejected a habeas challenge and upheld the government's power to hold
deportable lawful permanent residents without bond pending removal
proceedings on the assumption that this prehearing confinement would
be a relatively short and finite period of time.[79] In 2005 the government
abandoned its policy of releasing illegal immigrants caught at the border
pending their hearings and replaced it with a mandate that they be detained until removed.[80] And the Justice Department stepped up prosecution of illegal aliens for federal crimes generally. By 2007, 37 percent
of offenders sentenced for federal crimes were illegal aliens, up from
23 percent in 1991. Most were subject to deportation following the completion of their sentences.[81]

Between 2001 and 2007, the number of detainees more than tripled,[82]
and as figure 2.1 indicates, the number of habeas petitions increased as
well. From the time the Court decided *Zadvydas* and *St. Cyr* in June
2001 through March 2006, the agency in charge of removing aliens recorded 2,152 habeas corpus petitions. Remarkably, nearly half of these—
958, or about 45 percent—resulted in the release of the petitioner, either
because the government opted not to defend the detention or because a
court ordered the release.[83] This success rate is nothing short of astound-
ing compared with the extremely low success rate of less than 1 percent
for state prisoners challenging their criminal convictions or sentences in
habeas (as we will discuss in chapter 4).

Pro bono organizations that represented detainees reported that a habeas petition was the most effective way to obtain not only judicial review but also agency review. A report prepared by the Office of the Inspector General concluded that filing a habeas petition moved the detainee to the "immediate attention . . . list" and the "head of the CIA line" for clearance. The government's goal in many cases was to avoid a court decision addressing the merits of whether the detainee was held unlawfully. In some cases prosecutors were unwilling to defend detention because of workload priorities, in others there was "insufficient documentation in the file to support continued detention."[84] For example, shortly after the 9/11 attacks, two young Israeli men had been swept up as suspected terrorists. They were ordered released by an immigration judge who found no evidence of any threat whatsoever, but the United States refused to give two of them permission to leave. Only after their attorney filed a habeas petition demanding an explanation were the two allowed to go home.[85]

Accepting the invitation in *St. Cyr* to be crystal clear about its intent to restrict habeas corpus jurisdiction, Congress passed the Real-ID Act of 2005, which expressly barred district courts from reviewing removal orders in habeas[86] and provided that the sole and exclusive avenue to challenge an administrative order of removal was an appeal filed in the court of appeals. In some circuit courts, immigration appeals have become a crushing burden, representing nearly 40 percent of the entire docket.[87]

The dialogue between the judiciary and Congress over the constitutional protections due to immigration detainees during this latest threat to the nation's security has not yet fully played out. Lower courts are presently considering whether, by vesting exclusive jurisdiction in the courts of appeals over constitutional claims and questions of law arising from final orders of removal, Congress provided in the 2005 act an "adequate substitute" to the habeas writ that would withstand challenge under the Suspension Clause. Because the act did not explicitly bar *all* habeas review of immigration custody, some district judges have persisted in reviewing claims that did not arise from a removal order but instead involved a different question, such as a question of law defining eligibility for removal or a detention issue that developed after a removal order.[88] And the Tenth Circuit upheld new regulations for continued detention of dangerous removable aliens that fail to provide for an Article III judge at the hearing in which dangerousness is determined, precisely because that determination may be challenged by seeking a writ of habeas corpus in federal court.[89]

When, periodically, threats to the nation's security escalate, Congress tends to join with the executive to summarily detain and remove groups of potentially dangerous people from our midst, groups that almost inevitably include noncitizens. From the Chinese immigrant cases of the late nineteenth century to the terrorism cases of today, the judicial branch has consistently reined in this understandable impulse. So far, at least with immigration, Congress has chosen not to bypass judicial review entirely. So far, it has stopped short of stripping federal courts of their habeas jurisdiction to review all issues of detention in immigration proceedings. But Congress has come much closer to eliminating habeas review in immigration cases than it has in criminal cases. Indeed, the very first Court decisions involving the Suspension Clause in more than a century occurred after the executive's attempts to deport masses of people slowed to a crawl in a backlog of habeas cases and Congress responded by depriving the courts of jurisdiction over key issues.

Our successful nation, built by immigrants, will continue to attract foreigners from around the world. The government will, and should, seek to remove those who are demonstrably dangerous. And the courts will, and should, be available to ensure that the process the executive employs to identify and remove dangerous people complies with federal law. Because national security threats are episodic and unpredictable, that process will never stand still. Whenever it changes, the primary means for courts to ensure its legality has been, and will continue to be, habeas corpus.

Habeas as Structural Safeguard of Democracy: Military Detention

War is a particularly risky time for freedom, not only because the government and its interests are vulnerable to attack, but also because military detention of both citizens and aliens becomes an available option to supplement all of the peacetime regulatory detention options outlined above. Perhaps the most ominous threat to liberty is posed by military detention of U.S. citizens alleged to be conspiring to overthrow the government. In every such conflict, the Court has overseen the use of military detention, checking the power of Congress and the executive to incarcerate and execute suspected enemies, both citizens and aliens here and abroad. Habeas corpus has served as the primary means by which controversies over the legality of military detention are resolved. And it is only during times of war that Congress has expressly suspended the writ so that martial law could function unchecked.[90]

Habeas and Military Detention before September 11

Before the Civil War, Congress had authorized military detention but had never eliminated habeas review of that detention. In enacting the Alien Enemy Act of 1798, a response to fears that French spies had infiltrated the country, Congress permitted the confinement and deportation of "enemy aliens" whenever there is "a declared war between the United States and any foreign nation or government, or any invasion or predatory incursion is perpetrated, attempted, or threatened against the territory of the United States by any foreign nation or government, and the President [makes] public proclamation of the event."[91] During the War of 1812, Congress authorized the incarceration of enemy aliens, including British loyalists and foreign seamen. The federal courts, through the writ of habeas corpus, supervised the use of this power, granting the writ when grounds for detention were lacking.[92]

It was not until the Civil War that Congress invoked its power under the Suspension Clause to strip the courts of authority to review detentions by the president. Congress first took this step in its act of March 3, 1863, ratifying an earlier suspension of the writ already announced by President Lincoln on his own in 1861.[93] The president's suspension of the writ without Congressional authorization was unconstitutional, Chief Justice Roger Taney had declared, granting a writ of habeas corpus. But Taney's decision was deliberately ignored by Lincoln and quickly mooted by the 1863 act.[94] Within ten months, Secretary of State William H. Seward, who became "notorious for his alleged ability to exceed the king of England in his power to have any citizen arrested simply by ringing a little bell on his desk,"[95] ordered the detention of nearly nine hundred people. Lincoln's hope was that the roundup "would keep them in prison awhile to keep them from killing the Government."[96] By the end of the war, Seward's successors had arrested about thirteen thousand people. Most were detained without charges and then were released after a few months. Military commissions tried more than two thousand cases. Those convicted were sentenced to death or to lengthy prison terms.[97]

One such case was that of Lambdin Milligan, an Indiana resident and leader in the Order of the Sons of Liberty, a group of Confederate sympathizers. In 1864, federal authorities infiltrated the group and learned of a plot to release and arm Confederate prisoners of war from Union prison camps. Rather than try Milligan and his fellow conspirators for treason before a jury of Indiana citizens, federal authorities used a military commission to try, convict, and sentence him to hang. President Andrew Johnson, who succeeded the slain President Lincoln, commuted the sentence to imprisonment, but Milligan sought a writ of habeas corpus. The Supreme Court held Milligan's detention unlawful, reasoning that even though the writ had been validly suspended by the 1863 act, Milligan's detention in Indiana was not authorized by that act. Martial rule, reasoned the Court, "can never be applied to citizens in states which have upheld the authority of the government, and where the courts are open and their process unobstructed."[98]

The decision was widely criticized by Republican supporters, who backed the use of military commissions to combat Southern opposition. An estimated 1,500 or more military commission trials of those accused of violence against blacks, unionists, federal officials, and federal troops took place between 1865 and 1870.[99] Anticipating that the Supreme Court would be more likely than the lower federal courts to find that *Milligan* prohibited the use of military commissions in the South, Congress in 1868 withdrew the Court's appellate jurisdiction over the habeas decisions of the lower federal courts and did not restore it until 1885.[100] And in the 1871 Ku Klux Klan Act, Congress expressly authorized the suspension of the writ until the end of its next regular session, so that President Ulysses Grant could continue to combat the Klan through military commissions and bypass local juries.[101] Grant invoked this suspension authority only once, in nine South Carolina counties during November 1871.

Habeas was called into service again to review the military detention of U.S. citizens during World War II.[102] Following the bombing of Pearl Harbor, with Japanese submarines attacking shipping offshore and a newly minted commission finding that the bombing of Pearl Harbor was facilitated by Japanese spies in Hawaii, fear of imminent Japanese attack on the West Coast gripped the nation. First aliens and then American citizens of Japanese descent were detained without hearings, forced into internment camps, and imprisoned there for, on average, nearly three years. More than 110,000 people, at least half of them U.S. citizens, were forced from their homes and confined in camps.

One of these was Mitsuye Endo, a clerical worker for the California Department of Motor Vehicles who had been raised a Methodist, had a brother serving in the army and had never been to Japan.[103] Her lawyers filed a petition for habeas corpus, arguing that *Milligan* required her release. In *Ex parte Endo*, the Court agreed, concluding that the War Relocation Authority had no statutory authority to detain anyone, like Endo, whose loyalty to the United States had been conceded or otherwise established.[104] The *Endo* decision prompted the termination of the internment program and the immediate release of fifty thousand citizens from detention, while the war was still raging in Europe and the Pacific.[105] At the same time that the Court decided that the executive lacked authority to detain *without conviction* persons like Mitsuye Endo, it also upheld as constitutional, in two now widely condemned decisions, the *convictions* of Japanese Americans for failing to register or comply with curfews.[106]

Meanwhile, in Hawaii, martial law remained in effect, and two civilians convicted and sentenced by military courts for assault and embezzlement—crimes that would have otherwise been handled by state criminal courts—sought and received writs of habeas corpus on the ground that they should have been tried in civilian courts. The Supreme Court agreed, finding that the use of military commissions in Hawaii was unlawful at the time, when no imminent threat required their use. As Chief Justice William Rehnquist later wrote, "an embezzling stockbroker and a brawling shipyard worker in Hawaii could not possibly be dressed up as threats to national security."[107]

The Court has not always asserted the habeas power whenever the president and Congress have sought to deny it during wartime. In July 1942, during "the darkest days of World War II,"[108] the Court in *Ex parte Quirin*[109] distinguished *Milligan* and upheld the secret military trials of eight German submarine saboteurs, including at least one U.S. citizen, who were captured after landing on Long Island. When habeas petitions reached the Court from noncitizens detained by military authorities overseas, the justices refused review.[110] Nor has the president used all of the detention power Congress has offered. After the war, in 1950, Congress authorized the president to combat the communist threat with military detention, by locking up in the vacant World War II internment and prisoner of war camps "persons as to whom there is a reasonable ground to believe that such persons probably will engage in, or conspire to engage in acts of sabotage or espionage." The authority was never used, and the statute was repealed in 1971.[111] The basic pattern, however, remains. During armed conflicts, the risk of military detention and the importance of habeas review escalate in tandem.

War on Terror

The present war on terror has presented new challenges for the federal courts in habeas cases testing military detention of alleged "enemy combatants." Just who is or is not an enemy, and just what would be an end to the "war," are issues difficult to determine. As many have recognized, these uncertainties raise the risk that innocents will be imprisoned, as well as the possibility that detention could last indefinitely.[112]

Although the details of military detention in the war on terror are novel, the primary means used to challenge the constitutionality of that detention is not. Once again, habeas has served as a lever for adjusting the balance of power between the branches. The Suspension Clause alone, however, is too blunt an instrument for the ongoing regulation of something as complex as wartime detention. The Court cannot itself draft legislation that would comply with the clause; it can only declare whether the legislation Congress has written has gone too far. In a series of cases beginning in 2004, the Court has done just that.

This latest showdown between the branches began when the Department of Defense ordered that certain foreign nationals captured abroad after the September 11 attack be detained at hastily erected facilities at the U.S. Naval Base at Guantanamo Bay, Cuba. One of the many reasons for choosing this particular location was to exclude intervention by the federal courts. To determine whether Guantanamo Bay detainees were indeed enemy combatants, the deputy secretary of defense established combatant status review tribunals (CSRTs). Each detainee's CSRT, relying on an administrative record compiled by a military officer to support the government's case for detention,[113] concluded the person was an enemy combatant. Hundreds of those imprisoned filed petitions for writs of habeas corpus in the United States District Court for the District of Columbia.

United States citizen Yasir Hamdi was swept into military custody as well after he had been seized in Afghanistan on the battlefield and confined by the military within the United States. In 2004, the Supreme Court upheld his military detention but in doing so refused to endorse the president's position that the judiciary was limited to reviewing the legality of the detention scheme and could not examine individual cases of detention.[114] On the same day, in a clear rebuke to the executive branch, the Court in *Rasul v. Bush* rejected the government's position that habeas corpus would not apply to noncitizens held at Guantanamo.[115]

In 2005, the district judge before whom most of the Guantanamo habeas cases were consolidated denied the government's motion to dismiss the petitions for failure to state a claim and granted petitioners' counsel access to the unredacted classified factual returns filed by the government in support of detention.[116] While the government appealed those orders, Congress twice amended the habeas statute in an effort to deny the Guantanamo detainees habeas review. Each attempt was rejected by the Supreme Court.

First, Congress passed the Detainee Treatment Act of 2005, which provided that "no court, justice, or judge shall have jurisdiction to . . . consider . . . an application for . . . habeas corpus filed by or on behalf of an alien detained . . . at Guantanamo" and gave the U.S. Court of Appeals for the D.C. Circuit "exclusive" jurisdiction to review CSRT decisions.[117] The Supreme Court quickly accepted a habeas case that challenged the act. In *Hamdan v. Rumsfeld* it held that the provision depriving courts of jurisdiction over the detainees' habeas petitions did not apply to cases already pending when it was enacted. This gave a green light to the habeas cases already pending in the lower courts, and it allowed the Court to reach the merits of the case before it. The petition had been filed by Salim Hamdan, Osama bin Laden's driver. The Court found that the closed proceedings and secret evidence permitted by the military commission rules deviated from the procedural guarantees provided in regular courts and courts martial. Because the president had failed to adequately justify why these departures were necessary, as required by both the Uniform Code of Military Justice and the Geneva Convention, the Court held that the commissions were illegal.[118]

Undaunted by the Court's ruling in *Hamdan*, Congress tried again to bypass habeas, enacting the Military Commissions Act (MCA) of 2006. The MCA barred habeas review of claims by Guantanamo detainees held as enemy combatants and allowed such detainees a limited ability to challenge their designation as an enemy combatant in one court only, the U.S. Court of Appeals for the D.C. Circuit.[119] When attorneys for

Lakhdar Boumediene asked the Supreme Court to declare whether this procedure amounted to a suspension of the writ, the Court agreed to review the case.

The personal story of Lakhdar Boumediene was recounted in chapter 1. As a legal matter, the *Boumediene* decision was historic. It struck down the military detention scheme, declaring that the jurisdiction-stripping provision of the MCA was an unconstitutional suspension of the writ. The Court specifically focused on the role of the writ in preserving the balance of powers among the branches of the federal government. It emphasized that among freedom's first principles

> are freedom from arbitrary and unlawful restraint and the personal liberty that is secured by adherence to the separation of powers. It is from these principles that the judicial authority to consider petitions for habeas corpus relief derives. . . . Within the Constitution's separation-of-powers structure, few exercises of judicial power are as legitimate or as necessary as the responsibility to hear challenges to the authority of the Executive to imprison a person.

The Court explained that "[t]he separation-of-powers doctrine, and the history that influenced its design . . . must inform the reach and purpose of the Suspension Clause."[120]

The *Boumediene* Court concluded that the truncated judicial review process that Congress had provided was an inadequate substitute for habeas review. Congress had failed to provide petitioners with the opportunity to challenge the president's detention authority, to contest the CSRT's findings of fact, or to introduce exculpatory evidence discovered after the CSRT proceedings, all features that the Court found to be part of the minimum level of alternative judicial review required in order to satisfy the Suspension Clause, given the risk of error in CSRT findings. The case left unanswered many other questions, among them whether federal courts must entertain similar claims from aliens held in other U.S. detention facilities overseas; what procedures are required by the Constitution in various military detention proceedings; what procedures are required in habeas cases reviewing detainee claims when classified information is at stake; whether orders releasing prisoners from Guantanamo can mandate that they be released within United States borders;[121] and what impact the Court's analysis of the Suspension Clause may have on Congressional efforts to limit habeas review for civilian prisoners serving criminal sentences. We will take up this last issue in chapter 5; the other issues remain the subject of ongoing litigation.[122]

After the *Boumediene* decision, the lower courts have continued to review individual habeas petitions filed by those taken into military custody after September 11. In July 2008, the Fourth Circuit granted relief to Ali Saleh Kahlah al-Marri, who had been held as an enemy combatant in the Navy brig at Charleston for six years. The court concluded that, even crediting the government's allegations that "al-Marri, like Milligan, is a dangerous enemy of this nation who has committed serious crimes and associated with a secret terrorist organization that has engaged in hostilities against us," al-Marri had "not been afforded sufficient process" to challenge his designation as an enemy combatant. Shortly after the Supreme Court accepted the Bush administration's petition to review al-Marri's case, the political winds shifted. The new Democratic administration of President Barack Obama, which swept into office on a platform that included closing the Guantanamo prison, decided not to contest the Fourth Circuit's decision. The case was dismissed after al-Marri was charged with providing and conspiring to provide material support to al-Qaeda and was transferred to civilian custody. He subsequently pleaded guilty.[123]

In the D.C. District Court, where some 250 habeas cases had been filed on behalf of Guantanamo detainees, judges held hearings constantly for weeks on end, just as Judges Shoob and Hoffman had decades earlier when hearing the cases of Cuban and Chinese detainees. And just as those habeas petitions of long ago eclipsed other cases—by, for example, shutting down access to regular trials for months—some judges put off all civil trials until spring 2010 in order to resolve the Guantanamo habeas cases.[124] By mid-2010 these judges had ordered the release of thirty-seven petitioners, including Boumediene.[125] Others have been denied release, when the government proved, to the satisfaction of the habeas court, that they had joined or supported al-Qaeda and thus were lawfully detained. More than one hundred petitioners' habeas cases were dismissed as moot once the government released them or transferred them to the custody of other nations.[126]

As for Salim Hamdan, whose case first paved the way for so many others to seek habeas relief, he was tried under revised military commission procedures in August 2008 and convicted of providing material support for terrorism. The commission, recognizing Hamdan's minor role, surprised defense officials by imposing a sixty-six-month sentence that gave Hamdan credit for the more than five years he had already spent at Guantanamo Bay.[127] After years of imprisonment as a person supposedly too dangerous to remain at large, he was released and returned to Yemen, his home country.[128]

Of the more than 770 detainees who were confined at some point at Guantanamo, more than 550 have been released without formal charges or trial. As this book went to press, 180 remain in detention, twenty have been formally charged, four have been convicted by military commission, and one is facing criminal charges in federal court in New York City. Six died in custody.[129] The Obama administration is continuing its attempts to release detainees to willing host countries outside the United States. Those not released will be prosecuted in federal court, tried by military commissions, or detained elsewhere. Habeas will continue to play an important role in this ongoing controversy until all of the Guantanamo detainees have had their legal status properly resolved.

Military detention has created, and will continue to create, constitutional showdowns like the one over the Guantanamo detainees, played out in habeas cases before the Supreme Court. These cases are inevitably controversial, forcing the Court to balance individual liberty against infringements on liberty that may be necessary for government's self-preservation. Reasonable people will disagree about what the Court should do. And each time, after the Court rules, the political branches will respond by taking additional steps designed to protect American lives—usually in compliance with the Court's commands, but occasionally in contravention of them, as with President Lincoln's actions during the Civil War. Seen in historical context, the tug-of-war between the political branches and the Court over habeas review of military detentions during the war on terror is just the latest iteration of a conflict that the Framers clearly anticipated.

*   *   *

Whenever government authority comes under attack, locking up the suspected attackers is an inevitable response. It is inevitable, as history shows, because swift incarceration can effectively silence and paralyze opposition, whether the threat is posed by citizens armed with dangerous plans or by alien invaders armed with bombs. When such threats appear imminent, due process can seem impossibly burdensome and idealistic, so political leaders often will turn to detention without conviction to fill the void. And the menu of legal options for locking up those seen as dangerous continues to grow. For example, several commentators recently have proposed, and President Obama has suggested, that instead of the military or criminal paradigm, a new system of long-term regulatory detention of those individuals found to pose a risk of terrorism should be created.[130] If and when these new detention programs take shape, the writ of habeas corpus will help ensure that they conform with the rule of law.

Habeas corpus, an obscure remedy developed by medieval courts, performs its most vital role in checking detention without conviction. Whenever a political or social crisis focuses the nation's fears and hostilities on certain individuals or members of a certain group, and whenever those targeted persons are imprisoned without access to a criminal trial, our nation turns to habeas. For each new detention scheme, habeas review enables the judiciary to preserve individual liberty until other alternatives for judicial review are developed. And when Congress and the executive attempt to circumvent judicial scrutiny, habeas, protected by the Suspension Clause, helps to restore the balance of powers on which our divided government rests.[131] The Great Writ has played this starring role in preserving our democracy for more than two centuries and should continue to do so in the future.

CHAPTER THREE

The History of Habeas Review of State Criminal Cases

The value of habeas corpus is greatest when an individual has been taken into custody with no access to any court or with access so limited as to be totally inadequate. This was the bleak situation facing Chinese immigrants in the 1880s and accused enemy combatants confined at Guantanamo Bay over a century later. When habeas is invoked to allow a judge to ensure that a detainee not serving a criminal sentence is being held lawfully, the writ protects not only the constitutional rights of the individual but also the carefully established balance of government powers that helps to guarantee liberty for all.

Yet arbitrary imprisonments are not necessarily limited to those that occur outside the criminal justice system. As Alexander Hamilton noted in *The Federalist*, judges administering the criminal law also can overstep the Constitution:

> Arbitrary impeachments, arbitrary methods of prosecuting pretended offenses, and arbitrary punishments upon arbitrary convictions, have ever appeared to me to be the great engines of judicial despotism; and these have all relation to criminal proceedings. The trial by jury in criminal cases, aided by the *habeas corpus* act, seems therefore to be alone concerned in the question.[1]

In the next several chapters, we turn to the use of habeas corpus to review criminal convictions and sentences. By far the most common version of habeas corpus encountered in the federal courts today is the review of state criminal cases, pursuant to 28 U.S.C. § 2254, for the purpose of ensuring state court compliance with federal constitutional standards of criminal procedure. This particular use of habeas corpus has grown dramatically since the early 1940s, when federal judges encountered on average only one habeas petition from a state prisoner in every three hundred civil cases filed. In the year 2000, state prisoners seeking habeas relief filed one of every twelve civil actions in federal district courts, and today in some districts the proportion is even higher.[2]

This chapter outlines the evolution of federal habeas review of state criminal cases. Those familiar with this history will recognize its essential chronology—the limited role that habeas review played in the late nineteenth century, its expansion by the Warren Court during the 1950s and 1960s, and the subsequent retrenchment efforts of the Burger and Rehnquist Courts and Congress. What is most important about this historical account, however, is how closely the story mirrors the one recounted in chapter 2. For detentions outside of the criminal justice process, the federal courts historically have used their habeas authority as a temporary means to address periodic disruptions in the balance of power within the federal government. For state-convicted prisoners, the federal courts have used habeas in a similar way, expanding habeas review as a response to disturbances in the balance of power. In this context, however, the power struggle has been between the federal and state governments.

In the chapters that follow, we explore the implications of this basic understanding of the role of habeas. In chapter 4, we present the findings of a pathbreaking empirical study of federal habeas review of state criminal cases today.[3] The study reveals that, with the exception of cases in which the defendant is sentenced to death, these petitions almost never succeed. We explain how the ridiculously low success rate of noncapital habeas petitioners today is linked with the dramatic expansion of state judicial review of federal claims between the 1960s and the 1980s—a structural change that habeas review actually helped to bring about. In light of the study findings, we conclude—contrary to the conventional account—that habeas review cannot serve as an effective means of correcting or deterring error in individual state criminal cases. In chapter 5, we trace the significant changes that have occurred in state criminal justice over the past half-century and argue that the enormous and wasteful consumption of resources now devoted to habeas review of noncapital cases can no longer be justified. The particular federalism crisis that led the federal courts in the mid-twentieth century to expand habeas review of state criminal cases has now passed, and the habeas remedy must be reshaped to meet the needs of today.

Expanding the Habeas Remedy for State and Federal Prisoners under the 1867 Act

Despite Hamilton's concern in *The Federalist*, early in our nation's history the writ of habeas corpus was generally unavailable to a person who had been found guilty in a criminal proceeding and was serving a criminal sentence. As outlined in chapter 1, Congress first granted broad authority to federal courts to use the writ of habeas corpus to review the constitutionality of both state and federal convictions and sentences in the Habeas Corpus Act of 1867.[4]

The 1867 act had its origins in the battle of federalism that raged during the Reconstruction era. The ongoing political and social crisis, although no longer manifested in a shooting war, continued to deeply divide the nation. Congress hoped that federal judicial review would protect federal Reconstruction officials and their families from persecution by unrepentant state officials—including state judges—who refused to shift their loyalties from the defeated Confederacy to the ideals of equality and due process as expressed in the newly enacted Thirteenth Amendment and recently proposed Fourteenth and Fifteenth Amendments to the federal Constitution. The 1867 act also protected the recently emancipated slaves from suffering a similar fate.[5]

In this sense, the 1867 act served what we have identified as the core purpose of habeas: it expanded the availability of the writ in response to a major political and social crisis that created a serious risk of abuse of the government's power to detain. In 1867, the nature of the particular crisis, including the people targeted for detention, differed from other crises to which the writ had previously responded. The threatened imbalance was not among the branches of the federal government but between the federal and state governments. And the people whose liberty was jeopardized were the freed slaves, only recently granted federal citizenship, as well as the federal officials who sought to help and protect them. But the fundamental structural problem—overreaching by the government at the expense of individual freedom—was exactly the same.

Federalism, as contemplated by the Framers and implemented in the Constitution, is one of the most enduring and valuable features of the

American system of government. The genius of James Madison recognized that, paradoxically, individual liberty will be more secure when there are two sovereign governments, each pitted against the other in a perpetual struggle for power, than when there is only one.[6] The Constitution thus divided sovereign power, granting to the new federal government only that authority enumerated in the Constitution itself and leaving everything else to the states. The Framers achieved a new nation in which each level of government, state and national, would be sovereign within its own sphere of authority.[7]

Ever since the Framing, this balance between state and federal power has been in constant motion. During several crucial periods in American history, when problems arose that seemed too great for the states to solve, the federal government has been allowed to claim additional powers—powers eventually authorized by expanded judicial interpretations of the constitutional text.[8] These expansions have produced a federal government that is immensely more powerful today than the Framers probably would ever have imagined. During other periods, however, the president or Congress has been willing to reverse this general trend and voluntarily relinquish certain powers back to the states from whence they came.[9] And the U.S. Supreme Court also has at times opted to read more narrowly some of its prior expansive constitutional rulings, thereby reviving state powers.[10]

Throughout the periods of expansion and contraction of federal power one element of federalism has always remained constant, however: the supremacy of the federal Constitution, as interpreted and applied ultimately by the U.S. Supreme Court.[11] Notwithstanding the never ending tug-of-war that is American-style federalism, it is the Supreme Court that has the last word on any disputed question concerning the constitutional scope of federal power. Once the Court has spoken on a question of federal law, the states must obey.

The 1867 act was intended to allow the federal courts to enforce the supremacy of federal law against potentially recalcitrant Southern states and state officials. But, ironically, one of the very first invocations of the 1867 act was by a southerner and former Confederate soldier, James McCardle, who had been imprisoned by federal authorities under the Military Reconstruction Act of 1867 after he published "incendiary" newspaper articles advocating resistance to the federal government. The U.S. District Court for the Southern District of Mississippi ruled that McCardle's imprisonment was legal, but Congress feared that the U.S.

Supreme Court—perhaps viewing the more radical aspects of Reconstruction as an overstepping of constitutional bounds—might reverse the district court's decision. So, in 1868, shortly before the Court could rule, Congress stripped it of jurisdiction to hear all appeals in habeas corpus cases, thereby ensuring that it could not overturn the interpretation and enforcement of federal law by the lower federal courts sitting in habeas.[12]

The *McCardle* saga was a reminder that, notwithstanding the centrality of habeas corpus to maintaining the balance of powers, and the corresponding need for the judiciary to retain primary control over the scope of habeas, Congress retains the power to define and change many of the particulars of habeas litigation. Congress's constitutional authority to define the Court's appellate jurisdiction, as it did in *McCardle*, and to legislate many other changes to habeas as well, so long as these changes do not represent a suspension of the writ, is generally acknowledged. In the litigation over whether the 1868 act eliminated the Court's jurisdiction over McCardle's appeal, the Suspension Clause was not even raised, presumably because the writ remained available to prisoners in the lower federal courts. In addition, as the Supreme Court made clear only a few months later in *Ex parte Yerger*, the Court also retained its so-called original writ jurisdiction and could grant relief in a habeas action filed directly with the Court.[13]

The Supreme Court's jurisdiction over appeals from habeas corpus cases was finally restored in 1885.[14] By then, Congress was ready to rein in lower federal court judges whom it had come to view as meddling inappropriately in the administration of criminal justice by the states.[15] Congress saw the Court as a mediating influence capable of limiting the overeager use of habeas by the lower courts. Indeed, in its first decision under the newly restored appellate jurisdiction, the Court imposed a limit on habeas review of state criminal judgments that exists to the present day—the requirement that a habeas petitioner generally must exhaust available state remedies before turning to the habeas courts for relief.[16]

In the earliest decades of the twentieth century, federal habeas review of state criminal cases remained relatively limited in practice. The federal courts continued to follow the traditional rules that habeas courts should neither allow the introduction of new evidence or testimony contrary to the record in support of a habeas petition[17] nor overturn a facially valid criminal conviction entered by a court with proper jurisdiction. Both rules would be transformed, gradually, over a period of forty years.

In 1915 the Supreme Court first acknowledged the possibility that a convicted prisoner seeking habeas relief could not only supplement but also contradict the record of proceedings underlying his detention. In a habeas petition challenging his Georgia conviction for the rape and murder of a thirteen-year-old girl,[18] Leo Frank claimed that his state court trial had been dominated by an anti-Semitic mob and that he had not waived his right to be present when the verdict was delivered.[19] The Court refused to issue the writ but in the course of doing so stated that a prisoner seeking habeas relief was entitled to a "judicial inquiry in a court of the United States into the very truth and substance of the causes of his detention, although it may become necessary to *look behind and beyond the record* of his conviction to a sufficient extent to test the jurisdiction of the state court to proceed to judgment against him."[20] By 1923, the Court wrote, "[I]t does not seem to us sufficient to allow a Judge of the United States to escape the duty of examining the facts for himself when if true as alleged they make the trial absolutely void."[21] And by 1938, the Court stated that although a judgment collaterally attacked in habeas carries a "presumption of regularity," if the petitioner "convinces the court by a preponderance of evidence" that the alleged deprivation of due process occurred, "it is the duty of the court to grant the writ."[22]

During the same period, the Court not only expanded the authority of habeas courts to question factual findings but also transformed the scope of error considered serious enough to deprive a state court of proper jurisdiction and warrant habeas review. A similar expansion had begun in habeas cases arising from federal criminal convictions during the late 1800s[23] but was slower to develop in the context of federal review of state criminal cases. This was largely a political matter. As Reconstruction gradually gave way to a period of greater solicitude for state sovereignty, the federal courts reverted to their historic reluctance to intrude in the affairs of the states. This reluctance was particularly strong in the area of criminal justice, which was one of the areas of sovereign power explicitly identified by the Framers as belonging to the states.[24]

The Supreme Court nevertheless edged toward broader habeas review of state convictions beginning in the *Frank* case in 1915, where the Court stated in dicta that it would violate due process if a trial were to be so dominated by a mob that a "jury is intimidated and the trial judge yields."[25] Eight years later, in *Moore v. Dempsey,* an appalling example of the abuse many black defendants suffered in Southern courts, the Court held that federal courts had the power to grant relief from a state conviction resulting from mob violence,[26] and in 1935 in *Mooney v. Holohan*, the Court announced that a prisoner convicted on the basis of perjured testimony would deserve habeas relief.[27] By 1942, the Court declared that " . . . the use of the writ . . . is not restricted to those cases where the judgment of conviction is void for want of jurisdiction. . . . It extends also to those exceptional cases where the conviction has been in disregard of the constitutional rights of the accused, and where the writ is the only effective means of preserving his rights."[28]

It would be decades before the Warren Court would discard the jurisdictional limitation entirely and allow prisoners to seek habeas relief for all constitutional errors in state and federal prosecutions whether or not those claims could have been raised on appeal. But by 1942, the Court had already expanded the scope of "jurisdictional error" well beyond its former meaning, extending habeas review to several additional constitutional errors and to claims not reviewable on appeal. Habeas review had become a means for explaining and enforcing constitutionally guaranteed rights of criminal procedure, in both federal and state cases.

By the 1940s, this shift contributed to a marked increase in the number of habeas petitions filed by both state and federal prisoners. It is at this point in our chronology that the story of habeas review for convicted prisoners divides into two separate paths, one for federal prisoners and the other for state prisoners. In 1948, responding to the increase in habeas filings and the concomitant burden on federal courts, Congress split habeas review of criminal cases into two separate federal statutes. For federal prisoners, Congress enacted a substitute for habeas, 28 U.S.C. § 2255, that allowed collateral review of federal convictions and sentences to proceed in a more efficient manner. For state prisoners, Congress preserved traditional habeas review as authorized by the 1867 act, but enacted a new statute, 28 U.S.C. § 2254, that introduced revised rules of habeas procedure. The remainder of this chapter traces the post-1948 development of habeas review under Section 2254 for prisoners serving state sentences. We will pick up the story for federal prisoners in chapter 6.

The Warren Court and the Expansion of Federal Habeas

In 1948, habeas review of state criminal cases, although described as a "flood" at the time,[29] was a relatively minor source of federal litigation.[30]

Within less than two decades, however, everything changed. During the Warren Court era, habeas became a crucial federal weapon in a new war of federalism. The dramatic expansion of habeas during the Warren Court years transformed the writ from an extraordinary remedy, invoked only in exceptional cases, into a routine component of the day-to-day criminal justice process.

The Warren Court's transformation of habeas corpus was deeply interwoven with the Court's extension to state criminal defendants of most of the constitutional protections already enjoyed by federal defendants under the Bill of Rights. From the late 1930s through the 1950s, the Court gradually became convinced that criminal "justice" was woefully lacking in many communities. Treatment of poor and minority defendants that would be considered appalling and illegal under federal standards was standard practice in many state courts. Police obtained confessions through brutality, sleep deprivation, drugs, and threats, confident that state courts would admit such statements as evidence. State courts refused to provide attorneys to defendants who could not afford them and denied defendants access to jury trials. State courts excluded nonwhites and women from juries, tolerated trials tainted by extreme prejudicial publicity, and failed to remedy prosecutors' use of perjured testimony.

Over time, the Supreme Court began to regulate such offensive practices by finding that they violated the Fourteenth Amendment, which prohibits the states from depriving any person of "life, liberty, or property without due process of law."[31] Building upon similar changes that it had already made in the scope and meaning of "due process" as applied to federal criminal cases under the Fifth Amendment, the Supreme Court construed the Fourteenth Amendment to place the same kinds of constitutional limits on the administration of criminal justice in the states.

By the 1960s, the so-called Warren Court Revolution in criminal procedure was in full force, producing such famous cases as *Gideon v. Wainwright*, which established the right of an indigent criminal defendant charged with a state felony to receive appointed defense counsel at state expense;[32] *Mapp v. Ohio*, which required the exclusion from a state criminal trial of evidence seized in violation of the Fourth Amendment;[33] and *Miranda v. Arizona*, which mandated the delivery of the now-familiar set of warnings before a state or local police officer could conduct a custodial interrogation of a suspect.[34]

These decisions, and many more, predictably provoked consternation, frustration, and even outrage on the part of many state officials, who perceived them as impermissible federal intrusions into a traditional state function. Calls were heard to "Impeach Earl Warren," on the basis of both these criminal procedure cases and the many equally controversial Supreme Court decisions dealing with civil rights issues.[35] The new federal constitutional rules of criminal procedure were resisted, either covertly or with open defiance, by many police, prosecutors, and state judges.[36]

At the very dawn of the Warren Court Revolution, Justice William Brennan—one of the revolutionary leaders on the Court—foresaw that the Court's new initiative would generate resistance. Brennan recognized that the Court was about to become embroiled in a new war of federalism with state governments and that the Court lacked both the time and the resources to police the states effectively and thereby ensure their compliance with its new (but often highly controversial) constitutional rules of criminal procedure.[37] Under Brennan's leadership, therefore, the Court armed the lower federal courts with expanded habeas corpus jurisdiction, essentially deputizing them to assist in the enforcement effort.

The expansion of federal habeas corpus took place primarily through four landmark decisions. The first was handed down in 1953, only five years after the two new habeas statutes went into effect. In *Brown v. Allen*,[38] the Supreme Court addressed the issue of whether a federal habeas court should be required to treat the prior adjudication of a federal constitutional issue by a state court as res judicata, precluding reconsideration of the same issue by the habeas court. In the collateral review of federal criminal cases under Section 2255, the answer to this question would be clear: the reviewing court generally would be prohibited from revisiting a prior decision on the merits. After all, why should one federal judge second-guess another? But in *Brown*, the Supreme Court reached a different conclusion with respect to habeas review under Section 2254. It held that whenever a state prisoner files a federal habeas corpus petition raising a claim that was previously denied on the merits by the state court, the habeas court is not bound by the state court decision. State court decisions on the merits should be treated as persuasive but not binding authority.

The fulfillment of the Warren Court's expansion of habeas corpus review of state convictions occurred in the spring of 1963, when the Court issued its famous "trilogy" of habeas decisions: *Townsend v. Sain*,[39] *Sanders v. United States*,[40] and *Fay v. Noia*.[41] *Townsend* involved the question of when, if ever, a federal habeas court must grant an evidentiary hearing to determine facts disputed by a habeas petition, instead of merely relying on the state court's prior determination of those facts. The Supreme Court in *Townsend* held that the federal habeas court must grant an evidentiary hearing if (1) the merits of the factual dispute were not, in fact, resolved in the state court; (2) the state court's factual determination is not fairly supported by the record as a whole; (3) the procedures followed in the state court did not constitute a "full and fair hearing" on the disputed factual issue; (4) there is newly discovered evidence; (5) the facts were not adequately developed in the state court; or (6) for any other reason, the state court did not provide the petitioner with a "full and fair fact hearing."

Sanders was actually a Section 2255 case involving a federal prisoner, although as in many such situations the Court applied the same rule to Section 2254 habeas corpus cases. The case dealt with the validity of a claim raised in a second or subsequent petition for collateral review. According to the Court in *Sanders*, federal courts must review claims in repeat petitions unless (1) the claim is identical to one that was already denied in connection with a previous petition, (2) the previous denial of the same claim was on merits, and (3) the "ends of justice" would not be served by reaching the merits of the claim in connection with the subsequent petition.

Both *Townsend* and *Sanders* were groundbreaking expansions of federal court power over state courts. But it was in *Fay v. Noia* that federal review of state cases received its most significant boost, in both legal and rhetorical terms. The issue in *Fay v. Noia* was one that had been a major concern of Justice Brennan for several years: should a person who has been convicted of a crime in state court but who asserts that his conviction was obtained in violation of his federal constitutional rights be precluded from litigating that federal claim in habeas because of his defense lawyer's previous failure to comply with a state procedural rule requiring the constitutional claim to be raised in state court in a certain way? In other words, if a state court refused to review a claim because of the defendant's failure to raise that claim properly under state procedural law—a situation known as "state procedural default"—should the federal courts be barred from considering that claim as well? Many had assumed the answer was yes, reasoning that such a state procedural default meant that the state court's decision was based on state law, not federal law, and that as a result there was no federal legal issue for the federal courts to review.

This topic had been the subject of a speech delivered by Justice Brennan at the University of Utah in 1961.[42] At that time, Brennan criticized state courts for failing to provide meaningful remedies to prisoners who had valid constitutional claims. According to Justice Brennan, the failure was twofold. Many states did not offer effective judicial review for convicted defendants whose direct appeals had been concluded, meaning that such prisoners had no meaningful opportunity to obtain relief from state courts for violations of new federal rights, such as the *Gideon* right to counsel, that were retroactively applicable. And even where modern and effective postconviction proceedings existed, the state courts often refused to review violations of federal rights if the defendant failed to comply with state procedural rules for raising that claim at prior stages of the litigation—even if the procedural misstep was not voluntary or was the fault of the defense lawyer and not the defendant himself.

In *Fay v. Noia*, for example, the state had convicted Noia and his co-defendants of murder even though little evidence tied any of them to the crime except for their individual confessions. These confessions were coerced; each defendant had been interrogated without rest, incommunicado, for over twenty-seven hours by relays of detectives using deceptive techniques, including practices the federal court of appeals had termed "satanic." Noia's codefendants had challenged their convictions on appeal and were eventually freed. Noia, however, had not appealed, fearful that a retrial might lead to a death sentence. By the time he decided to challenge his conviction in state court under the only postconviction review process still available to him, it was too late. The state court held that state procedural law did not permit postconviction review of a claim that could have been, but was not, raised on direct appeal.

When Noia sought habeas relief in federal court, the state argued that there was no federal law issue to decide because the state court's refusal to review the merits of Noia's claim was based on his violation of state procedural law. The Supreme Court disagreed, concluding that such a state procedural default generally should not bar federal habeas review and relief. The Court held that federal habeas courts possess the discretion to reach the merits of federal claims that state courts choose under state law not to review. The only situation in which the habeas court might decline to exercise such discretion is where the prisoner himself knowingly and voluntarily made the choice to avoid raising the federal claim in state court. Because Noia would have run "a substantial risk of electrocution" by raising his claim on appeal, the Court found that his refusal "to play Russian roulette in this fashion" was not "a deliberate circumvention of state procedures." The Court's narrow definition of the so-called deliberate bypass situation ensured that, as a practical matter, virtually all defaults would be overlooked. The decision obliterated one of the states' most potent barriers to federal judicial review of state convictions.

In rhetorical terms, Justice Brennan's opinion for the Court in *Fay v. Noia* contains one of the Court's most eloquent odes to habeas corpus. The language in the opinion soars. A brief excerpt (with quote marks omitted) will suffice to convey the overall content and tone:

> We do well to bear in mind the extraordinary prestige of the Great Writ, *habeas corpus ad subjiciendum*, in Anglo-American jurisprudence: the most celebrated writ in the English law. . . . It is a writ antecedent to statute, and throwing its root deep into the genius of our common law. . . . It is perhaps the most important writ known to the constitutional law of England, affording as it does a swift and imperative remedy in all cases of illegal restraint or confinement. It is of immemorial antiquity. . . . We repeat what has been so truly said of the federal writ: there is no higher duty than to maintain it unimpaired . . . and unsuspended, save only in the cases specified in our Constitution.
>
> These are not extravagant expressions. Behind them may be discerned the unceasing contest between personal liberty and government oppression. It is no accident that habeas corpus has time and again played a central role in national crises, wherein the claims of order and of liberty clash most acutely. . . . Although in form the Great Writ is simply a mode of procedure, its history is inextricably intertwined with the growth of fundamental rights of personal liberty. For its function has been to provide a prompt and efficacious remedy for whatever society deems to be intolerable restraints. Its root principle is that in a civilized society, government must always be accountable to the judiciary for a man's imprisonment: if the imprisonment cannot be shown to conform with the fundamental requirements of law, the individual is entitled to his immediate release.[43]

Brennan's majority opinion concludes with the emphatic statement, "Habeas corpus is one of the precious heritages of Anglo-American civilization. We do no more today than confirm its continuing efficacy."[44]

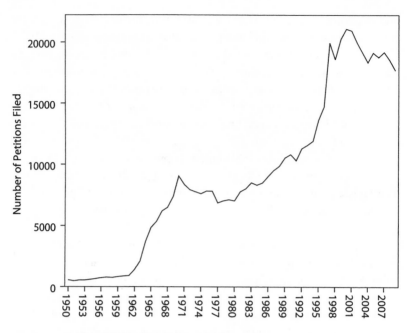

FIGURE 3.1. Petitions Filed by State Prisoners, 1950–2009

As a result of the decisions in *Brown v. Allen* and the "trilogy" cases, federal habeas corpus was transformed into a potent weapon in the hands of the lower federal courts. Sitting in habeas, federal judges could in theory review, and reverse, almost any state judicial decision that either failed or refused to enforce the Warren Court's new constitutional pronouncements in the realm of criminal procedure law.[45] Moreover, the expansion of habeas review and the dramatic rise in the number of petitions filed between 1962 and 1970 (see fig. 3.1) gave the lower federal courts the opportunity to make their own legal pronouncements about the scope and application of federal constitutional rights in state criminal cases. These lower court rulings further contributed to the Warren Court Revolution in criminal procedure and helped to inform the Supreme Court's final resolution of these same issues.[46] Just as they had during Reconstruction, the federal courts during the civil rights era used habeas corpus to make sure that the state courts complied with dramatic changes in the scope and content of federal constitutional rights.

Justice Rehnquist, the Antiterrorism and Effective Death Penalty Act of 1996, and the Decline of Federal Habeas

In the 1960s, Justice Brennan emerged as the Supreme Court's leading champion of expansive federal habeas corpus review of individual state criminal cases. Brennan's view of federal habeas, as expressed in *Fay v. Noia*, was unabashedly romantic: habeas, according to Brennan, should provide the federal courts with the broad and unconstrained authority to intervene, on a case-by-case basis, in state criminal cases to ensure that no individual defendant is ever denied a right guaranteed to him by the federal constitution.

Justice Brennan's archnemesis, consistently and forcefully advocating the traditional prerogative of the states to run their own criminal justice systems free from federal interference, was Justice (later Chief Justice) William Rehnquist. Rehnquist joined the Supreme Court in 1972, after a stint in the U.S. Justice Department during which he once wrote a memo bemoaning the broadening of federal habeas corpus.[47] Within a few years, he left his mark on the Court's habeas doctrine.

In 1977, Rehnquist authored the majority opinion in *Wainwright v. Sykes*.[48] Sykes's defense lawyer had failed to object at trial to the admission of incriminating statements that Sykes had made to the police. Sykes was convicted of murder, and on direct appeal, his lawyer again failed to challenge the admissibility of his statements. Sykes himself then sought to raise such a claim, based on alleged *Miranda* violations, in a federal habeas petition. The question before the Supreme Court in *Sykes* was whether the petitioner's prior failures to assert his federal claim in state court should bar him from obtaining relief in federal habeas.

Rehnquist's majority opinion opened with a review of the history of federal habeas, mostly for the purpose of "illustrat[ing] this Court's historic willingness to overturn or modify its earlier views of the scope of the writ, even where the statutory language authorizing judicial action has remained unchanged."[49] Having thus "explained" why stare decisis would not bind the Court, Rehnquist went directly after Brennan's *Fay v. Noia* position:

> [I]t is a well-established principle of federalism that a state decision resting on an adequate foundation of state substantive law is immune from review in the federal courts. . . . The area of controversy . . . has concerned the review-

ability of federal claims which the state court has declined to pass on because
not presented in the manner prescribed by its procedural rules. . . . [50]

Rehnquist cited two recent Supreme Court cases in which the petitioners had failed to complain about alleged grand jury discrimination before trial, in violation of applicable court rules, and then tried to litigate
the issue in federal habeas.[51] The Court held these claims to be procedurally defaulted and thus barred from federal habeas review, unless the
petitioners could show cause (a sufficient excuse) for and prejudice (resulting harm) from their failure to raise the claim in accordance with
state rules. In *Sykes*, the Court tackled the issue of whether this two-part
requirement—clearly inconsistent with the deliberate-bypass test of *Fay
v. Noia*—should also apply to the waiver of an alleged *Miranda* violation
by failure to make a contemporaneous objection at trial. Rehnquist's answer was a resounding yes:

> The contemporaneous-objection rule . . . deserves greater respect than *Fay*
> gives it, both for the fact that it is employed by a coordinate jurisdiction
> within the federal system and for the many interests which it serves in its own
> right. . . . We believe the adoption of the . . . rule in this situation will have the
> salutary effect of making the state trial on the merits the "main event," so to
> speak, rather than a "tryout on the road" for what will later be the determina-
> tive federal habeas hearing.[52]

Without attempting to define the precise contours of the cause-and-
prejudice exception to the procedural default bar, Rehnquist concluded
that petitioner Sykes—who offered "no explanation whatever" for his failure to object at trial and who was proven guilty by substantial evidence
other than his challenged statement—could not possibly meet the test.[53]

Sykes proved to be a formidable barrier to federal review. The Court
soon held that a petitioner could establish cause sufficient to excuse default only by showing (1) that the claim not raised was too "novel" to
recognize earlier,[54] (2) that the state concealed the evidence needed to
raise the claim,[55] or (3) that his attorney's mistake in failing to raise the
claim at trial or on appeal was so egregious that he was deprived of his
constitutional right to the effective assistance of counsel.[56] And the second requirement—prejudice—was held to mean that there was a "substantial likelihood" that he would not have been convicted or sentenced
as severely had the constitutional error not occurred.[57] Petitioners un-

able to meet both of these demanding standards, including those petitioners whose attorneys' mistakes fell short of constitutional ineffectiveness, were simply out of luck. The only exception at that time, and still today, was the case in which the petitioner could demonstrate a "fundamental miscarriage of justice" by proving that it was more likely than not that he was innocent of the crime and that he was convicted as a result of the alleged constitutional violation.[58]

Whereas *Fay v. Noia* contained Brennan's most eloquent, heartfelt, and rhapsodic endorsement of federal habeas corpus as a case-by-case remedy for the deprivation of federal constitutional rights, *Wainwright v. Sykes* represented Rehnquist's vigorous counterattack on behalf of states' rights federalism. Today, *Fay v. Noia* is long dead,[59] while *Sykes* lives on as a key limitation of federal habeas relief for state prisoners.

In addition to dismantling *Fay v. Noia*, Rehnquist's majority opinion in *Sykes* set the stage for additional assaults on Brennan's broad vision of federal habeas corpus. Rehnquist laid out two key conceptual issues, in addition to the "state procedural default" problem, that he saw as central to defining the proper scope of federal habeas: what types of federal claims may a habeas court properly consider? And, even assuming that a federal claim is cognizable by a habeas court, to what extent must that court defer to a resolution of the claim in prior state proceedings?[60] Rehnquist's majority opinion left little doubt as to where he stood on these two issues. Influenced by a strong states' rights view of federalism, Rehnquist's answers—albeit in dicta—were straightforward: (1) federal habeas should be available only for the most fundamental constitutional claims; and (2) habeas courts generally should defer to prior state court adjudications of federal claims.

Over time, the issue of the substantive scope of federal habeas corpus would be the subject of several Supreme Court opinions. As a general matter, Rehnquist's view—that habeas should be limited to certain fundamental claims—did not prevail. The lone exception, in which the Court decided to limit the substantive scope of habeas review, was *Stone v. Powell*.[61] There the Court held that Fourth Amendment claims of allegedly unconstitutional searches or seizures generally should not be cognizable in habeas, because the deterrent effect on state officials of habeas reversals is insufficient to justify the release of factually guilty prisoners. No other constitutional claims have been barred in habeas.[62]

On the other hand, Rehnquist's view that federal habeas corpus courts should defer to the prior resolution of federal claims in the state courts ultimately was partially vindicated. First, the Court in 1989 held in *Teague v. Lane*[63] that, with only rare exceptions, federal courts cannot disturb state decisions that fail to anticipate new rules not yet dictated by federal precedent. This meant that state courts could construe federal law quite narrowly and get away with it. It also meant that extensions of constitutional rights could be declared only by the Supreme Court on direct appeal and that lower federal courts could no longer use habeas as a forum to enlarge the scope of constitutional protections. In this way, *Teague* essentially shut down the main engine of the Warren Court's expansion of criminal procedure. Second, in 1996, Congress enacted the Antiterrorism and Effective Death Penalty Act of 1996 (AEDPA),[64] which adopted, among other habeas limitations, the deferential standard of review of state decisions that Rehnquist had advocated in *Sykes*. Under AEDPA, a state court decision that errs in applying existing federal law must nevertheless be upheld, so long as the error is "reasonable." Specifically, AEDPA provides,

> (d) An application for a writ of habeas corpus . . . shall not be granted with respect to any claim that was adjudicated on the merits in State court proceedings unless the adjudication of the claim—
>
> (1) resulted in a decision that was contrary to, or involved an unreasonable application of, clearly established Federal law, as determined by the Supreme Court of the United States. . . .[65]

In other words, under AEDPA, a federal habeas court is limited to determining whether the state court applied "clearly established" federal law—as expressed solely in the decisions of the Supreme Court— "unreasonabl[y]" to the facts of the case. This may not be the literal definition of "deference," but it comes pretty close.[66]

A Crisis Long Since Passed

In the context of state criminal cases, federal habeas corpus has twice been pressed into service during major crises of federalism. Federal habeas review of such cases was first authorized in the late 1860s as a way to vindicate important federal interests and federal policies during the Reconstruction era following the Civil War. Congress expanded the scope of federal habeas and then stripped the appellate jurisdiction of the Supreme Court to ensure that the lower federal courts would be able to force the former Confederate states to obey federal law. Once the resistance had waned, however, this aggressive federal habeas review of state criminal justice was no longer needed. Congress restored the Court's appellate jurisdiction in order to permit the Court to moderate the use of the writ by lower federal courts.

In the late-twentieth-century war of federalism, the Supreme Court's reinvigoration of federal habeas corpus had much the same effect as the habeas expansion of the 1860s, allowing the lower federal courts to force recalcitrant states to obey federal law. Brennan's vision of habeas as an individual remedy for any prisoner whose federal rights were trampled was never truly realized; reversal rates in federal habeas were never very high.[67] Yet over time, habeas review did fulfill its principal function—it served as a catalyst for institutional change. As we will discuss in the chapters that follow, federal judicial review of state criminal judgments prompted the states to provide better access to appellate review and to develop new postconviction proceedings that gave defendants the chance to vindicate their federal claims in state court. And the state courts were forced—by reversals on certiorari review from direct appeal and by writs of habeas ordering release—to accept the binding nature of federal constitutional decisions with which they originally may have vehemently disagreed. Eventually state judges, prosecutors, and legislators acknowledged, however grudgingly, the inevitability that the administration of criminal justice would no longer be governed primarily by state law but instead by federal constitutional law. Previously unpopular Supreme Court decisions gradually became accepted as a way of life in the states, to the point where, in 2000, when the Court considered overruling *Miranda*, state police and prosecutors asked that it be retained.[68] Habeas may never have provided relief to every state prisoner who arguably deserved it, but habeas did facilitate the Court's dramatic changes in the scope and content of federal constitutional law and helped to bring about a seismic shift in the structure of state judicial remedies for state-convicted defendants nationwide.

Today, the second war of federalism between the federal courts and the states, a war fought so vigorously during the Warren Court era, is long over. There remains frequent disagreement, to be sure, over the appropriate scope of many federal constitutional rights in the area of criminal procedure. Sometimes, these disagreements continue to pit state courts on one side and federal courts on the other. The disagreements, however, no longer stem from a serious dispute over the legitimacy of the Supreme Court declaring such rights as a matter of federal constitutional law. Nor are the disagreements about whether federal law or state law is supreme. Those matters are settled. Moreover, today's disagreements over criminal procedure, contrary to those of the 1960s, sometimes find state courts on the side of granting more protection to criminal defendants and federal courts on the side of granting less.[69] The times have surely changed.

In any event, any disagreements over criminal procedure rights that may still persist today are all about the content and scope of those rights and not about their source. The battle, in other words, is now about the rights themselves and about how to balance those rights against the equally strong interests of law-abiding society in enforcing the criminal law. It is no longer about the restoring the balance of federalism.[70] Federal courts today no longer provide the only meaningful opportunity for state prisoners to assert their federal constitutional rights; state courts now routinely enforce those rights as well.

The Rehnquist Court and Congress, through the enactment of AEDPA, tried to define a narrower vision of federal habeas corpus, one that would free the states to carry out their desired penal policies (especially, as we will see in chapter 7, the death penalty) and would also show the state courts the respect properly due them as an equal partner in federalism. As a matter of legal doctrine, very little remains of the grand edifice of federal habeas law that was constructed by Justice Brennan during the 1960s.

These legal retrenchments of habeas, however, have not produced the hoped-for efficiencies in the administration of state criminal justice. As we will see in the next chapter, state prisoners—like Ronald Graham—continue to file federal habeas corpus petitions, in numbers that continue to impose a substantial burden on the federal courts and diminish public respect for the Great Writ. The war of federalism that raged in the 1960s has ended, but the habeas law designed to fight it still stands, devoid of meaning.

CHAPTER FOUR

The Costly Charade:
Habeas and State Prisoners Today

It is satisfying to believe that the most untutored and poorest prisoner can have his complaints or petitions considered by a federal judge and ultimately by the Supreme Court of the United States. But we are in truth fostering an illusion. —1972, Federal Judicial Center Study Group

Half a century ago habeas corpus played a crucial role in ensuring that federal constitutional law would be properly applied in state criminal cases. At about that time, the Supreme Court began to announce new federal rules of constitutional criminal procedure that would revolutionize the way that the states handled such cases. Predictably, many police, prosecutors, and state judges resisted the imposition of those new federal rules. What's more, in many states, defendants whose new federal rights were violated had little if any opportunity to challenge their tainted convictions in the state courts.

The Court responded to this serious crisis of federalism by expanding federal habeas review of constitutional claims by state prisoners. Expansive habeas review facilitated the development of modern federal criminal procedure law, spurred the states to create new and improved avenues for judicial review where convicted defendants could litigate claims in state court based on that federal law, and helped to overcome the initial reluctance of state judges to take responsibility for enforcing that federal law. These systematic achievements, however, have been overshadowed by much of the modern rhetoric about habeas, which continues to focus on the vision of habeas as a means of correcting and deterring, through case-by-case litigation, individual constitutional violations that state courts fail to find or fix.

This common understanding of habeas as a routine error-correcting and error-deterring mechanism has become so entrenched that even those justices who have sought to limit habeas review have often based their opinions on the same premise. For example, in *Teague v. Lane*,[1] the Court held that most new rules of constitutional criminal procedure should not be enforceable in habeas because the purpose of habeas is to deter constitutional error and the retroactive application of new law to old cases—cases that were decided properly by the state courts under the federal law that prevailed at the time—would not serve that deterrent purpose.

In this chapter, we challenge the conventional wisdom about the role of habeas as a means for reviewing and correcting constitutional error in individual state criminal cases. Drawing upon the latest empirical study of habeas litigation, we explain why expansive habeas review makes no sense as a case-by-case method of enforcing federal law in noncapital cases. Federal habeas review for state noncapital prisoners has become, in essence, a lottery. This lottery, funded at great expense by taxpayers, is open almost exclusively to the small group of convicted felons who are sentenced to the longest prison terms. It is wholly incapable of producing any substantial increase in the enforcement of federal constitutional rights. Habeas simply does not matter enough to have any meaningful impact on the police, lawyers, and state judges who determine the course of state noncapital cases today—and *it never will*.

Habeas review in the context of state criminal cases can best be understood as playing the same role that it has historically served in other detention contexts—restoring the balance of powers and facilitating the development of new judicial review procedures during times of social and political upheaval. Almost fifty years ago, broad habeas review made it possible for the Supreme Court to federalize most of the law that governs the day-to-day investigation and adjudication of state criminal cases. At the same time, broad habeas review prompted the states to develop better methods of reviewing compliance with these new rules in the state courts. But those institutional and structural transitions are now complete. The new empirical study of habeas that we will discuss in this chapter shows that the primary function of habeas review for state prisoners today is to waste resources that could be better used elsewhere. If it is true that state criminal justice continues to fall short of the federal constitutional mark—and we will argue in the next chapter that it often does—then a new and different strategy is needed.

The Transformation of State Judicial Review of Criminal Judgments and the Inaccessibility of Federal Habeas

We begin with the claim that federal habeas courts cannot police constitutional error in individual state noncapital cases because too few defendants will ever have meaningful access to federal habeas review.

Our explanation for this state of affairs starts with figures 4.1 and 4.2, which illustrate changes in the rate at which state prisoners have filed federal habeas petitions over the past several decades. In 1950, before the Warren Court's revolution in criminal procedure, only a small fraction of state prisoners ever sought habeas relief—about forty petitions were filed for every ten thousand state prisoners nationwide. After the Warren Court began to establish new federal criminal procedure rights

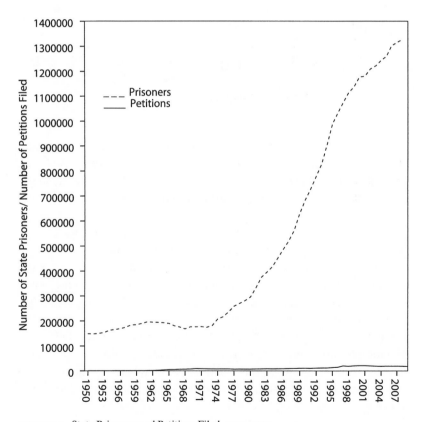

FIGURE 4.1. State Prisoners and Petitions Filed, 1950–2009

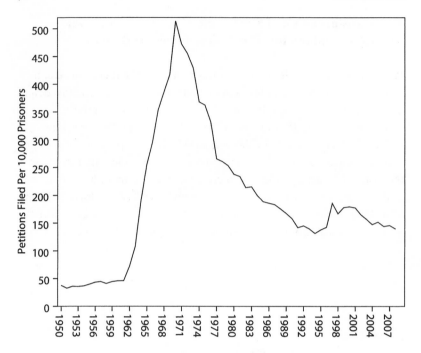

FIGURE 4.2. State Prisoner Petitions Filed per 10,000 State Prisoners, 1950–2008

and to expand the scope of federal habeas review, the rate of habeas filings increased dramatically. From 1962 (the year before *Fay v. Noia* and
the other trilogy habeas cases) to 1970, the annual filing rate increased
more than tenfold, to more than five hundred petitions per ten thousand
prisoners.

Beginning in the 1970s, however, another dramatic shift took place.
The filing rate dropped precipitously. Between 1970 and 2006, the number of petitions filed for every ten thousand prisoners plummeted from
five hundred to less than 150. From the perspective of federal judges
and the states' attorneys who had to respond to these petitions, the total number of petitions continued to grow, each year surpassing the number filed the year before, as Figure 3.1 from the last chapter illustrated.
But for state prisoners, habeas actually became less accessible, not more.
The modern explosion in state prisoner populations overwhelmed, and
masked, a long and gradual decline in the rate of habeas filings per
prisoner.

The rate of habeas filings today seems to be returning to a level more typical of the period before the expansive habeas decisions of the Warren Court, when no one expected federal habeas review to enforce a complex assortment of new federal constitutional rules of criminal procedure in the state courts. For most state prisoners today, habeas review of their convictions and sentences is nearly as inaccessible as it was back then—but for different reasons.

The Transformation of State Judicial Review of Constitutional Claims in Criminal Cases

What changed around 1970 was not the Court's approach to habeas law. At that time, the Court was still expanding habeas review and had not yet started to restrict its scope. Neither Congress nor the Court had added any major procedural or substantive barriers to filing habeas petitions that might explain why fewer state prisoners chose to seek relief in federal court.[2] Instead, the primary reason for the dramatic decline in the rate at which state prisoners sought federal review is that, beginning in the early 1970s, more and more of them were able to litigate their federal constitutional claims in the state courts.

In the 1950s, any judicial review of a state conviction or sentence was more theoretical than real, particularly for indigent defendants. Although most states provided a right to appeal a criminal conviction, record keeping in trial courts was spotty, particularly for the vast majority of cases that were resolved by guilty plea. Until 1956, there was no constitutional right to a transcript of trial proceedings.[3] Prison practices of the 1950s and 1960s often discouraged prisoners from filing legal challenges.[4] More importantly, states were not required to provide inmates with the assistance of counsel at trial or on appeal until 1963[5] or with access to legal materials until 1977.[6] And appeals of sentences were, as a general matter, simply unavailable.[7]

For prisoners in the 1950s and 1960s who completed their direct appeals, most states also provided an opportunity for so-called state post-conviction review, or state habeas, a separate procedure whereby the prisoner could return to state court and file a petition to "collaterally" challenge his conviction. But until the late 1960s, in many states these proceedings were not designed for, nor capable of, reviewing alleged violations of the new federal constitutional rules of procedure that were then being applied to the states by the Supreme Court. Two reports issued in 1967, one by the American Bar Association (ABA) and the other by the President's Commission on Law Enforcement and Administration of Justice, found that state postconviction review was "grossly inadequate" and that many states were relying on "a faulty and antiquated system of ill-defined common law remedies. . . ."[8]

By the mid-1970s, however, the situation had dramatically changed. For one thing, state appellate review of federal constitutional claims in criminal cases became routine. States began to provide attorneys for indigent defendants on trial and appeal, as required by the Supreme Court in 1963.[9] The result was "a much higher rate of appeal than American courts have ever experienced," including a sharp rise in the proportion of guilty plea cases that were appealed. Several states also added intermediate appellate courts during the 1960s and 1970s.[10] And as sentencing laws changed in the late 1970s, sentencing appeals increased.[11] The overall expansion of federal rights had a "pervasive" effect on the state courts, according to the authors of a leading text on appellate review in 1976. Because almost any objection could be cast in federal constitutional terms, they observed, "state appellate courts must deal regularly with federal law as well as their own."[12]

The same period also witnessed a substantial increase in postappeal, collateral attacks on convictions filed in state trial courts, with a corresponding increase in appeals from those decisions.[13] Throughout the 1960s, many states amended their laws to provide those convicted of crimes with more uniform and easier access to postconviction judicial review of federal constitutional claims, although some states did not do so until the late 1970s.[14] In short, state convicts who entered state prisons in the 1970s, unlike those in the 1950s, enjoyed a much greater opportunity to pursue wide-ranging federal constitutional challenges to their convictions and sentences in multiple layers of state court proceedings.

These transformative changes in state judicial review made it inevitable that a smaller percentage of prisoners would file federal habeas petitions, for two reasons. First, as the state courts gradually became more familiar with, and began to apply more consistently, the Warren Court's new federal constitutional rules in appellate and postconviction proceedings, undoubtedly more of those prisoners with valid constitutional claims would have received relief in state court and therefore would have had no reason to file a habeas petition in federal court.[15] But even when these new state proceedings did not meet such high expectations, their

very existence would have contributed to the falling rate of federal habeas filings because of two longstanding habeas doctrines—the requirements that petitioners must exhaust their state remedies and be in custody in order to seek habeas relief.

Since 1886, federal habeas review has been available only to those
state prisoners who have already used up, or "exhausted," their state appellate and postconviction remedies and who are still in "custody" (either in prison or on probation or parole) at the time when they file their
petitions in federal court.[16] The longer that it takes for review proceedings in state court to be completed, the more likely it is that a prisoner's
sentence will expire before he can exhaust his state remedies and seek
habeas relief in federal court. A study in 1977, for example, found that in
three of the four states studied no more than eleven percent of prisoners
had filed a state postconviction motion and attributed this "small number of filers" to "the fact that a vast majority of prisoners do not stay in
prison long enough to become filers at all. . . ."[17]

Because of the combined effect of the exhaustion and custody requirements, the major expansion of state post-trial remedies that began
in the late 1960s effectively choked off federal habeas review for all but
the small and shrinking portion of state criminal defendants who are
sentenced for longer than it takes the state courts to review their cases.[18]
Since 1970, greater access to state judicial review of constitutional claims
has meant more time spent litigating those claims in state court. And as
state review proceedings have lengthened, the chance to obtain an additional round of judicial review in federal court has faded, except for those
prisoners serving the very longest sentences. Today, the majority of this
nation's convicted felons are either released with a short term of probation or incarcerated in local jails and released well before their state appeals and state postconviction proceedings (if filed at all) are completed;
only two of every five people convicted of felonies in state court are actually sentenced to state prison.[19] And among those who are sentenced
to prison, most will still never have the chance to seek a writ of federal
habeas corpus because they will be sentenced to less than five years and
actually will serve less than three.[20]

The declining rate of habeas filings beginning in the 1970s may also
reflect yet another development—the simultaneous drop in the proportion of state criminal defendants convicted after trial and the corresponding increase in the proportion of guilty pleas. Defendants who
contest their guilt at trial are probably more likely to file habeas peti-

tions than those who plead guilty,[21] and after the Supreme Court actively
endorsed plea bargaining in several decisions during the early 1970s, the
proportion of prisoners opting for a trial—representing already less than
10 percent of all felonies in many states—decreased even further.[22] Yet
the essential underlying point here is the same for both plea-convicted
and trial-convicted defendants: the transformation in state review of
criminal judgments rendered federal habeas a meaningless remedy.
Most state felons who are sentenced to incarceration after trial receive
sentences of less than six and a half years[23] and will not have the opportunity to seek federal habeas review if their state review proceedings
drag on past the end of their custody.

Empirical Evidence of the Effect of State Judicial
Review on Habeas Today

The findings of a pathbreaking nationwide study of habeas litigation,
completed in the fall of 2007, are consistent with this account. They confirm that the rule mandating the exhaustion of state remedies has meant
that only those with the longest prison sentences are able to file habeas
petitions.[24] The study was the first to examine contemporary federal habeas cases filed under the current Antiterrorism and Effective Death
Penalty Act of 1996 (AEDPA) statute. It followed nearly 2,400 noncapital cases through the district courts, cases that were randomly selected from among the over thirty-six thousand federal habeas cases that
had been filed during the years 2003 and 2004 by state prisoners across
the nation.[25] Approximately two thousand of those cases were filed by
prisoners challenging a noncapital criminal conviction or sentence.[26]

The data show that habeas petitioners appear to be fulfilling the requirement that they pursue all available avenues of review in state court
before filing in federal court. Of the habeas cases for which this information was available, more than 83 percent were filed by a petitioner who
had previously appealed the convictions or sentences he was challenging, and in three-quarters of the cases, the petitioner had already sought
postconviction relief in state court. Most filers had pursued both kinds
of state remedies. Of terminated habeas cases, only about one in ten
was dismissed for failure to exhaust all claims in state court[27] (see Table 5.1). In addition, the study found that "many prisoners simply list all
the claims raised earlier in state post-conviction proceedings" and that
the high proportion of petitions with four or more claims may be the re-

sult of a corresponding increase in the number of claims that are raised in state court.[28]

It also takes years for federal habeas petitioners to get through all of their state court proceedings. Current law sets a deadline for filing a federal habeas petition challenging a conviction or sentence. The prisoner has exactly one year to file, and that one-year clock starts either on the date the defendant was sentenced if he did not appeal, or on the date his direct appeal concluded, whichever comes later. The one-year time clock is stopped, or "tolled," for postconviction review proceedings in state court. Petitioners in the study who complied with the deadlines and filed their federal habeas petitions on time reached federal court, on average, more than five years after being sentenced in state court.[29] This finding suggests that—taking into account the one year of allowable delay before filing the habeas petition under AEDPA—appellate and postconviction proceedings in state court, for those who subsequently seek habeas review, are averaging four years or more to complete.

The sentences of habeas petitioners are also disproportionately severe. Although those sentenced to life in prison make up less than 1 percent of all who are sentenced to state prison,[30] the study findings suggest that in 2003 and 2004 nearly 30 percent of all federal habeas petitions challenging state criminal judgments were filed by prisoners serving life sentences. This is an even higher proportion than was found by a study of habeas filers conducted just twelve years earlier.[31] One in four habeas challenges examined in the 2007 study were filed by prisoners sentenced to thirty years or more, and the median sentence of filers (excluding those sentenced to life) was twenty years. Only 12 percent of all noncapital habeas petitions examined in the study were filed by prisoners who had received a sentence of five years or less, even though that group makes up the majority of those admitted to prison.[32] And most of those who sought habeas review had been convicted at trial; only about a third of habeas filers in the 2007 study had pled guilty.[33]

For all but a very small proportion of the millions of those convicted of crime every year in the United States, the Great Writ is a pipe dream. It is available only to those prisoners whose prison sentences are so long that they are still in custody even after the state courts have finished reviewing, and rejecting, their constitutional claims. For everyone else, habeas provides no remedy at all.

This situation is structural and highly unlikely to reverse. With corrections costs overwhelming state budgets, it is doubtful that states will choose to significantly increase the proportion of convicted defendants who serve prison terms that extend beyond the duration of their state court remedies. Nor are significant improvements in the speed with which state courts review convictions and sentences on the horizon. In 1993, the ABA Commission on Standards of Judicial Administration reviewed the research into delay on appeal in state courts and concluded that even in an ideal system the appellate process in a criminal case would take at least two years.[34] At the time, most states were nowhere near this goal.[35] Since then the number of appeals filed in many states has increased, while judicial resources have struggled to keep pace.[36] The scant research on the duration of postconviction litigation in state court suggests that such litigation probably takes as long as direct appeal, particularly since evidentiary hearings are available and granted more often than in federal habeas review.[37]

Moreover, any potential deterrent effect on police, prosecutors, defense attorneys, and trial judges of case-by-case enforcement of criminal procedure rules in habeas is seriously undercut by plea bargaining. For the more than 90 percent of defendants whose convictions are obtained by settlement, prosecutors will willingly trade reductions in charge or sentence for a defendant's waiver of the opportunity to raise constitutional claims—including ineffective assistance of counsel claims—and defense lawyers and trial judges will eagerly approve these bargains.[38]

In short, as a means of enforcing federal law in individual state criminal cases, federal habeas review is doomed to fail. The unavailability of habeas effectively ensures that it does not, and cannot, provide any meaningful correction of error or deterrence of constitutional misconduct by state officials in the vast majority of state criminal cases. Any hope of invigorating habeas review will necessarily be in vain if police, prosecutors, and state judges know—from the very outset of a criminal investigation through the conclusion of the case—that most convicted prisoners will never be in a position to file a petition to begin with.

Complexity and Delay in Federal Habeas Proceedings

There is a second problem that has disabled federal habeas review from correcting or deterring constitutional error in state criminal cases. Far too much of the time and effort that federal courts and states' attorneys devote to habeas litigation has nothing to do with whether the petitioner is actually guilty or has been convicted or sentenced in violation of the Constitution. As a result, habeas cases take far too long to resolve.

A significant amount of the briefing, argument, and judicial decision making in habeas cases addresses whether the convoluted rules of habeas procedure allow a federal court even to consider the merits of a prisoner's constitutional claims at all. Judges, lawyers, and prisoners in habeas cases today labor within an increasingly complicated procedural maze.

Many of the procedural rules that have multiplied since habeas was expanded fifty years ago are byzantine, and needlessly so. Most of these rules were not even designed for the more than seventeen thousand noncapital habeas cases filed each year, the kind of habeas cases to which the rules are applied day in and day out. Instead, as we discuss later in chapter 7, most of the procedural restrictions on habeas that were adopted by the Supreme Court or by Congress beginning in the late 1970s grew out of frustration with federal habeas review of capital convictions and sentences. For example, the title of the 1996 statute that amended the habeas statute for all state prisoners was "The Antiterrorism and Effective *Death Penalty* Act of 1996." Protests that these changes were not needed in noncapital habeas cases fell on deaf ears.

Even the briefest summary of some of these procedural requirements will convey their mind-numbing complexity. If a habeas petition is filed before the prisoner gave the state courts a "fair opportunity" to rule on his claims, it will be rejected as "unexhausted" and filed too early. If the petition is filed more than a year after a conviction becomes final, however, it will be barred as having been filed too late, unless the filing period was suspended for "properly filed" state postconviction review proceedings or for "equitable tolling." Courts keep changing what all those standards mean.

The prisoner must also file the petition in the right place. Normally that is the district where he is incarcerated, but if his petition is considered "successive," he must file instead in the court of appeals, which must first give him permission before he may seek a writ of habeas in the district court.[39] There is continuing confusion about which petitions are "successive" and which are not, as well as about the statutory exceptions that allow some petitioners, under some conditions, more than one shot at habeas review.

A federal court will not consider a claim if the prisoner failed to raise the claim properly in state court,[40] as discussed in chapter 3, but this so-called state procedural default rule has several exceptions. It does not apply if the state's procedural rules for raising the claim are "inadequate."[41] A prisoner's default will also be excused if the state actively prevented the prisoner from raising the issue or if the lawyer who should have raised the claim at trial or on appeal was so incompetent that the representation is considered a denial of the constitutional right to the effective assistance of counsel. But in order to use that excuse, the prisoner must have objected to the misconduct of his lawyer in state court proceedings. If he did not, he must be able to show that the state prevented him from doing so. And there is an exception to this exception. A prisoner can persuade a federal habeas court to reach a claim that he did not raise in state court if he can show that he was probably innocent, but it is not clear whether she must show innocence of the crime itself or whether he can claim to be "innocent" of one of the facts used in setting his sentence.[42]

Even if these habeas procedural barriers are cleared, a federal court will not reach the merits of a petitioner's constitutional claim if the rule on which the petitioner relies is "new" and was not dictated by decisions of the Supreme Court at the time the state court last rejected the claim.[43] This rule has exceptions as well: review is available for new constitutional rules that limit the state's authority to define substantive crimes or penalties (such as the constitutional ban on the death penalty for the crime of rape) or for new procedural rules that are as fundamental as the right to appointed counsel established in *Gideon*. These two narrow exceptions have turned out to have virtually no practical application in noncapital cases.

Assuming a federal court resolves these and other habeas procedural questions in the petitioner's favor and concludes that the merits of his claim should be addressed, there remain the thorny questions whether and when new evidence may be introduced in support of the claim. Only after struggling through this vast procedural morass may a habeas court finally turn to whether or not the state actually violated the Constitution in the prisoner's case. Not surprisingly, the 2007 study found that about half of all noncapital habeas cases are dismissed or denied without reaching the merits of any claim[44] (see table 4.1).

Each one of these procedural limitations barring habeas review or relief may have been intended to reduce the burden of habeas on the states and on the federal courts. Indeed, the implementation of most of these limitations has roughly coincided with a drop in the rate at which con-

TABLE 4.1. **Litigating Noncapital Cases: Selected Findings of the 2007 Study**

Petitioners and representation:	
% Cases petitioner without counsel	92.3
% Cases filed by petitioners who pleaded guilty or nolo	32.2
Petitions, claims raised[a]:	
Average/median number claims raised per case	4/3
% Raising claim of ineffective assistance of counsel	50.4
% Raising a claim of innocence of conviction	3.9
% Challenging sentence/sentencing proceeding only	12.9
% Challenging sufficiency of evidence of guilt	18.9
Litigation:	
% Cases with amended petitions	11.8
% Answer or motion to dismiss filed by state	58.2
% Cases including a stay for exhaustion	2.6
% Cases with discovery ordered	0.3
% Cases with evidentiary hearing held	0.4
Average/median number of docket entries	18/15
Disposition type and reason:	
% Cases dismissed as time barred[b]	21.7
% Cases dismissed as successive[b]	6.8
% Cases all claims dismissed as unexhausted[b]	10.9
% Cases including at least one procedurally defaulted claim[b]	13.3
% Cases including at least one *Teague*-barred claim[b]	0.4
% Cases dismissed or denied, without reaching merits	42.0[c]
% Granted relief on any claim[b]	0.35
% Of grants on sentence only	0.0

[a] Of 1,521 cases with claims information available (63.8 percent of the 2,384 cases in sample).

[b] Of 1,986 nontransferred, terminated cases.

[c] Of the 1,979 cases that had terminated without grant or transfer, 1,311 had claims information.

victions and sentences have been overturned in habeas. As we will soon see, the percentage of petitioners who obtain relief has decreased over time. But it is not clear that these various restrictions have actually reduced the burden of litigating those cases to conclusion.

At least one of the procedural screening mechanisms appears to have lengthened, rather than reduced, the time it takes federal courts to process these cases. In particular, the current rules governing state procedural default may actually add to the burdens of habeas litigation rather than streamline it. Procedural default is a defense that may lead a habeas court to dismiss a claim without reaching the merits, based on the state court's conclusion that the petitioner failed to raise the claim in compliance with state law. As Table 4.1 reports, the 2007 study found that about one out of seven noncapital habeas petitions attacking a conviction or sentence includes at least one claim that is eventually dismissed because of procedural default. Presumably, it should be speedier to dismiss such a claim because it was not raised properly in state court than it would be to resolve the claim on its merits. But the study indicated that, controlling for other factors, it takes habeas courts up to 17 percent longer, on average, to complete cases in which a claim was dismissed as defaulted than it does to complete cases in which no claims were dismissed for this reason.[45] Among the cases studied, not a single court found that the petitioner had managed to establish one of the exceptions to procedural default, such as ineffective assistance of counsel, interference by the state that prevented the defendant from raising his claim, or actual innocence of the crime. In several of the cases, judges simply skipped over the question of procedural default to deny the petition on the merits, presumably to save time and effort. In noncapital habeas cases, litigation over whether procedural default applies or should be excused appears to be a time waster, not a time saver.[46]

Turning to the time and effort it takes to finish these cases, the study revealed that few noncapital habeas cases are summarily dismissed. Every pleading submitted by the state or petitioner, and every order entered by the court, is entered on each case's docket sheet. Noncapital habeas cases average eighteen docket entries per case, more than a third of the average number of docket entries in capital cases. Six in ten noncapital cases included at least one responsive motion and brief by the state and a reply by the petitioner. More than one of every eight cases included an amended petition, and amended petitions generally required an additional responsive pleading. In more than half of the cases, the district judge first forwarded all of the pleadings to a magistrate judge for disposition. This generated a report and recommendation from the magistrate judge back to the district judge, which provided the opportunity for the petitioner to file yet another pleading objecting to that report and often required yet another response from the state. Among terminated cases, referral to a magistrate accounted for an increase of 10 to 49 percent in the number of days required for disposition.[47]

And federal courts actually take longer to resolve habeas petitions today than they did before the 1996 AEDPA statutory reforms that were designed to shorten the process. Noncapital habeas cases that terminated in 1992 averaged six months from filing to disposition. By contrast, nearly one out of every ten noncapital cases filed during the years 2003 and 2004 were still pending at the end of 2006, and after taking these pending cases into account, the average disposition time had stretched to a year.[48] One year is not a very long time for a court to resolve a civil case. But in a habeas case, the petitioner is not seeking damages; instead, he is claiming that his incarceration is in violation of the Constitution. Speedy resolution would seem particularly important when a person's liberty is involved and when the state may be ordered either to retry the petitioner or to release him.

The Futility and Wastefulness of Habeas Review When Obtained

Notwithstanding the complexity and delay apparent in this cumbersome review apparatus and its irrelevance for all but the most serious prosecutions, we might decide that we nevertheless should preserve federal habeas as a safety net to allow those bearing the most severe penalties to challenge the validity of their convictions and sentences. But it would make sense to do so only if habeas actually corrected or deterred enough error to be worth its cost. At present, federal habeas review of noncapital cases completely fails this test.

An Illusory Remedy

At the end of the long procedural tunnel, the ultimate chance of a noncapital federal habeas petitioner obtaining any habeas relief is very close to zero. Of the thousands of randomly selected cases examined in the 2007 study, only seven habeas petitioners actually received any relief from a district court (Figure 4.3). At that rate, we can estimate that fewer than sixty of the more than seventeen thousand habeas cases filed each year in the federal courts will result in the order of a retrial, resentencing, new opportunity for appeal, or release.[49] That is about one-third of 1 percent (0.35 percent) of all federal habeas cases filed each year challenging state criminal judgments. As a percentage of individual claims raised, the odds of habeas relief are less than one-tenth of 1 percent (0.1 percent). As a percentage of all felony cases prosecuted, the probability that a writ will be granted is truly microscopic: less than two-thousandths of 1 percent (0.002 percent) of felony cases started each year in state court will ultimately result in habeas relief.[50]

Given these astonishingly low success rates, the expectation that federal habeas review will either correct or deter constitutional violations in any individual state criminal case is absurd. Even if a defendant is convicted of murder and sentenced to life in prison, and is therefore among

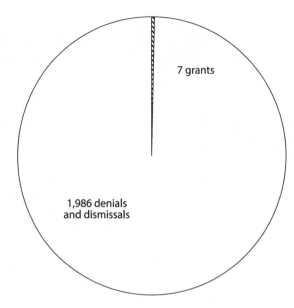

7 grants

1,986 denials
and dismissals

FIGURE 4.3. 2007 Study, Noncapital State Prisoner Petition Terminations

those few prisoners most likely to end up filing a habeas petition, habeas relief is so improbable that the possibility can easily be ignored.
If state judges, prosecutors, and police are deterred from violating the
Constitution in noncapital criminal cases, that deterrence cannot be the
result of federal habeas litigation. Constitutional rules will be enforced
in the state courts—at trial, on direct appeal, and in state postconviction
review—or they will not be enforced at all.

In other forms of civil litigation, a low rate of plaintiff victories may
mask a higher success rate through settlement. Meritorious cases that
get settled before they ever go to trial never show up as recorded wins for
the plaintiff. But habeas cases do not settle. In 2006, Anup Malani published a survey finding that, in most jurisdictions, habeas settlements are
completely unheard of.[51] He suggested that this was because most prisoners had no lawyers and also no incentive to settle, since to them the
cost of habeas litigation was nearly zero.

We believe there is an even better explanation: states likewise have
no incentive to settle habeas cases. Certainly states might prefer to avoid
the cost of litigating in habeas court, which, as we point out above, is not
insignificant. This may lead state prosecutors to trade charging or sentencing concessions for defendant waivers of postconviction remedies.

But once a habeas petition challenging a conviction is actually filed, the only meaningful concession a state could possibly make, in return for the petitioner's agreement to drop the case, would be to agree to retry or release the prisoner. No rational prosecutor would ever exchange a new trial, or a get-out-of-jail-free card, for the petitioner's agreement to voluntary dismiss a habeas case that the state has a more than 99.96 percent chance of winning.[52] This would be a bizarre trade-off, especially considering the nature of the crimes most habeas petitioners have been convicted of committing. Based on the 2007 study, about 31 percent of all habeas petitions challenging state criminal judgments are filed by prisoners whose most serious offense of conviction was homicide, 15 percent by those convicted of sexual assault, and 14 percent by those convicted of robbery. Assault, burglary, kidnapping, and arson account for the most serious offenses of an additional 19 percent of habeas filers, with drug offenses being the most serious offense for 14 percent.[53]

The High Cost of Futility

The microscopically low rate of habeas relief might also mean that there are hardly any meritorious claims left to grant after the prisoner has had his chance at state judicial review. But if that is true, then why should society continue to pay for this elaborate legal apparatus to solve such a tiny problem? This wasteful effort means that habeas review today disappoints not only those who wish it could actually provide individual prisoners a remedy but also those who believed that the recent doctrinal and statutory restrictions would help reduce the toll that habeas litigation takes on state and federal resources.

The proportion of the federal judiciary's workload taken up by habeas litigation today is larger than it was in the 1960s, even though the proportion of prisoners who can access habeas is much smaller. In 1950, federal habeas petitions were both more common among state prisoners and less common within federal dockets. At that time, habeas petitions filed by state prisoners made up only about 1 percent of all civil cases started in federal district courts nationwide. A habeas petition was relatively unusual, and a federal judge presumably could find the time to focus on the merits of the claims that it raised. In 1963, the Court let loose its full assault on state intransigence by announcing its habeas decisions in *Fay*, *Townsend*, and *Sanders*. Even so, during the next year, only about 3,500 habeas petitions were filed by state prisoners nationwide, or about 5 percent of the federal courts civil caseload.[54]

Today, with state prison populations many times bigger than they were then, even the miniscule percentage of state prisoners who are incarcerated long enough to file federal habeas petitions gives rise to a habeas caseload that now represents 7 percent of the total civil caseload in the federal district courts nationwide. In several districts with large state prison populations, 17 percent or more of all federal civil cases are habeas petitions filed by state prisoners.[55] These petitions have become relentlessly, monotonously routine for the federal judges who are required to consider them. Surely this gives new force to the observation by Justice Jackson, in 1953, that "[h]e who must search a haystack for a needle is likely to end up with the attitude that the needle is not worth the search."[56]

Whether federal judges must search in vain for the meritorious needle in the meritless haystack, or whether the very few habeas cases that do result in relief are the tip of a much larger iceberg of valid constitutional claims that are forever submerged under an ocean of habeas procedure—or a little of both—federal habeas review today is a futile exercise. Habeas is not now, and will never be, a significant deterrent for garden-variety constitutional mistakes. Relief comes far too little and far too late to make a difference. Federal habeas corpus review of state noncapital criminal cases once helped to transform the institutional structure of judicial review of constitutional claims; today it is an almost completely wasted effort.

*   *   *

In the 1960s and 1970s, federal habeas review of state prisoners' constitutional claims made a difference. Habeas mattered because it expanded the opportunity for the federal courts to develop new rules of constitutional law, and it prompted the states to provide judicial review of alleged violations of those rules in their own courts. The relationship between state appellate and postconviction review and federal habeas review was clear and immediate to state legislatures. Improving the structural mechanisms of state judicial review was an obvious response for state officials seeking to reduce the intrusiveness of federal judicial review. For police, prosecutors, defense attorneys, and trial judges involved in the day-to-day administration of state criminal cases today, however, the remote risk of habeas reversal can hardly make an impression.

Some have responded by arguing that Congress and the Supreme Court should attempt to fix federal habeas so that it provides more relief to more prisoners more often. The best way to repair habeas, they argue, would be for the Court to remove the many restrictions it has adopted,[57] for Congress to repeal AEDPA,[58] and for the federal government to provide lawyers and evidentiary hearings to habeas petitioners so that they can more effectively litigate their federal claims.[59]

This is one possible way to respond to this failed system, but it is not a sensible response. The cost of providing a lawyer to every habeas petitioner, increasing habeas litigation activity, and slowing down even further the resolution of more than seventeen thousand habeas cases filed every year in federal district courts would be steep. Even with a large investment of new resources in federal habeas review, it will remain out of reach, with habeas grants few and far between, and thus unlikely to bring about any meaningful reduction in constitutional error in state criminal justice. The fact is that no matter how much money Congress and the states may sink into it, federal habeas will continue to be an inaccessible remedy that state law enforcement agents, prosecutors, judges, and legislatures can easily ignore. For this reason, as we will argue in the next chapter, society's resources would be much better spent on reforming state criminal justice at the front end, by improving the quality of defense representation that can help to secure fair trials, plea proceedings, and sentences for all defendants.

Investing even more resources in futile case-by-case habeas review of state criminal judgments could even backfire as a strategy for correcting and deterring constitutional error in noncapital cases. If the cost to the states of defending criminal judgments were to increase, it would drain even more resources that might otherwise be spent more effectively, in the first instance, to address the same goal.

In the 1960s and 1970s, expansive habeas review of state criminal cases was needed to help achieve the writ's traditional goals. Habeas served as a stopgap in the absence of reasonable alternatives for judicial review and influenced the development of institutional and structural reforms to provide such alternative review. Even if most habeas petitioners never actually obtained release, expansive habeas review sent a clear message to state legislatures and state courts that they needed to take greater responsibility for the effective enforcement of federal constitutional law in state criminal cases.

Today, the situation is different. The institutional and structural reforms of state judicial review have long since occurred, and convicted defendants generally now have access to state appellate and postconviction review processes in which they can litigate their federal constitutional claims. Moreover, as a general matter, state courts no longer resist enforcing the criminal procedure decisions of the Supreme Court simply because they are federal rules rather than state rules. Given these changes, habeas litigation in state noncapital cases today, involving more than seventeen thousand petitions filed each year, is an appalling waste of resources, despite numerous efforts by the Supreme Court and Congress to cut back on both access and relief.

It is time to recognize that case-by-case habeas review of state criminal cases never was intended to become a permanent and routine aspect of the American criminal justice process. In the next chapter, we will explain how a return to the core principles of flexibility and prudence can restore habeas to its proper place and preserve it for when it may once again be truly needed.

CHAPTER FIVE

The Future of Habeas Review of State Criminal Cases

The 2007 habeas study described and detailed in chapter 4 demonstrates that, whatever we may think in theory about the importance of providing convicted state defendants with an opportunity to vindicate their federal constitutional rights in a federal judicial forum, the opportunity provided by federal habeas is nothing more than a costly charade. The charade squanders scarce societal resources that could be put to much better use, both within and outside of the criminal justice system. Moreover, and perhaps more importantly, the futility of federal habeas corpus review of state criminal cases cheapens the currency of habeas itself, leading federal judges to view habeas as a worthless waste of their time and energy and diminishing public respect for the writ.

Requiring the federal courts to review state noncapital criminal cases for federal constitutional error, routinely and case-by-case, is an idea whose time has come and gone. To be sure, serious problems in state criminal justice persist. But litigation after the fact, in an effort to find and fix problems with the way that police, prosecutors, defense attorneys, judges, and juries handled a particular state criminal case, can never be as effective as well-designed and well-funded preventive measures to avoid those problems in the first place. Prudent use of the extraordinary power of federal habeas corpus calls for pursuing a radically different, proactive approach to addressing the problems that continue to affect state criminal defendants today.

In this chapter, we propose a solution: Congress should amend Section 2254 to limit habeas review of state noncapital criminal cases to those few situations in which the value of the habeas remedy would be the greatest. And whatever resources are saved by doing so should be re-deployed instead to a new federal initiative designed to help the states improve their defense representation systems—a front-end reform that promises to do more good, in terms of protecting the constitutional rights of individual state criminal defendants, than any amount of post hoc habeas litigation ever could.

This proposal might seem, at first glance, to violate the core principle that federal habeas must remain broadly available as a flexible remedy for unanticipated governmental intrusions on fundamental liberty. However, as we will argue below, the Suspension Clause ensures that, notwithstanding the limits contained in our proposed new statute, the Supreme Court will retain the authority to reinvigorate federal habeas review in state criminal cases if, in the future, it should once again be needed.

The Problem: A Lack of Prudence

When the Supreme Court originally expanded the scope of federal habeas corpus review of state criminal cases in the 1950s and 1960s, the expansion was described by Justice Brennan, who largely orchestrated it, as temporary in nature. According to Brennan, once the states had reformed their own appellate and postconviction review procedures, and once the state courts had accepted the responsibility of vindicating federal constitutional criminal procedure rights, there would no longer be a need for searching federal habeas review of state criminal cases. Everything could go back to normal.[1]

In the decades since the 1960s, both of Justice Brennan's conditions have been fulfilled. As noted in the last chapter, the states have adopted and implemented modern appellate and postconviction remedies. These remedies generally allow convicted state defendants to raise and litigate both record and nonrecord claims of federal constitutional error. And the judges, prosecutors, and police who work in state criminal justice have become completely acclimated to the once controversial idea that criminal procedure is regulated by a host of federal constitutional rules that must be enforced by state courts in state criminal cases.[2] State judicial review of criminal judgments today may not be as extensive or as generous as many would hope,[3] but it is available and routinely used to review federal constitutional claims. This is much more than could be said decades ago when Justice Brennan and his fellow justices enlisted the lower federal courts to step into the breach. That particular crisis in the balance of power between federal law and state governments no longer exists.

These important institutional and structural changes in state criminal justice were prompted, in large part, by the expansion of federal habeas corpus. To be sure, even after habeas was expanded, habeas relief in state noncapital criminal cases remained very rare. Excluding capital cases, success rates for state prisoners in habeas probably never approached double-digit percentages, even during the late 1960s and early 1970s.[4] But the importance of the Warren Court's habeas expansion cannot be measured by the relatively small number of individual state prisoners who received new trials or were released from custody through habeas. Instead, as with the assertions of habeas power reviewed in chapters 2 and 3, the Court's expansion of habeas review mattered most in this context because it helped facilitate the creation of new judicial review mechanisms for an entire class of prisoners. The Warren Court's habeas expansion sent a shot across the bow of the states, signaling to state legislators and judges the need to revamp the mechanisms for judicial review of criminal cases in the state courts.

As we have already seen, throughout history the most important role of habeas has been to provide the judiciary with the authority to intervene whenever the balance of governmental powers has been seriously disrupted and alternative mechanisms of judicial review to meet the new detention challenges have not yet emerged. At such times, habeas serves as a flexible but necessary stopgap. Over time, however, habeas prompts the development of new and improved judicial review procedures— alternative review procedures that, once fully implemented, obviate the need for habeas review itself. In other words, when habeas review works well, it brings about its own obsolescence.

This cycle has yet to be completed in the context of habeas review of state criminal cases. The particular circumstances that originally led the Supreme Court to expand federal habeas in the 1950s and 1960s receded as soon as the institutional and structural deficiencies in state judicial review of criminal cases were repaired. But Justice Brennan's promised rollback of federal habeas review of state criminal cases never happened. Neither the Court nor Congress returned the writ to its traditional role of intervening only in situations of extraordinary need.[5]

Since the late 1970s, numerous restrictions have been imposed by the

Supreme Court on federal habeas review of state criminal cases. These include the *Wainwright v. Sykes* procedural default doctrine, under which habeas courts must refuse to review claims that were defaulted by virtue of the petitioner's failure to follow applicable procedural rules in the state courts, and the *Teague* rule of nonretroactivity, under which habeas courts generally cannot upset state convictions based on new rules of constitutional law declared after those convictions became final in the state courts. But these restrictions did not substantially reduce the total amount of habeas litigation; instead, they simply diverted it onto different paths, forcing litigants to contest whether the restrictions apply in each individual habeas case. Nor did Congress succeed, through Antiterrorism and Effective Death Penalty Act of 1996 (AEDPA), in restoring habeas to its historically limited role in state criminal cases. The 2007 study confirms these assessments.

As a result, the federal courts continue to struggle with a huge volume of habeas petitions filed by state prisoners. Every one of these petitions must be examined by the courts, even though, except in capital cases, they almost never lead to relief. As the Supreme Court itself has explained, in a related context: "Every paper filed . . . no matter how repetitious or frivolous, requires some portion of the institution's limited resources. A part of the Court's responsibility is to see that these resources are allocated in a way that promotes the interests of justice."[6] Yet time-consuming and wasteful habeas litigation continues, largely unabated.

We believe that the main problem in federal habeas corpus review of state criminal cases today stems from a lack of prudence in the exercise of habeas jurisdiction. During the federalism battles of the Warren Court era, the Supreme Court decided that it needed to expand the scope of habeas. In light of the core principle that habeas must be flexible to allow for an appropriate judicial response to the unforeseen challenges of a particular time, this expansion was justified. But neither the Court nor Congress has sufficiently constrained access to habeas even though the crisis that led to its expansion has now passed.

During the 1960s and 1970s, there were important reasons to support a system of duplicative postconviction litigation. Even Professor Paul Bator, famously critical of expansive federal habeas review for state prisoners, observed in 1963, "The existence, notorious and oft-exhibited, of grave inadequacies in the states' criminal procedures, both original and post-conviction, makes the federal habeas corpus jurisdiction a present necessity."[7] But those justifications are no longer compelling. The states have developed modern judicial review procedures that provide defendants with the opportunity to litigate their constitutional claims in state court that was sorely lacking during earlier decades, state review procedures that today result in the reversal of a significant percentage of convictions and sentences.[8] And even if federal oversight of the state courts were still viewed as desirable, case-by-case habeas review does not, and cannot, effectively serve that role. Habeas should, instead, be reserved for the role it performs best: temporarily providing judicial review of claims of unlawful imprisonment during periodic political or social crises until adequate alternatives for judicial review are created.

The Proposal: Curtail Federal Habeas Review of Noncapital Cases

We propose to conserve most of the resources that are currently spent on ineffective federal habeas litigation and to cut off the endless stream of habeas petitions that causes federal judges, politicians, and the public at large to view habeas as a worthless burden rather than a revered remedy for fundamental injustice. Congress should take the lead to implement this shift toward a more prudent exercise of federal habeas review in state criminal cases. New statutory restrictions on the application of the writ to state criminal cases should limit habeas review to those situations in which its potential value can justify its cost.

We propose, specifically, that Congress amend the federal habeas corpus statute applicable to state prisoners, Section 2254, so that in noncapital cases, habeas courts retain jurisdiction over only two limited and especially important categories of federal claims. The proposed amendments would provide that—subject to any limits that may be imposed by the Suspension Clause and with the special exception of capital cases (which we will discuss in chapters 7 and 8)—an application for a writ of habeas corpus on behalf of a person in custody pursuant to a judgment of conviction entered by a state court shall not be granted unless the court finds that

(1) the petitioner is in custody in violation of a new rule of constitutional law, made retroactive to cases on collateral review by the Supreme Court; or
(2) the petitioner is in custody in violation of the Constitution or laws or treaties of the United States, and has established by clear and convincing new evidence, not previously discoverable through the exercise of due diligence,

that in light of the evidence as a whole, no reasonable fact finder would have found him guilty of the underlying offense.

This proposal would limit federal habeas corpus review of state noncapital criminal cases to those two situations in which collateral review in federal court can prove most valuable: first, a conviction based on a violation of newly declared, but retroactively applied, federal constitutional rule for which there may be no other judicial remedy; and second, the conviction of a probably innocent person in violation of the Constitution.[9] These two situations may be rare, but when a credible allegation is made along such lines and is not addressed or properly resolved by the state courts—to which a habeas petitioner would still have to present his claim first, so long as there is any state remedy still left to exhaust— habeas courts should be able to review the claim and, if necessary, grant the writ. In all other cases, however, habeas review should be denied.

Claims of Retroactive New Law

Under our proposal, the first category of permissible habeas claims would allow for the postconviction enforcement of new federal constitutional rules that have been held to apply retroactively to cases already final on direct appeal.[10] Without this opportunity, a convicted defendant whose direct appeal had already concluded by the time a new constitutional rule was declared and held to be retroactive might be unable to obtain the benefits of that new rule, if the courts of the state provided no forum to raise this sort of claim.

Fortunately, most state courts today do possess the general authority to revisit final criminal judgments based on a violation of a new and retroactively applicable constitutional rule. Our proposal would preserve federal habeas review of such claims despite the fact that the federal courts in such cases are likely to be second-guessing prior state court decisions about the proper application of these new constitutional rules. We believe that federal habeas review should remain available for these extraordinary claims, despite the potential for duplicative effort, for one simple reason: the Supreme Court has made it very clear that new constitutional mandates will be applied retroactively to disrupt settled criminal judgments only if the new rule is of truly exceptional importance to fundamental fairness.

The Court has held that only two kinds of new rules should be given retroactive application in habeas: (1) new substantive rules that place certain conduct totally beyond the bounds of punishable behavior or that prohibit a particular sanction for a particular crime;[11] and (2) new procedural rules that are so important that they rise to the level of the fundamental right, announced in *Gideon*, that all indigent defendants facing felony charges are entitled to the assistance of counsel at state expense. As to the first kind, if a defendant's conduct turns out to be constitutionally protected, so that it never should have been made a crime in the first place, then it seems appropriate to make the extraordinary remedy of habeas available to vindicate such a claim. As to the second kind, the Court has not yet identified any other right, other than the *Gideon* right, that it thought sufficiently fundamental to deserve this status. Because the two kinds of federal claims encompassed within this first portion of our proposed new habeas statute are both extremely rare and exceptionally compelling, habeas jurisdiction—when properly invoked—will be well worth the effort.

Claims of Innocence

Under our proposal, the second statutory category would preserve habeas review for federal constitutional claims that had been rejected, or that can no longer be raised, in state court, when the petitioner can bring forward newly discovered evidence of his innocence of the crime of conviction or of a sentencing factor that is treated as the functional equivalent of an element of the crime.[12] If a petitioner can make such a strong showing of innocence, based on new evidence, then the habeas courts should be allowed to reach the merits of his constitutional claims. Without such new evidence, however, the original criminal judgment would serve as a legally sufficient answer to the petitioner's claim of innocence.

Cases of wrongful conviction of the innocent involve the most fundamental kind of unjust incarceration, as federal courts recognized well before the Warren Court years. They justify the extraordinary expenditure of resources to allow habeas courts to provide a last-chance remedy. Moreover, the numerous DNA revelations of the last several years, combined with reluctance by some state officials to act quickly to correct and prevent such mistakes,[13] could well be characterized as a new and growing crisis warranting federal intervention into state criminal justice.

These cases present a novel challenge that the Supreme Court is still in the process of addressing.

There are at least two different ways that a petitioner's claim of innocence might impact access to habeas relief. As under current habeas law, a sufficient showing of innocence could be held to allow a petitioner to avoid certain procedural restrictions on habeas review that would otherwise block the habeas court from reaching the merits of his claim of constitutional error. Alternatively, a strong enough showing of innocence could conceivably provide a sufficient basis for habeas relief even without any additional showing of constitutional error. Our proposal embraces the first possible role for innocence and is designed to accommodate future Supreme Court decisions concerning the second.

Innocence as Gateway

As the Supreme Court and Congress have erected new barriers to habeas review of the merits of constitutional claims, the Court has also declared exceptions to most of those new restrictions for petitioners who can demonstrate a strong likelihood of factual innocence.[14] For example, a showing of innocence can provide the means to avoid the preclusive effect of the *Wainwright v. Sykes* "state procedural default" doctrine. The Court has defined the so-called miscarriage-of-justice exception to require the petitioner to show "a fair probability that, in light of all the evidence, including that alleged to have been illegally admitted [and evidence that could have, but was not, produced and admitted], . . . the trier of the facts would have entertained a reasonable doubt of his guilt."[15] The Court has also said that this exception applies "where a constitutional violation has probably resulted in the conviction of one who is actually innocent."[16] Given the narrowness of the exception, it is perhaps not surprising that even Justice Rehnquist joined every one of the Court opinions that created and defined it.

Few convicted habeas petitioners can make a showing of innocence strong enough to meet the Court's current test for the miscarriage-of-justice exception. But on rare occasions, it does happen. In 2006, the Court held that Tennessee death row inmate Paul Gregory House passed the miscarriage-of-justice test, which meant that House could litigate his federal constitutional claims—including the claim that his defense lawyer at trial was constitutionally ineffective—in the habeas courts, despite the fact that he had not raised the claims on time in the state courts and therefore would normally be barred from raising them in habeas under the *Sykes* procedural default doctrine. House's strong showing of innocence allowed him to get around the *Sykes* procedural barrier and obtain habeas review of the merits of his claims—and he eventually prevailed, gaining a new trial and ultimately his release from custody.[17] A strong showing of innocence may provide the only hope for a habeas petitioner who, like Paul Gregory House, otherwise would be unable to work around a procedural barrier to habeas review. And even when a petitioner raises procedural claims unrelated to innocence, a showing of innocence may help to persuade a federal judge to take a closer look at the merits of those claims.[18]

Our proposal includes a requirement that is similar to this existing "gateway" role for innocence, but it is even more stringent in operation. Under the second part of our proposal, a strong showing of innocence based on new evidence would be a prerequisite to obtaining habeas review of any constitutional claim, not merely those that would otherwise be procedurally barred. In other words, under the second part of our proposal, federal habeas review of state noncapital criminal cases would be reserved for those habeas petitioners who can show a strong likelihood that they might be factually innocent of their crimes.[19]

As demonstrated by the track record of the current miscarriage-of-justice exception, few habeas petitioners will be able to make even a facially plausible showing of factual innocence sufficient to meet the standard contained in our proposed statute. As a result, habeas courts will rarely need to spend significant time reviewing the merits of habeas petitions making such innocence claims; most petitions will be summarily dismissed. The end result—very few grants of habeas relief—will resemble the current habeas situation. The process, however, will be much less complicated and much less wasteful. And the few cases that do receive meaningful habeas review in the federal courts will be those involving the most compelling of potential injustices—the conviction of a defendant who is likely innocent.

Innocence as Independent Claim

There is a second possible role for innocence in habeas cases, and it is an extremely important one. This is the role of innocence as an independent federal constitutional claim. The Supreme Court has never held that a strong showing of factual innocence alone, unrelated to any underlying claim of procedural error, states a federal constitutional claim. For this reason, such a claim of "bare innocence"—sometimes referred to as a "naked," "stand-alone," or "actual" innocence claim—is currently insufficient to justify federal habeas relief. This subject has been the subject of frequent debate, both on and off the Court.

In 1993, the Court decided a controversial case involving a capital habeas petitioner who raised a claim of factual innocence.[20] Leonel Torres Herrera was convicted and sentenced to death for the September 1981 murder of a police officer near Brownsville, Texas. The conviction and death sentence were affirmed on direct appeal and in state postconviction proceedings, and a federal habeas petition was denied. In 1992, Herrera filed another federal habeas petition, claiming that the case was one of mistaken identity—that his brother, Raul, who had recently died in prison, was the real killer. Herrera supported his claim with affidavits from witnesses who had heard Raul confess his guilt before he died. This new evidence was of no avail in the Texas state courts, because Texas law at the time prohibited any challenge to a conviction based on new evidence filed more than thirty days after the imposition of sentence.

In his federal habeas petition, Herrera alleged no procedural violation of the Constitution at his trial or capital sentencing hearing. He simply argued that it would violate either the Eighth Amendment's "cruel and unusual punishments" clause or the Due Process Clause to punish, by execution, one who is factually innocent of the crime. Herrera's stand-alone claim of innocence was the first such claim to reach the Supreme Court.

The Court held that Herrera was not entitled to habeas relief. The Court assumed, "for the sake of argument in deciding this case, that in a capital case a truly persuasive demonstration of 'actual innocence' made after trial would render the execution of a defendant unconstitutional, and warrant federal habeas relief if there were no state avenue open to process such a claim."[21] Given the disruption that would be caused by habeas courts routinely reviewing the accuracy of jury verdicts, however, the Court noted that "the threshold showing for such an assumed right would necessarily be extraordinarily high."[22]

The Court's opinion in *Herrera* also highlighted the historic role of executive clemency, as opposed to habeas litigation, in addressing post-trial claims of innocence. According to the Court, "Executive clemency has provided the 'fail safe' in our criminal justice system. . . . It is an unalterable fact that our judicial system, like the human beings who admin-

ister it, is fallible. But history is replete with examples of wrongfully convicted persons who have been pardoned in the wake of after-discovered
evidence establishing their innocence."[23] The Court noted that "Texas
clemency procedures contain specific guidelines for pardons on the
ground of innocence."

In the end, the Court concluded that under any standards that might
be applied to such a bare-innocence claim, Leonel Herrera could not
qualify for habeas relief. The facts that the slain officer before his death,
as well as his partner, had both identified Herrera as the killer; that the
killer drove a car belonging to Herrera's girlfriend; that Herrera had the
keys to that car in his pocket at the time of his arrest; and that Herrera
pled guilty to murdering another police officer in a separate incident
earlier on the same night all undermined his claim of factual innocence.
Given the weakness of Herrera's innocence claim, the Court declined to
issue any further guidance about what would happen if a capital habeas
petitioner actually made a "truly persuasive" showing of innocence.

As a result, at the present time, factual innocence alone—meaning
a *Herrera*-type claim of bare innocence unconnected with any alleged
violation of constitutional criminal procedure law—does not yet state a
federal constitutional claim and therefore cannot provide a basis for habeas relief. This may seem shocking, but it is true. In at least two post-
Herrera cases, both decided within the past six years, the Supreme Court
has continued to entertain the possibility that stand-alone claims of factual innocence might be constitutionally cognizable and thus an appropriate subject of habeas litigation.[24] But the Court has yet to find such a
claim plausible enough to require even resolving the basic constitutional
issue, let alone explicating the specific legal standards that would apply
to such a claim.[25]

Habeas corpus is a potentially powerful remedy for violations of federal law—primarily, violations of the U.S. Constitution. But the habeas
remedy does not create the federal rights it vindicates. The federal guarantees upon which habeas petitioners must rely to challenge their state
convictions and obtain relief from the federal courts must be established
independently by Supreme Court decisions interpreting and applying
the Constitution. Indeed, given the limited constitutional authority provided to Congress in the area of criminal justice, it is doubtful that any
federal habeas statute could manufacture a new federal right, cognizable
in habeas, on behalf of state prisoners who claim to be factually innocent.[26] We therefore have not included such a provision within our stat-

utory proposal for habeas reform. At the same time, we have drafted
our proposal so that, if the Supreme Court eventually does recognize
such a bare-innocence claim as an independent constitutional violation,
the claim would fit squarely within the scope of the second part of our
proposed new habeas statute and would thus be preserved for habeas
review.[27]

Moreover, we believe that—at least under current circumstances,
where state post-trial remedies for wrongful convictions are still evolving and often clearly deficient—such claims of bare innocence do belong in federal habeas. Since *Herrera*, and especially since the advent
of widespread DNA analysis, the American criminal justice system has
advanced significantly in its treatment of claims of factual innocence
made by convicted defendants. But the situation remains confusing and
far from settled. The most effective reforms to protect against wrongful conviction are those that operate to prevent those convictions in the
first place, such as state law requirements that police videotape all interrogations and that judges give extra scrutiny to the testimony of notoriously unreliable "jailhouse snitches." Numerous states are already moving in this direction. Nevertheless, judicial review of post-trial innocence
claims must continue to play a crucial role.

States are only beginning to develop the postconviction processes
required to accommodate recent developments in post-trial access to
compelling new proof of innocence. A few states have even created, or
are considering creating, "innocence commissions," based on a model
currently in use in Great Britain and Canada. These new government
agencies generally have the power to investigate post-trial claims of innocence and to refer meritorious cases back to the courts for legal action.[28] Such developments are encouraging, because it is not uncommon for exonerations to be based on new evidence of innocence that
could not reasonably have been discovered until long after the original
conviction and sentencing. More states have eliminated or significantly
lengthened deadlines for filing legal challenges to convictions based
on new evidence. But not all states currently allow convicted inmates
reasonable access to the DNA evidence that could prove their factual
innocence.[29]

Given the likelihood that state remedies will continue for some time
to be inadequate to address and resolve all persuasive claims of factual
innocence filed by state prisoners, federal habeas review can and should
provide an additional layer of judicial protection for these unusual cases.

Although it is not properly a part of our statutory habeas reform proposal, we encourage the Court to resolve the uncertainty about the scope of constitutional protection engendered by *Herrera*. The Court should acknowledge, once and for all, the constitutional status of a narrowly defined, *Herrera*-type, bare-innocence claim and should proceed to develop an appropriate set of legal standards for such a claim.[30]

Eliminating Wasteful Litigation

Adopting our proposal would mean a huge reduction in the amount of habeas litigation by state prisoners in noncapital cases. In effect, the proposal would operate something like *Stone v. Powell*,[31] the Supreme Court decision that barred federal habeas review of Fourth Amendment claims so long as the petitioner had a full and fair opportunity to litigate those claims in state court. Our proposal would eliminate federal habeas jurisdiction over all federal constitutional claims raised by state prisoners challenging custody resulting from a noncapital criminal judgment, absent either retroactive application of new federal law or compelling new proof of innocence. Presently, only a small percentage of habeas petitions contain allegations of either kind of violation. In the 2007 study, for example, fewer than 4 percent of noncapital filers raised a claim of innocence based on newly discovered evidence.[32]

One might reasonably anticipate that, if our proposal were adopted, many more habeas petitioners would assert claims of factual innocence in an effort to obtain habeas review that would otherwise be unavailable to them. After all, any prisoner can file a petition claiming innocence. But this need not, and should not, generate a new tidal wave of wasteful habeas litigation. The proposal requires that claims of innocence be supported by compelling new evidence, something that only a tiny handful of habeas petitioners will be able to produce. And this defect will be apparent on the face of most petitions. So long as the habeas courts—led by the Supreme Court—exercise proper prudence in their handling and disposition of such claims, the likelihood that a court will have to spend significant time screening petitions raising undeserving allegations of innocence should be extremely small. And where such litigation proves necessary, it can hardly be termed "wasteful"; habeas litigation about a convicted defendant's compelling claim of factual innocence is exactly the kind of litigation we should want to encourage.

As we will explain, our proposal also relies on a judicially controlled escape hatch—the Suspension Clause—that can ensure the flexibility of federal habeas to respond if the states were unreasonably to withhold, in the future, judicial review for prisoners convicted in their courts. The Suspension Clause, in other words, can operate in much the same way as a safety valve, allowing the Court to retain needed control over the scope of habeas review.[33]

A Better Federal Approach: Encouraging Reform of State Defense Representation

In the end, our proposal would allow for the reallocation of resources currently wasted on futile federal habeas litigation toward the pursuit of more important societal goals. One such goal, as we have argued elsewhere,[34] should be to create a bold new federal initiative devoted to improving the quality of defense representation services in the states. Most knowledgeable observers would agree that ensuring the vindication of constitutional rights in criminal proceedings depends, more than anything else, on vigorous representation of the accused by a qualified and competent defense lawyer. Unfortunately, far too often, such representation is not available in state courts today.

Twenty-five years ago, the Supreme Court tried to fulfill the promise of *Gideon* and ensure the quality of defense counsel by creating an opportunity for defendants convicted in state court to complain in federal court, after the fact and case by case, that they had received ineffective assistance of counsel in violation of the Sixth Amendment.[35] But as so many others have made clear, after-the-fact litigation about defense counsel's effectiveness, which has now become routine in state postconviction proceedings as well as in federal habeas, has failed—and will always fail—as a means of ensuring competent defense counsel in criminal cases.[36] Systematic underfunding of criminal defense representation persists, resulting in repeated and widespread breakdowns in defense representation. State and local governments in fiscal distress continue to struggle to provide even the most minimal levels of representation to indigent persons who are accused of a crime.[37]

This is a particular kind of structural problem that, unfortunately, case-by-case habeas litigation is poorly designed to address.[38] Our proposal, therefore, would almost completely eliminate such litigation. What we need is an entirely new approach that focuses on prevention rather than cure. A proactive federal program with the clear mission, and the funding, to encourage the states to improve their defense representation services offers a realistic promise of reform that case-by-case habeas review cannot deliver.

The establishment of a new federal agency to promote quality defense representation in the states, along the lines of the Federal Center for Defense Services that was first proposed in 1979 by the American Bar Association (ABA), is long overdue. Through matching grants and other financial incentives, research programs to develop quality-of-counsel standards and summaries of "best practices" and similar initiatives, this new approach could help the states to improve the ways that defense counsel are trained, certified, appointed, compensated, supported, evaluated, and regulated. If such an agency is provided with the tools to succeed—including, especially, adequate funding—this could eventually lead to better compliance with federal law for all criminal defendants, not just those few lucky ones who manage today to win the habeas lottery.

For thirty years, the ABA's suggestion of a federal center has gone nowhere, mostly because of natural political resistance to any program that would benefit primarily criminal defendants. But our proposal to limit federal habeas corpus review of state criminal cases can help to transform this political dynamic. Linking the creation of a new federal initiative to reform state indigent defense with a companion proposal to dramatically reduce wasteful federal habeas litigation—perhaps even conditioning one upon the other as a quid pro quo in Congress—has both political and economic advantages.[39] And, in turn, the political viability of our proposal to restrict habeas is likely to be much greater than it might have been in the past because of the compelling new empirical evidence from the 2007 study, which reveals just how little of value habeas petitioners really have to lose. As Professor Daniel Meltzer surmised years ago, the limited societal resources that are currently wasted on futile federal habeas corpus litigation could, and should, be used for something of greater value.[40] Habeas review in noncapital cases costs more than ever and delivers almost no benefits. By clinging to a system of case-by-case enforcement that has long outlived its usefulness, Congress is pouring tax dollars down the drain.

Preserving Habeas Flexibility:
The Role of the Suspension Clause

We have proposed that Congress should amend the federal habeas statute, Section 2254, to curtail habeas review of state criminal cases and
thereby send a clear message to the Supreme Court about the need for
prudence in the use of habeas. In taking this step, however, Congress
cannot have the last word on the scope of federal habeas. The Court retains the power, through interpretation of both habeas law and the Suspension Clause, to control the extent to which any new habeas statute
can limit the authority of the federal courts to remedy unlawful detentions. We would not want our proposal to disable the Court from responding to an unforeseen political or social crisis that might once again
make broad habeas review of state criminal cases desirable. How can we
ensure that prudent restrictions on habeas review do not eliminate the
flexibility that is also a key component of the habeas remedy? The Suspension Clause provides the answer to this question.

The Suspension Clause, ratified in 1789 as part of the original Constitution, provides, "The Privilege of the Writ of Habeas Corpus shall not
be suspended, unless when in Cases of Rebellion or Invasion the public
Safety may require it."[41] Admittedly, the Court has never squarely held
that this Clause limits the suspension of federal habeas for prisoners
serving state criminal sentences. As noted in chapter 1, the Court has adopted the historical stance that federal habeas review for convicted state
prisoners was unavailable until provided by Congress in 1867. The Fourteenth Amendment, however, which—just one year after the 1867 act—
broadened both the definition of federal citizenship and the reach of federal law, arguably extended the protection of the Suspension Clause to
those incarcerated after conviction by the states.[42]

Interpreting the clause to limit suspension of the habeas remedy provided to state prisoners as of 1867 leaves the Court and Congress considerable leeway in which to contract habeas review without amount-
ing to a "suspension."[43] But under the recent decision in *Boumediene
v. Bush*, as discussed previously, it is also clear that substantial restrictions on the scope of habeas can survive a Suspension Clause challenge
only if an "adequate substitute" is available. As interpreted in *Boumediene*, the Clause requires that any adequate substitute for habeas review
must provide the prisoner with, at a minimum, "a meaningful opportunity to demonstrate that he is being held pursuant to 'the erroneous ap-

plication or interpretation' of relevant law" and must also provide the reviewing court with "the power to order the conditional release of an individual unlawfully detained—though release need not be the exclusive remedy."[44]

In *Boumediene*, the statute challenged as an unconstitutional suspension of the writ had stripped the federal courts of jurisdiction over any habeas petition filed by those incarcerated at Guantanamo. The Department of Defense had instead created Combatant Status Review Tribunals to adjudicate disputes over a detainee's status as an "enemy combatant," and Congress in the Detainee Treatment Act of 2005 had provided only limited judicial review of the tribunal's decision, in the Court of Appeals for the District of Columbia. Because the statute failed to provide to prisoners the opportunity to challenge the president's detention authority, to contest findings of fact, or to present new evidence to the federal court and also failed to authorize the court to order a detainee's release, the Supreme Court ultimately rejected the government's claim that such limited federal appellate review could be an adequate substitute for habeas.[45]

The *Boumediene* decision emphasized that the "adequacy" of any alleged federal "substitute" for habeas that is challenged as a possible suspension of the writ must be evaluated in light of the context of prior legal proceedings.[46] The defects in the Detainee Treatment Act's judicial review process proved fatal to the statute in large part because the military tribunals themselves provided very limited procedural safeguards, thus creating a "considerable risk of error in the tribunal's findings of fact."[47] The Court was careful, however, to distinguish the statutory scheme in *Boumediene* from judicial review of detention based on a criminal conviction. The Court emphasized that where the original detention proceedings themselves are more rigorous ("*e.g.*, in post-trial habeas cases where the prisoner already has had a full and fair opportunity to develop the factual predicate of his claims"[48]), substituting limited federal appellate review for broad access to habeas might be permissible.

If federal habeas corpus review were limited according to our proposal, only four narrow avenues of federal judicial review of state noncapital criminal cases would remain: (1) Supreme Court certiorari review of state direct appeal proceedings; (2) Supreme Court certiorari review of state postconviction proceedings; (3) statutory habeas review in the lower federal courts for those few cases that fall within the categories in which habeas would be preserved under the new Section 2254;

and (4) review pursuant to a petition for a writ of habeas corpus filed in either the lower federal courts or the Supreme Court as an "original writ" pursuant to 28 U.S.C. § 2241, an alternative form of the habeas remedy that our proposal would not alter. For most state prisoners, the likelihood of meaningful review of constitutional claims through these channels would be quite rare, and future habeas petitioners would surely challenge our proposal as a violation of the Suspension Clause.

Under *Boumediene*, however, which holds that the adequacy of any federal court substitute for habeas depends in part on the prior judicial proceedings mandating detention, our proposal will comply with the Suspension Clause so long as the states continue to provide not only an initial adjudication of guilt that is rigorous and compliant with Due Process but also reasonable levels of state appellate and postconviction review for constitutional claims.[49] Under *Boumediene*, state judicial proceedings themselves cannot serve as an adequate substitute for habeas, but those prior proceedings can provide the necessary litigation context in which even a severely limited federal judicial forum can nevertheless suffice as an adequate substitute for habeas.

The Suspension Clause in Action

The Suspension Clause, as interpreted in the *Boumediene* case, provides the Supreme Court with all of the flexibility the Court might need to deal with a future crisis. Under *Boumediene*, for example, if a state were to eliminate appellate or postconviction review entirely, the Court could hold that the proposed statutory curtailment of federal habeas, given the absence of a context of meaningful prior judicial review, represents a suspension of the writ. Similarly, if a state—in a reprise of the situation that prevailed in the 1950s and 1960s—were suddenly to foment a new crisis of federalism by abdicating its responsibility to enforce certain federal constitutional rights, then the Court could hold that the context of prior judicial review had changed and that any statute limiting federal habeas review to the narrow scope that we propose herein represents a suspension of the writ. The Suspension Clause, in other words, leaves the Court with the ultimate control over the scope of habeas review of state criminal cases. The Clause thus preserves the Court's ability to monitor state judicial enforcement of federal constitutional rights on an ongoing basis, just as the Clause protects the Court's ability to use habeas to monitor ever-changing schemes for military and immigration detention initiated by the political branches.

To be sure, the Court has yet to use its powers under the Suspension Clause in precisely this way. But Justice Brennan's 1961 Utah speech suggests the line of reasoning the Court should adopt. Brennan articulated two different reasons for expanding federal habeas review for those serving state sentences: (1) defiance by state judges in the face of what they considered an unjustifiable incursion of federal law into the traditional domain of the states and (2) the lack of state postconviction proceedings and remedies adequate to adjudicate defendants' constitutional claims.[50] If either or both of these two conditions were to recur in a particular state as a consequence of our proposal, this would give rise to a legitimate concern that our proposed habeas restrictions might constitute a violation of the Suspension Clause as applied to criminal cases from that particular state.

The idea of applying habeas corpus differentially, based on a particular state's handling of federal constitutional claims in its own state courts, may seem strange today. But in 1949 a somewhat similar situation arose. At that time, the Supreme Court decided that the Illinois state courts were refusing to enforce federal constitutional standards in criminal cases. It instructed federal district courts not to insist that Illinois prisoners exhaust their state remedies before filing their federal habeas corpus petitions because there were, essentially, no such state remedies to exhaust. This led the State of Illinois to adopt one of the very first modern state postconviction review statutes in the United States.[51]

The Supreme Court should take care not to encourage wasteful habeas litigation over alleged state-specific suspensions of the writ. But if a new crisis ever arose under our proposal, the Court would possess a flexible set of remedial options. The Court could leave the amended statute in place and avoid the constitutional problem by broadening habeas review under Section 2241, an alternative habeas statute untouched by our proposal. Section 2241 currently provides only a very limited opportunity for state prisoners to challenge their state criminal judgments,[52] but the Court could expand those opportunities—as it did, even in the absence of legislative changes, with respect to Section 2254 in the 1950s and 1960s. Or the Court could find our proposed amendments unconstitutional as a suspension of the writ and reinstate a former version of Section 2254. In any event, the Court should choose the particular remedy that best responds to the nature of the particular Suspension Clause crisis. This approach ensures the flexibility that is the historic hallmark of the habeas writ. Accordingly, we do not believe that Congress should try to include in the proposed amendments any provision specifying the particular legal regime that would take over if the amendments should ever be struck down as a suspension of the writ.

Two additional points are worth emphasizing about the operation of the Suspension Clause. First, as a general matter, states should not be required to adopt identical, cookie-cutter review procedures, nor should states be required to make significant changes to their existing review procedures. For example, the fact that some states make appellate review discretionary instead of providing an appeal of right should make no difference in assessing the constitutionality of the proposed restrictions under the Suspension Clause. Second, because the Court's analysis under the Suspension Clause is inherently flexible, and because the risk of constitutional error may change as the procedures associated with detention change, a ruling upholding the proposed cutbacks in habeas review should neither freeze current state review mechanisms in place nor stifle experimentation.

We believe that our proposal to curtail federal habeas corpus review of state noncapital criminal cases satisfies the Suspension Clause only because of the existing context of meaningful state appellate and postconviction judicial review of criminal cases. If that context were to change in the future, in a manner that substantially diminishes the opportunity for enforcement of federal constitutional rights by the state courts, then the Suspension Clause, as construed in *Boumediene*, would require that the Supreme Court step in and restore an appropriately broader habeas remedy.

*   *   *

The need for routine, case-by-case federal habeas review of state criminal cases has come and gone. The Warren Court's expansion of habeas served its purpose, which was to prod the states to reform their own judicial review processes and to compel state judges to accept federal law as if it were their own. As a remedy for case-specific constitutional violations, however, habeas review was never worth the cost. Today, it is even less so. It is high time for this charade to end and for habeas to be scaled back to its traditionally limited role in state criminal cases. This will help to ensure that habeas will remain available when it is needed to address the next recurrence of institutional imbalance and remedial gaps leading to large-scale arbitrary detentions. Our statutory proposal to curtail habeas review of state criminal judgments relies on Congress to initiate a more prudent use of habeas. It also relies on the Supreme Court as the ultimate authority to decide, pursuant to the Suspension Clause, whether or not criminal defendants in a particular state have a reasonable opportunity to litigate in state court the constitutionality of their custody.

This proposal is consistent with both good policy and the long history of habeas corpus. It is consistent with good policy because it conserves societal resources that would otherwise be wasted on ineffectual case-by-case review. These resources can, and should, be devoted instead to a new federal initiative designed to encourage the states to reform their defense representation systems—a front-end reform that can deliver much greater benefits. The proposal is consistent with habeas history because the Court has long viewed the statutory version of habeas applicable to state prisoners as a special kind of statute, resting upon a foundation of common law dating back centuries and therefore subject to the Court's interpretation and control—both to expand and to contract the scope of the statute—to a much greater extent than most other federal statutes.[53]

The Court's longstanding practice of exercising control over the scope of the writ, including its frequent adjustments of that scope in response to changing conditions, strongly suggests that the Court, and not Congress, must have the final say in deciding whether the circumstances warrant either the curtailment or the expansion of federal habeas review of state criminal cases. We have proposed Congressional action as a catalyst to reduce the scope of habeas review. The Court, however, must retain the ability to adapt the habeas remedy to meet the specific needs of the time. The Suspension Clause, as construed in *Boumediene*, provides the constitutional authority for the Court to do exactly that. As a result, our proposal can achieve both prudence and flexibility at the same time.

CHAPTER SIX

Collateral Review for Prisoners Convicted of Federal Crimes

In this chapter we turn from habeas review for prisoners convicted of noncapital crimes in state courts to habeas review for prisoners convicted of noncapital crimes in federal courts. In this context, the federal courts are essentially supervising themselves. Collateral review here does not preserve the supremacy of federal law in the states, nor is it a means for the federal courts to maintain or restore the balance of powers among the president, Congress, and the judiciary. Collateral review in federal criminal cases serves a different role, and our policy prescriptions for its future are thus entirely different from the reforms that we have outlined for habeas review for federal detainees or convicted state prisoners. What we recommend here is not a contraction but a modest expansion of federal judicial review of federal criminal cases.

Section 2255—an Alternative to Habeas for Federal Prisoners

We pick up the story of federal prisoners at the crucial juncture in the 1940s, after the Supreme Court had begun to use habeas under the 1867 act to assure that both state and federal courts were complying with its initial expansions of constitutional rights in criminal cases but before its modern criminal procedure revolution was in full swing. As recounted in chapter 3, during the decades leading up to 1948 the Court had handed down several decisions interpreting the 1867 act more broadly than before. The Court had held that habeas courts could reach claims by convicted prisoners that they had been denied procedural protections guaranteed by the Constitution and had abandoned the former approach of limiting review to the narrower category of "jurisdictional error." Because the Court had not yet held that most of the specific constitutional protections in the Bill of Rights were included within the scope of due process, which the Fourteenth Amendment required the states to provide to state criminal defendants, this shift in the scope of habeas review had its most immediate effect on petitions from federal prisoners. By 1938, for example, the Court had declared that an indigent federal prisoner convicted of a felony without a defense lawyer could claim in his habeas petition that he had not validly waived his right to counsel under the Sixth Amendment,[1] but it was not until *Gideon* in 1963 that the Court recognized a similar constitutional right to counsel for indigent state felony defendants.[2]

During the 1940s, the number of habeas petitions filed by federal prisoners grew rapidly.[3] Only a few of these petitions had any merit, however, once they were compared with the record in the court of conviction.[4] Unfortunately, making this comparison was no easy matter, and resolving prisoners' allegations became an overwhelming burden for some district courts. Because a petitioner had to file his habeas petition in the district in which he was incarcerated, districts that contained federal prisons received hundreds of petitions each year, while other districts received none. Federal prisoners from across the nation were concentrated in just six major federal prisons—some located far from the districts in which most of the inmates had been convicted. These prisons included Alcatraz near San Francisco, Leavenworth near Kansas City, and McNeil Island off the coast of Washington State. In the District Court in Kansas, 65 percent of the court's workload entailed resolving habeas petitions filed by Leavenworth prisoners.[5] The Supreme Court also had made clear in 1941 that the habeas statute required the court to produce the petitioner for a hearing whenever substantial issues of fact existed.[6] Litigating a habeas petition in the district in which the petitioner was incarcerated made it easier to deliver the prisoner to court, but it complicated access to everything else that was needed to resolve the case.

Records in criminal cases from distant courts of conviction were difficult to obtain, and in most cases, there were no records at all. No mandatory system for reporting proceedings in federal criminal cases existed until after World War II. Instead, as an administrative office report bemoaned in 1943, in most criminal cases—and in almost all cases decided by guilty plea—there was "no reliable evidence of what actually occurred at the time of the defendant's arraignment and sentence." As the report explained, "The defendant often asserts that he was not properly advised of his right to counsel, or that his rights in other respects were not properly safeguarded. The only way to establish the facts satisfactorily is to have a verbatim record of what occurred at the trial, and that is not obtainable except rarely under present conditions. . . ."[7]

Reconstructing what happened in the absence of a record sometimes required deposing the district judge who had presided over the original proceedings or ordering witnesses to travel long distances to the district where the prisoner was being held. Typical was the case of Jack Walker, imprisoned at Alcatraz, who filed his habeas petition in the federal district court in California. He claimed that before pleading guilty to bank robbery in federal court in Texas, he had not been advised of, nor waived, his right to counsel. The habeas court initially denied Walker's petition without a hearing, relying on affidavits from prosecutors in the Texas district in which Walker had been convicted, including one stating that Walker "told the judge in open court that he had no counsel and did not desire any as he was guilty and intended to plead guilty." The Supreme Court, however, remanded the case, explaining that Walker deserved an opportunity to support his claims by evidence, that he had a "right to be heard," and that the federal officials from Texas whose affidavits were challenged "must be subjected to examination . . . as are all other witnesses."[8]

By 1945, a committee of judges appointed by the Supreme Court proposed new legislation to address the "practical difficulties" created by these petitions from federal prisoners. The same proposed legislation also responded to the sea change in federal habeas petitions filed by state prisoners raising new constitutional claims.[9] These reforms were enacted into law in 1948, dividing habeas into three separate federal statutes. The new statutory remedy for federal prisoners, 28 U.S.C. § 2255, required that federal inmates file their postconviction challenges in the district of conviction, not in the district in which they were incarcerated, a clear break from habeas corpus practice under both the common law writ and its statutory offspring, the 1867 act. This change promised better and quicker access to trial court records and witnesses, but it also meant more decisions without the presence of the petitioner. The new statute expressly provided, "A court may entertain and determine such motion without requiring the production of the prisoner at the hearing." Supporters of the legislation argued that "[t]he writ . . . is not a plaything of penitentiary inmates to accomplish temporary vacation visits to the federal courts,"[10] and Congress agreed. Every federal prisoner attacking his conviction or sentence was required to use the new Section 2255 remedy unless it was "inadequate or ineffective to test the legality of his detention," a statutory phrase that became known as the "savings clause."

To the disappointment of reformers, in the first eleven months after its passage, only 102 applications under Section 2255 were filed.[11] Most federal prisoners continued to file traditional habeas petitions, as they always had under the old habeas statute, which was now recodified at 28 U.S.C. § 2241.[12] The new statute's less than auspicious debut had two possible explanations. First, prisoners may simply have missed the statutory changes, particularly since even more important legislation affecting the federal courts was enacted the same year, including a comprehensive revision of both the federal criminal code and the Judicial Code. The new statutory substitute also was challenged in the courts as unconstitutional, on the theory that forcing a petitioner to litigate the legality of his custody in a district far from where he was imprisoned, and without his physical presence, was such a break from the common law habeas writ that it amounted to a violation of the Suspension Clause.[13] Not until 1963 did the Court finally uphold as constitutional the discretion granted to district courts to dispense with the prisoner's presence in Section 2255 proceedings, stating, "Not every colorable allegation entitles a federal prisoner to a trip to the sentencing court."[14]

Expanding Rights, Expanding Remedies, and the Temporary Advantage of Parallel Rules for State and Federal Prisoners

After the 1948 enactment of Sections 2254 and 2255, habeas corpus review of state prisoner claims and collateral review of federal prisoner claims were no longer governed by the same statute, yet the Court continued to interpret the two statutory remedies together. As the Court gradually expanded habeas review to enforce new constitutional rights, it often adopted the same interpretation under both statutes, so that the two remedies grew in lockstep. As Justice William Brennan explained in 1959, the two remedies were to be construed to have equal scope in reaching constitutional claims, as they both rested "fundamentally upon a recognition that adequate protection of constitutional rights relating to the criminal trial process requires the continuing availability of a mechanism for relief."[15]

For example, similar limitations on successive habeas petitions were established for both state and federal prisoners, despite different statutory language.[16] The Court likewise adopted the same rules regarding access to an evidentiary hearing to challenge a guilty plea for state and federal prisoners. It acknowledged that the relevant statutes "differ somewhat in phrasing,"[17] but reasoned that the remedy under Section 2255 was intended to be "exactly commensurate" with the habeas corpus remedy it replaced. And the definition of "custody" grew to encompass those who were under court supervision or subject to a consecutive sentence, first in state prisoner cases, then in federal cases.[18]

The two remedies were also narrowed simultaneously by the Burger and Rehnquist Courts in the late 1970s and 1980s, by the lower federal courts, and finally by Congress in 1996. As described in chapter 3, the Court in *Wainwright v. Sykes* borrowed a limitation on the review of claims that were procedurally defaulted in the state courts from the similar limitation it had already developed for claims by federal prisoners.[19] The Court's 1976 decision in *Stone v. Powell*, banning the habeas review of Fourth Amendment claims by state petitioners, was soon followed by lower court extension of the same ban to Section 2255 applicants.[20] And even the Court's 1989 decision in *Teague v. Lane* to bar state habeas petitioners from invoking most constitutional rules announced after their appeals had ended—a limitation based in large part on respect for state sovereignty—was later repackaged to limit collateral review of federal criminal judgments under Section 2255.[21] In its 1996 revision of the statutes governing collateral review, Congress too retained much of this parallel treatment.[22] Under the Antiterrorism and Effective Death Penalty Act of 1996 (AEDPA) both federal and state prisoners continue to face similar filing deadlines, as well as similar barriers to filing multiple petitions and appeals of orders denying or dismissing petitions.

One advantage of this identical twin approach to collateral review of criminal convictions was predictability and efficiency. Litigants and lower courts could look to decisions under one statute and adapt them for the other, without waiting for the Court itself to reach the same issue under both statutes. This shortcut made sense when, back in 1948, the single habeas statute was first subdivided. And it made sense even through the early 1970s, when constitutional rights of criminal defendants were still expanding, the scope of relief under the new statutes remained uncertain, and the procedures to be followed by courts in applying those statutes were a moving target. Most importantly, during the 1950s and 1960s, the parallel construction made conceptual sense. Both habeas review under Section 2254 and collateral review under Section 2255 were fulfilling the same function. Because of the deficiencies of state postconviction judicial review, many state prisoners, like their federal counterparts, had no other opportunity to litigate the constitutional claims they were raising in federal habeas.

Today, however, these justifications for parallel construction under Section 2254 and Section 2255 are no longer viable. Whatever efficiencies may still be gained by cloning these two similar remedies are not worth the cost of ignoring the fundamental differences between the functions each remedy now serves.

Realigning Section 2255 Review

The problem with Section 2255 review today is that it continues to be tied too closely to the wrong model of postconviction review—the federal review of state criminal judgments. The solution is to recognize that the role that Section 2255 plays in enforcing federal law in federal criminal cases is the very same role that state postconviction review now serves in state criminal cases.[23]

Collateral review under Section 2255 has always provided the very first opportunity for a federal prisoner to raise before any judge several important claims that generally cannot be meaningfully litigated on direct appeal. Back in 1948 before the development of modern state postconviction remedies, when Congress first enacted Sections 2254 and 2255, it made sense to assume that habeas proceedings in federal courts would provide the first opportunity for state prisoners to raise such constitutional claims as well, and that the two remedies should resemble each other. With the development of state postconviction review of constitutional claims, however, federal habeas review no longer represents the first bite at the apple of judicial review for state prisoners. We have argued in previous chapters that this evolution in state criminal justice requires rethinking federal habeas review for prisoners who are serving state criminal sentences. The same analysis reveals why the Section 2255 remedy for prisoners serving federal criminal sentences requires realignment as well. The first and only chance for judicial review should not be as limited as a second chance.

There are two important categories of claims that a person convicted of a crime usually will not be able to litigate on appeal and must raise instead in a collateral proceeding. The first category is made up of claims that could not be raised on appeal because the relevant law changed after appeal was concluded. The second category involves claims that could not be raised on appeal because the facts to support the claim are not part of the trial court record. State prisoners may raise both categories of claims in state postconviction proceedings—indeed, they generally must, as a precondition to seeking federal habeas review. For federal prisoners, however, an application for relief under 2255 is generally the first chance to raise both categories of claims.

Claims Based on Postappeal Changes in Federal Law

Federal prisoners need access to collateral review for two types of claims based on new pronouncements of law. The first type, discussed in chapter 5, consists of new rules of constitutional law. New constitutional rulings that apply retroactively to benefit even those prisoners who have completed their appeals are very rare. They are limited to new decisions holding that the Constitution forbids criminal punishment of certain conduct, prohibits a particular sanction for a particular crime, or guarantees a procedural right as fundamental as the right to appointed counsel that was first recognized for indigent state felony defendants in *Gideon*.[24] State postconviction review now provides a forum for state prisoners to take advantage of these retroactively applicable new rules.[25] Section 2255 provides federal prisoners with their first opportunity to do so.[26]

There is an additional type of claim that falls into the same category of changed legal rulings that federal prisoners generally cannot raise on appeal. Collateral review under Section 2255 may also be the first chance the federal prisoner has to raise an allegation that he was convicted for conduct that was never covered by the federal statute defining his offense (a nonexistent crime) or that he was sentenced more severely than the punishment authorized by federal statute (a nonexistent penalty).[27] Whenever the Supreme Court, or any other federal court whose decisions are binding on a lower court, unexpectedly announces a narrowing interpretation of the scope of a federal criminal statute, a defendant who had been improperly convicted or sentenced in the lower court under a broader, erroneous reading of that statute is entitled to the benefit of its correct interpretation, and collateral review under Section 2255 often provides his first opportunity to raise this claim.

For example, in 2008, the Supreme Court affirmed an order granting Section 2255 relief to Efrian Santos, a federal prisoner whose convictions for running an illegal lottery in East Chicago, Indiana, included two counts of laundering the "proceeds" of the gambling crime. The money-laundering convictions, which added more than twelve years to the five-year prison term Santos received for the gambling crime, were based on routine payments Santos had made to his employees and to the winners of his lottery. After Santos's appeal was denied, a new ruling by the U.S. Court of Appeals for the Seventh Circuit established that the proper definition of "proceeds" under the relevant money laundering statute included only the "net profits" of an illegal gambling operation and not the "gross revenues" that Santos used to pay his employees and his customers. In granting the Section 2255 application, the federal district judge remarked that "Santos is currently imprisoned for acts that are not now, nor ever have been crimes." The Supreme Court agreed, both with the Seventh Circuit's narrowing interpretation of the money-laundering statute and with the grant of Section 2255 relief.[28] Efrain Santos was guilty of running an illegal lottery, but he was never proven to be a money launderer, and thus he did not deserve to be punished as one.

Federal offense definitions are notoriously ambiguous, and a misunderstanding among the lower courts about the meaning of a statute can go uncorrected for years.[29] Perhaps the most disruptive correction in recent history took place after 1995, when the Supreme Court held that the federal statute making it a separate crime to "use" a firearm during a drug offense did not punish conduct that many lower courts had assumed it did—conduct such as keeping a gun, unloaded and holstered, locked in a footlocker at the defendant's apartment. The United States Sentencing Commission later estimated that between 1,500 and 2,200 federal defendants *per year* had been convicted under the broader reading of the statute that was ultimately rejected by the Court.[30] When these prisoners sought relief, claiming they were convicted of a nonexistent crime, there was a dramatic spike in Section 2255 filings that is visible in figure 6.1.[31]

Whenever controlling interpretations of a criminal statute turn out to be narrower than the lower courts anticipated, some prisoners may be stuck serving sentences for conduct that was never a crime. It is essential that collateral review for federal prisoners under Section 2255 continue to provide a forum for sorting out the consequences of unanticipated pronouncements about the proper reach of federal criminal law. State postconviction review provides a parallel forum for managing the

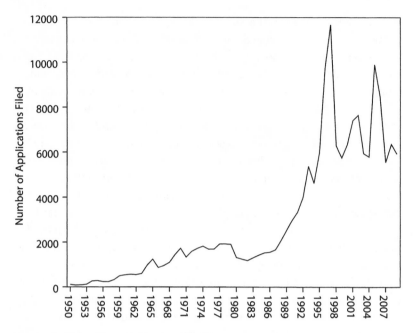

FIGURE 6.I. Federal 2255 Applications Filed, 1950–2009

fallout from decisions of state appellate courts that narrow the scope of the state's own criminal law statutes.[32]

Claims Based on Facts outside the Record

Section 2255 also provides the first opportunity for federal prisoners to obtain any judicial review of claims that could not be raised on appeal because they rest on facts that are not part of the trial record. For example, Section 2255 is the only vehicle available to a federal prisoner to attack a sentence that was based on prior convictions if those convictions are later vacated.[33] It is also the first chance a federal defendant has to raise a claim of ineffective assistance of counsel.[34]

Consider the case of L. B. Smith. What happened to Smith is a classic case of being in the wrong place at the wrong time. Police discovered over twenty-five pounds of cocaine in a car driven by a man named Vargas, and Vargas agreed to help them catch the buyer. Working with the authorities, Vargas told the buyer to meet him at a hotel where Vargas explained that his car had broken down. Surveillance revealed that at the appointed time, a car arrived at the hotel driven by Smith and carrying a passenger, Burks, who alone went in to meet with Vargas. Later Vargas and Burks were talking near enough for Smith to overhear, and when Vargas mentioned "the drugs," Smith showed no reaction. Smith and Burks were arrested for drug trafficking. Burks pleaded guilty, but Smith elected to go to trial.

At trial, the government offered testimony that cell phone calls linked to the drug transaction were made from the phone that was found in Smith's possession at the scene. Prosecutors also argued that Smith was carrying a gun to protect himself during the drug deal and that he did not react to the mention of the drugs was because he was not surprised. Burks, who had pleaded guilty and admitted setting up the drug deal with Vargas, testified for the defense. Smith was a childhood friend, Burks said, who worked on cars and ran an auto-detailing business, and he had asked Smith that morning to help him check out a car that was not running. Smith drove him to the hotel without knowing anything about the drug transaction because, Burks said, he never mentioned any drug deal to Smith. The defense pointed out to the jury that the surveillance tape showed Smith attempting to start Vargas's car in the parking lot, that Smith was arrested before he could possibly react to the mention of the drugs, and that he had told the police on the spot, truthfully, that he had purchased his gun lawfully a month earlier. The defense also argued that there were innocent explanations for the allegedly incriminating calls from Smith's cell phone. The jury convicted Smith of conspiracy to distribute over twenty-five pounds of cocaine, and he was sentenced to prison for twelve and a half years.

After his conviction was affirmed by the Fifth Circuit in 2004, Smith sought relief in the district court in which he had been convicted, under Section 2255, alleging that he had been denied the effective assistance of counsel at trial and that the prosecution had presented false testimony. At an evidentiary hearing, Smith presented evidence corroborating Burks's testimony about why he was at the hotel. He also proved that there were actually three different cell phones recovered at the scene, that both the prosecution and the defense were aware of this before trial, that the government presented false testimony that the suspicious calls were made with Smith's phone, and that it was actually Burks who used both of the phones discussed at the trial. In fact, Smith had a different cell phone with an entirely different area code, a fact that was never mentioned and that defense counsel had completely overlooked.

The judge vacated Smith's conviction and sentence, finding that if the true facts had been presented to the jurors, they probably would have acquitted Smith.

If L. B. Smith, the unlucky auto detailer, had been convicted of a state crime, he could have raised his claims of ineffective assistance and prosecutorial misconduct in the state courts. As we have argued, federal habeas review under Section 2254 today need not duplicate this opportunity, an opportunity that was not available to state defendants at the time when the Warren Court expanded habeas relief. But because Smith was convicted in federal court, review under Section 2255 was Smith's first and only chance to bring his ineffective assistance and prosecutorial misconduct claims to the attention of any judge. For prisoners like L. B. Smith, Section 2255 review in federal court is not at all like federal habeas review of state criminal judgments under Section 2254; instead, it is the functional equivalent of state postconviction review in the state courts.

The Future of 2255

From 1948 through the 1960s, when the Court used collateral review under the new Sections 2254 and 2255 to implement its modern revolution in constitutional criminal procedure, it made sense to treat these two statutes as clones. But federal and state prisoners are no longer similarly situated. Today, a habeas petition under Section 2254 has become the state prisoner's second chance to seek judicial enforcement of constitutional rules that cannot be raised on appeal, but an application under Section 2255 remains the federal prisoner's first and only chance to do so.

The difference in function is reflected in filing trends for both sets of prisoners. The establishment of state postconviction review coincided with a dramatic and sustained decrease in the rate at which state prisoners sought habeas relief after 1970, as illustrated in Figure 4.2. Figure 6.2 tells a very different story for federal prisoners. Section 2255 filing rates exhibit no pronounced long-term trend similar to that in the rate of state filings, and federal prisoners continue to apply for relief at a higher rate than state prisoners. It is time to abandon parallel rules for collateral review for state and federal prisoners—rules that were developed under circumstances that no longer exist—and to think anew about how col-

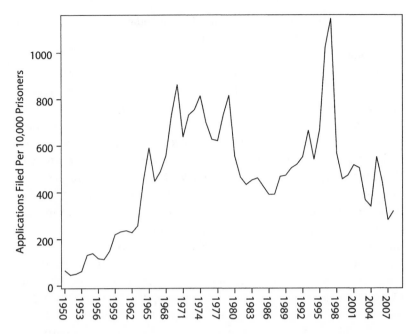

FIGURE 6.2. Federal 2255 Applications Filed per 10,000 Federal Prisoners, 1950–2009

lateral review of federal criminal cases can best perform its most vital functions.

Our starting point for the policy recommendations with which we conclude this chapter is the general principle examined in chapter 2, that federal judicial review should be safeguarded whenever it provides a prisoner with the first and only opportunity for any kind of judicial review of an alleged violation of federal law. Collateral review of criminal convictions and sentences under Section 2255 routinely performs this key function, whereas habeas review for state prisoners under Section 2254 rarely does. Claims that could not reasonably be raised before conviction or on direct appeal—including claims seeking retroactive application of new legal rules and claims based on facts outside of the record, such as ineffective assistance of counsel, prosecutorial suppression of exculpatory evidence, and challenges to sentences based on subsequently vacated prior convictions—are all examples of claims that generally must be reviewed collaterally, after appeal, or they will not be reviewed at all. Consequently, the limitations on access to review under Section 2255 should not be as restrictive as those we have recommended for habeas review of state prisoner petitions, where federal habeas today represents, for most claims, the state prisoner's second bite at the apple of postappeal judicial review.

This framework suggests that Section 2255 should be spared the restrictions on habeas review of state noncapital cases that we recommended in the previous chapter. In addition, however, Congress should loosen some of the current restrictions on Section 2255 review that were put in place to mirror similar restrictions on habeas review for state prisoners. For example, among the 1996 statutory amendments to Section 2255 were severe restrictions on new claims in successive petitions filed by federal prisoners, restrictions very similar to those Congress placed upon state prisoners. A federal prisoner can file a second application for relief under Section 2255 only if he presents clear and convincing proof that he is innocent of the offense he is convicted of committing and shows either that he could not have discovered the factual basis for his claim earlier or that he is seeking relief under a new rule the Supreme Court announced after his appeal and that applies retroactively.[35] This leaves no opportunity for a federal prisoner to seek relief if he learns well after his first Section 2255 application that what he was convicted of doing was not a proper crime. This could easily have been the situation facing the aforementioned Mr. Santos, if the Seventh Circuit ruling that narrowed the interpretation of "proceeds" under the money-laundering statute had been made after, instead of before, the disposition of Santos's first application for relief under Section 2255. Because a prisoner in this situation has no "newly discovered *evidence*," but only a new court decision announcing that a criminal statute punishes less than what was previously believed, review under the current version of Section 2255 would be unavailable to him.

Until Section 2255 was amended in 1996, the statute actually authorized review in such situations.[36] But the new limitation added by AEDPA meant that courts have had to review these claims under Section 2241 instead.[37] It would be better for the federal courts to turn to Section 2241, an all-purpose statutory version of the writ that essentially dates back to what existed in 1867, only as a backup emergency remedy. The main problem, as we will explain later in chapter 9, is that the procedural rules governing Section 2241 habeas petitions are not the same as those governing applications filed under Section 2255—nor should they be. When operating under the all-purpose Section 2241 habeas statute, courts must retain the flexibility to respond to unanticipated legal challenges to detention schemes not yet imagined. The habeas substitute in Section 2255, on the other hand, was designed specifically to deal with the particular situation of a federal prisoner convicted of a federal crime. Section 2255 should be expanded so that it does not unreasonably exclude any categories of claims that such federal prisoners may still need to raise after their appeals have been concluded.

It may have been reasonable, back in 1948, for Congress to restrict successive filings by both state and federal prisoners by means of the same statutory regulation. Sixty years later, however, the two contexts are no longer similar, and habeas law should not continue to operate as if they are.[38] Neither habeas review under Section 2254 for state prisoners nor Section 2255 review for federal prisoners has changed to reflect the twentieth-century transformation in state court review of criminal judgments. This transformation, as we have argued in previous chapters, signals an end to the crisis of federalism underlying the expansion of federal review for state prisoners and supports a much more judicious use of federal habeas review in that context. The same transformation suggests an entirely different approach for the collateral review for federal prisoners, who are not similarly situated. An efficient statutory remedy must be maintained for the review of challenges to federal criminal judgments that prisoners cannot raise anywhere else. Providing a reasonable first bite at the apple of judicial review means loosening, not tightening, some of the present restrictions on Section 2255 review.

CHAPTER SEVEN

Habeas and the Death Penalty

In previous chapters we have recounted the behind-the-scenes story of habeas corpus in noncapital cases, both state and federal. We turn now to what is more often found in the front-page news: habeas corpus review of capital cases. America has a troubled history when it comes to the ultimate criminal punishment, the penalty of death. And nowhere does that sorely troubled history become more apparent than in the seemingly endless litigation of death penalty cases. Such litigation typically becomes particularly intense during the final few days before a scheduled execution, at which point it is taking place mostly in federal habeas proceedings. For this reason, criticism of the habeas remedy often focuses on the role played by federal courts in the late stages of capital cases.[1]

Indeed, the modern evolution of federal habeas corpus for state prisoners under 28 U.S.C. § 2254 has been dominated by pitched battles over capital punishment. As evidence in support of this claim, consider the title of the most significant piece of habeas corpus legislation enacted since Reconstruction: the Antiterrorism and Effective Death Penalty Act (AEDPA) of 1996.[2] As noted earlier, this act changed the rules of federal habeas for all state-convicted prisoners. But the main motivation behind the act—as is eminently clear from its title—was to eliminate impediments to state executions imposed by federal habeas litigation.[3]

The expansion of habeas corpus implemented by the Warren Court, and discussed in chapter 3, was not motivated primarily by concerns about capital cases. Instead, that expansion was part of a much broader conflict of federalism; it was intended to marshal the lower federal courts to help force the states to provide judicial remedies for new (and often unpopular) federal criminal procedure rights that applied to all criminal cases. But the subsequent retrenchments of habeas that occurred under Chief Justices Warren Burger and William Rehnquist, and especially Congress's dramatic revision of the habeas statute through AEDPA, were chiefly designed to reduce the amount of habeas litigation in state capital cases and to speed up its pace. We examine in this chapter how habeas litigation in capital cases became what it is today, before turning in the next chapter to our recommendations for reform.

The Death Penalty and the Evolution of Eighth Amendment Law

Capital cases involve the highest stakes and have the highest public profile of any litigation in the entire American legal system. Decisions in capital cases determine whether a petitioner lives or dies. A capital case can influence the outcome of elections for the judges and state officials. Capital cases hog the criminal justice headlines and consume a hugely disproportionate share of scarce criminal justice resources when compared with noncapital cases, which are vastly more numerous.[4] The cost of litigating a capital case to execution dwarfs that of almost any other category of state court litigation.

Capital cases have received extraordinary attention from the U.S. Supreme Court for decades. The death penalty has cast a long shadow over the development of American criminal procedure law. In these cases, the Court has hammered out many of the constitutional rules that govern the behavior of state officials in all criminal cases. Death penalty cases have often served as catalysts for major reforms in criminal procedure. Many well-established and broadly applied rules of criminal procedure were either first developed, or subsequently advanced, during the litigation of capital cases. These include standards for effective performance by defense attorneys, requirements that prosecutors turn over exculpatory evidence to the defense, prohibitions on race discrimination in jury selection, and many other rules and standards.[5]

At the same time, however, capital cases also have developed their own special rules, rules that do not apply at all (or that apply quite differently) to noncapital cases. Capital cases are governed by two completely different sets of criminal procedure rules. One set has broad, general application in noncapital cases as well, the other set applies only to capital cases. This unusual situation originated with the Supreme Court's modern jurisprudence of the Eighth Amendment.

Regulation under the Eighth Amendment Begins

The modern era of the American death penalty began in the latter half of the 1960s. During that turbulent time, public support for capital punishment waned, only a few defendants were sentenced to death, and even fewer were executed. In fact, from 1967 to 1972, there was a de facto moratorium on executions in the United States.[6] Many observers believed that the Supreme Court would soon follow the lead of Great Britain and other European countries in abolishing the death penalty altogether.[7]

In 1972, the Court did just that. In *Furman v. Georgia*, the Court, by a 5 to 4 vote, held that the death penalty violated the Eighth Amendment's ban on "cruel and unusual punishments."[8] But among the majority, only Justices William Brennan and Thurgood Marshall took the position that the death penalty itself was unconstitutional. The other three—Justices William Douglas, Potter Stewart, and Byron White—found the death penalty to be unconstitutional because of problems with its application, including that the punishment was applied arbitrarily, discriminatorily, and too rarely to serve any deterrent purpose. As a result of *Furman*, all inmates then on death row had their capital sentences commuted.

Because three of the five justices in the *Furman* majority did not absolutely rule out the possibility of a constitutional death penalty, and because American society in general turned in a more conservative direction in the mid-1970s, advocates of capital punishment were able to rally public support to revive it. Within a few years after the *Furman* decision, at least two-thirds of the states had adopted new statutes designed to solve the particular procedural problems that led Justices Douglas, Stewart, and White to vote against the death penalty in *Furman*. That set the stage for the Court to revisit the constitutional issue and to decide whether the death penalty could resume under these new state statutes.

In 1976, in *Gregg v. Georgia*, the Court upheld the constitutionality of three of the new statutes: those enacted in Georgia, Florida, and Texas.[9] These three statutes differed slightly in their procedural approaches to capital sentencing. Georgia and Florida both sought to implement a system of so-called guided discretion by providing the capital sentencer[10] with lists of "aggravating circumstances" that militated in favor of death and "mitigating circumstances" that pointed in the other direction. Texas, by contrast, posed three specific questions to the capital sentencer; only if the answer to all three questions was "yes" would the death penalty be imposed. The Court in *Gregg* held that all three statutes achieved a reasonable balance between rationality and predictability, on the one hand, and individualized treatment of each capital case, on the other, thus complying with the dictates of the Eighth Amendment. Although numerous procedural issues remained to be resolved with respect to each particular state statute, a lengthy legal process that would delay the resumption of actual executions in most states for several more years, the *Gregg* decision meant that the states were generally free to get back into the business of capital punishment.

Procedural Requirements under the Eighth Amendment: Super Due Process

In the years immediately following *Gregg*, defendants sent to death row under the new state statutes continued to challenge their death sentences under the Eighth Amendment. It was no longer legally viable, in light of *Gregg*, for these inmates to challenge the death penalty itself as cruel and unusual punishment in violation of the Eighth Amendment. But they continued to argue that their death sentences were cruel and unusual in light of the specific facts and circumstances of their particular cases.

In several such cases, including *Lockett v. Ohio*[11] and *Godfrey v. Georgia*,[12] the Supreme Court granted review. But after oral argument, the Court declined to decide the question posed in the certiorari petition, which was whether the Eighth Amendment barred the use of the death penalty given the specific circumstances of the crimes and the defendants' personal backgrounds. Instead, the Court overturned the death sentences on procedural grounds. In *Lockett*, for example, the Court held that the defendant should have been allowed to introduce evidence to support any mitigating circumstances that she might have wished to present to the sentencing jury. And in *Godfrey*, the Court held that the instructions provided to the jury explaining the "aggravating circumstance" supporting the death sentence were not sufficiently clear. These procedural rulings were based on the Eighth Amendment, not on any other constitutional criminal procedure standards that the Court had previously applied in noncapital cases. The Court, in these cases, held that the death penalty was cruel and unusual, not because it was inherently so on the underlying facts but instead because of the procedural manner in which the punishments were determined.

Lockett, *Godfrey*, and other similar cases gave rise to what is now called the "super due process" interpretation of the Eighth Amendment.[13] This interpretation essentially transforms the cruel and unusual punishments clause from a substantive limit on punishments (either in the abstract or in particular cases based on the facts and circumstances of the case) into a Due Process Clause on steroids. The super due process interpretation means that capital cases must be administered in a manner that complies not only with all of the usual due process requirements that apply to all criminal cases but also with a host of special procedural rules that are necessary in order to satisfy the Eighth Amendment. If these special rules are satisfied, then the death penalty is constitutional; if not, the death penalty—as administered—violates the cruel and unusual punishments clause.

In the past three decades, the super due process interpretation of the Eighth Amendment has generated dozens of new procedural rulings from the Supreme Court, all of which were presumably intended to promote greater reliability and greater rationality in capital sentencing. One impact of these Eighth Amendment procedural rulings has been to produce an ever-changing constitutional landscape, frustrating those state trial and appellate judges who try diligently, but without success, to keep up with the Court's evolving dictates.

This constant churning of the governing constitutional standards that govern the death penalty has been, in retrospect, inevitable. Capital cases necessarily generate many special constitutional rules. Not only do these cases include a special, separate sentencing phase that most other cases lack, they tend to be much more legally complex than other felony criminal cases. Just as there are more things that can go wrong at a jury trial than with a guilty plea, the potential for error in a jury proceeding on the death penalty is generally much higher than at a judicial sentencing to a term of years.

There has never been a clear blueprint for the states to follow when filling in the details of the broad procedural outlines sketched by the Supreme Court in Eighth Amendment cases such as *Gregg* and *Lockett*. Like many other Warren Court expansions of the constitutional regulation of criminal procedure, the Court's regulation of capital cases went well beyond historical practice. But unlike the procedural rules in noncapital cases, there was no well-established practice in federal courts to which the states could turn for guidance. Congress did not enact an up-dated, post-*Furman* death penalty statute for most federal capital crimes until 1994, and the Court has yet to consider its first case testing that federal statute.[14] Defining, case by case and state by state, exactly which procedural rules for capital cases pass constitutional muster and which do not has been a slow, costly, and turbulent process for the Court.

More importantly, the special nature of capital cases has tended to breed procedural instability. In capital cases, the understandable goal of both the legal system and society at large is perfection. We want our le-gal procedures to ensure, to a 100 percent probability, that no innocent defendant will ever be convicted and sentenced to death and also that no death sentence will ever be imposed on one who does not truly deserve it. These goals are impossible to achieve in any legal system run by hu-man beings. No matter how perfect our legal procedures may be, there will always be some risk of human error in decision making.

Most of the Justices of the Supreme Court, however, seem not to have accepted the inevitability of error in capital cases.[15] Every time a capital case appears wrongly decided, the Court changes the procedural rules to make sure it does not happen again. But lurching from one new proce-dural rule to another is a cycle without end. It has led to massive instabil-ity in Eighth Amendment super due process law.

Substantive Limitations under the Eighth Amendment: Proportionality

At the same time, the Court has increasingly used the Eighth Amend-ment to impose substantive restrictions on the use of capital punishment, mostly through the so-called proportionality doctrine that requires the severity of a punishment to be roughly commensurate with the heinous-ness of the crime and with the moral responsibility of the defendant who commits the crime.[16] Although the Court has not elected to develop a robust proportionality doctrine for individual capital cases,[17] it has ap-plied the Eighth Amendment in categorical terms to strike down the use of the death penalty for juveniles, for the mentally retarded, for certain nontriggermen, and for rapists who do not kill.[18]

This has resulted in a jurisprudential approach that, at least until quite recently, diverged significantly from the approach taken in non-capital cases in which similar claims were raised. In the noncapital con-text, the Court has long stated that no proportionality claim will receive substantial scrutiny unless the Court itself finds the punishment to be grossly disproportionate to the crime and the criminal.[19] Even then, the Court will not invalidate the sentence unless there is clear evidence of a national consensus against the challenged application of the punishment. This highly deferential approach led the Court in 1991 to uphold a Michigan statute imposing a mandatory life sentence, without possibility of parole, for a first offense of simple possession of a substantial quantity of cocaine.[20] Using the same approach, the Court also upheld in 2003 a California law authorizing a life sentence, with a possibility of parole only after twenty-five years, for a third felony offense that involved stealing three golf clubs from a pro shop.[21]

Recent capital cases, by contrast, have utilized a much more aggressive Eighth Amendment proportionality analysis. In cases involving juveniles and the mentally retarded, the Court majority found a national consensus against the death penalty. It concluded that a discernible trend in the states toward abolition was sufficient, even though many states permitted its use.[22] And in *Roper v. Simmons*, the juvenile death penalty case, the Court even extended its inquiry to embrace international human rights law, relying in part on a brief against the juvenile death penalty filed by the European Union. Although Justice Antonin Scalia fumed about the irrelevance of European moral views to a question of American constitutional law, a majority of justices, per Justice Anthony Kennedy, responded that it is appropriate for the United States to behave in ways that are consistent with prevailing international norms.

Until 2010, it appeared that the Court was intent on creating two separate strands of Eighth Amendment proportionality doctrine—one for capital cases and another for noncapital cases. In May 2010, however, the Court ruled in *Graham v. Florida* that states may not impose life sentences without a possibility of parole upon juvenile offenders who are convicted of nonhomicide crimes.[23] *Graham* was the first case in more than twenty-five years in which the Court rejected a noncapital sentence as constitutionally disproportionate.[24]

It is possible that *Graham*—a decision that in many respects resembled that in *Roper*, including even a similar discussion of the relevance of international legal norms—may come to represent the beginning of an effort by the Court to reconcile the capital and noncapital doctrinal strands. We think it much more likely, however, that *Graham* eventually will be limited to a different aspect of its special facts—namely, the fact that the case involved an extremely severe (albeit nonlethal) punishment meted out to a juvenile offender. On the heels of *Roper v. Simmons*, the

Court clearly remains concerned that juveniles should be punished in a manner reflecting their immaturity and reduced moral culpability, as well as their greater possibilities for rehabilitation over an extended period of incarceration.

Graham, in short, is probably more about reinforcing the special nature of juvenile offenders than it is about denying the uniqueness of the death penalty. As Justice Kennedy wrote for the majority,

> Terrance Graham's sentence guarantees he will die in prison without any meaningful opportunity to obtain release, no matter what he might do to demonstrate that the bad acts he committed as a teenager are not representative of his true character, even if he spends the next half century attempting to atone for his crimes and learn from his mistakes. The State has denied him any chance to later demonstrate that he is fit to rejoin society based solely on a nonhomicide crime that he committed while he was a child in the eyes of the law. This the Eighth Amendment does not permit.

Such language would seem almost wholly inapplicable to adult offenders. At a minimum, it seems premature to conclude that *Graham* has, outside the juvenile context, undermined the doctrinal dichotomy between capital and noncapital proportionality cases. Pending further notice from the Court, death is still "different."

Habeas Review in Capital Cases before 1996

Habeas corpus has been the vehicle for the declaration and application of almost all of these new Eighth Amendment rules. Many of the Court's new Eighth Amendment rulings were, at least initially, applied retroactively, so that inmates who had completed their appeals could return to court and challenge their sentences again based on the new rule.[25] Every single person on death row, even those whose capital trial and sentencing had occurred many years earlier in compliance with all of the constitutional and legal rules then in effect, might suddenly and unexpectedly benefit from each new Court decision that changed those rules after the fact. Because traditionally habeas was not subject to fixed time limits and did not prohibit multiple filings, death row inmates could always turn to the habeas courts to try to vindicate their newly minted federal rights, even after the usual appellate remedies were no longer available. Even today, the Court's proportionality rulings limiting who can be put to death all apply retroactively, so that convicted murderers yet to be executed can seek habeas relief from their death sentences on these grounds no matter how many times they have sought relief before.[26]

In the years following the *Gregg* and *Lockett* decisions, the combination of new super due process and proportionality Eighth Amendment rules and the retroactive application of many such rules produced a no-win situation for the state courts. Indeed, in the late 1970s, the overall reversal rate for capital cases in federal habeas corpus often exceeded 50 percent.[27] Executions stalled. Repeated hearings greatly increased the total cost. Not surprisingly, some state courts, as well as victims, prosecutors, and legislators, chafed against the perceived excesses of federal regulation of state capital punishment.

This led, in turn, to growing calls to reduce or eliminate the barriers imposed by the federal habeas courts to the efficient administration of the death penalty by the states. Because federal habeas was the forum for most capital litigation involving the new Eighth Amendment rights, it became the prime target for reform initiatives. Curtailing access to federal habeas became an important, albeit indirect, method of limiting the impact of the Court's expansion of Eighth Amendment constitutional law.[28]

Many, if not most, of the Court's decisions restricting habeas corpus that were discussed in chapter 3 were prompted by the desire of a majority of justices to increase finality in capital litigation. In essence, what the Court gave to death row inmates with one hand, by creating a host of new Eighth Amendment super due process rights, it subsequently tried to take away with the other by restricting access to the procedural remedy usually used to assert those rights. The Court in *Wainwright v. Sykes*[29] discarded the rule in *Fay v. Noia*,[30] which had for nearly fifteen years allowed federal courts to reach the merits of issues that defendants had not raised properly in state courts, except for those issues the defendant had personally and deliberately withheld. After *Sykes*, habeas petitioners became responsible for the mistakes and poor judgment calls of their lawyers. The Court also limited the opportunity for habeas petitioners to file multiple petitions. It barred relief for claims that could have been raised, or that had already been raised, during the petitioner's first trip to federal court.[31]

In what was probably the Court's most significant restriction on habeas relief, it held in *Teague v. Lane*,[32] a capital case from Illinois, that new constitutional rules of criminal procedure generally cannot be applied retroactively by means of habeas corpus litigation. Once a criminal case has become "final," by virtue of completing the usual appellate review process, no further changes in the governing constitutional standards are allowed to upset the outcome. As discussed previously, the only exceptions are for (1) rules that limit the substantive reach of the criminal law, by placing certain primary conduct outside the scope of what the state can legally prosecute or punish; and (2) so-called watershed procedural rules, such as the *Gideon* rule guaranteeing indigent state felony defendants the right to appointed counsel, that are necessary to guarantee fundamental fairness and without which the accuracy of any resulting conviction would be seriously questioned. The first *Teague* exception arises only rarely; the second, almost never.

These steps were designed to eliminate the constant churning of new claims in new habeas proceedings so that finality (which in this context means execution) could be achieved in capital cases. Indeed, it seems clear that the Court would not have paid nearly as much attention as it did in the 1980s and 1990s to the rules of habeas if it were not for the special problem of capital cases. In noncapital cases, as we have already seen, habeas reversal rates were extremely low. The Court's restrictions on habeas surely were intended to address, and ameliorate, the much higher reversal rates in capital habeas cases. But as we will see in the next chapter, the Court's efforts had only limited success; petitions in capital cases continued to be granted at a relatively high rate.

In addition, the Court's decisions produced consequences that were probably unintended. The restrictions on defaulted, successive, and new claims were designed primarily to deal with capital habeas litigation, but those restrictions were not limited to capital cases. Nor were they limited to frivolous claims or to claims unrelated to the reliability of the petitioner's conviction. The doors to the habeas courthouse were closed to all.

To avoid what would otherwise be draconian results, the Court had to create exceptions to these new restrictions in order to allow habeas courts to reach the merits of the claims of exceptionally deserving petitioners. As noted in chapter 3, for almost every one of the habeas restrictions imposed by the Court, an exception was later recognized for fundamental "miscarriages of justice." This term of art has been interpreted to require a showing that an alleged constitutional violation probably resulted in the conviction of an innocent person or the imposition of a death sentence against a person who was legally ineligible to receive that sentence. The exception, while extremely narrow and almost never satisfied, preserved the authority of the habeas courts to control access to habeas as a remedy for serious substantive injustice.[33]

The exception, however, added yet another issue to contest, thus ensuring that habeas corpus litigation would continue to grow in complexity and cost, consuming an even greater share of the criminal justice system's limited resources. Each capital habeas case potentially involved at least four separate layers of procedure: (1) the procedural requirements of the Constitution applicable in all state criminal cases; (2) the special super due process requirements of the Eighth Amendment that applied only to capital cases (for example, the requirement of clear jury instructions about the meaning of certain aggravating circumstances); (3) the procedural rules of habeas, which in turn often depended on procedural issues that previously arose in the state courts (for example, the *Wainwright v. Sykes* procedural default doctrine); and (4) the exceptions to those habeas restrictions (that is, the fundamental miscarriage of justice exception). All provided opportunities for prolonged litigation, including the possibility of evidentiary hearings to develop and determine the relevant facts. Professor Jordan Steiker's term, "excessive proceduralism,"[34] captured perfectly the growing sense, throughout the 1980s and 1990s, that habeas litigation was becoming more and more burdensome on the states and on society and that such litigation—especially with respect to the proper application of habeas procedural rules—was making it harder and harder to reach the underlying question of the justice of the petitioner's conviction and sentence.[35]

The Latest Phase: Capital Habeas under AEDPA

By the early 1990s, Congress got involved. Years of legislative attempts, with political momentum generated by the Oklahoma City terrorist bombing in 1995 (which led to the first federal execution in nearly forty years),[36] resulted in the enactment of AEDPA,[37] which dramatically altered the rules of habeas corpus litigation for those convicted of state crimes.

The act imposed, for the first time, a statute of limitations for filing a habeas petition. Under AEDPA, a prisoner must file his petition within one year from the completion of the direct appeal process. The act tightened even further the existing restrictions on filing second or successive habeas petitions. The act made it more difficult for habeas petitioners to obtain evidentiary hearings on claims that had not been fully developed in the state courts. Most controversially, as we discussed in chapter 3, the act created a new and more stringent standard of review: under AEDPA, a habeas court may overturn a petitioner's conviction or sentence only if the state court made a decision that (1) was contrary to, or involved an unreasonable application of, clearly established federal law as determined by the U.S. Supreme Court; or (2) was based on an unreasonable determination of the facts in light of the evidence presented in the state court. This new standard of review was designed to ensure that fewer habeas petitions would lead to grants of habeas relief.

As if there were any doubts about the motivation behind the Effective Death Penalty Act, Congress also included an entirely separate, streamlined version of habeas corpus—with new and unprecedented time limits for the rulings of federal habeas judges. This version, which applied only to capital cases, also imposed on petitioners an even shorter statute of limitations (180 days from the time the state judgment became final on direct appeal). But this state-friendly version of capital habeas, based in part on recommendations issued several years earlier by the Powell Committee of the Judicial Conference, would apply only if the particular state became eligible for it by furnishing qualified and experienced defense counsel in state postconviction proceedings. The hope was that thorough and well-developed state review proceedings would narrow the issues for federal habeas, obviate the need for additional and lengthy evidentiary hearings, and make it easier and quicker for federal courts to resolve these messy cases. To date, no state has managed to convince a federal court that it qualifies for these so-called opt-in capital habeas rules, although many have tried. Congress amended the statute in 2005, adjusting some of the processing deadlines and potentially making it easier to qualify by shifting the eligibility decision from the federal courts to the U.S. attorney general. But implementing regulations for the amended statute have yet to be put in place.[38]

Finally, although the main focus of this chapter (and the one that follows) is on capital punishment as administered by the states, most of the same observations apply equally to the federal death penalty. The first attempt by Congress to respond to *Furman*, and to legislate a death penalty that would meet the Supreme Court's new constitutional standards, was the so-called drug kingpin criminal statute, enacted in 1988;[39] six years later, Congress adopted new procedures designed to revive several pre-*Furman* capital statutes.[40] Only three federal prisoners have been executed in the modern era, and the Court has not yet reviewed any of the new federal capital statutes. But the entire corpus of Eighth Amendment law, both procedural and substantive, applies to federal as well as state capital cases. The pattern of litigation in federal capital cases under Section 2255 tends to mirror that in federal habeas review of state capital cases. Collateral review of federal capital cases may involve federal statutory issues; it involves only one layer of postconviction proceedings instead of at least two; and it will not, of course, raise any issues of federalism. But these differences are overwhelmed by the similarity in the fundamental dynamics of capital litigation: futile attempts to define perfect legal procedures, producing an imperfect and constantly changing situation. In this sense, federal and state capital cases turn out to be nearly identical.

*   *   *

The story of habeas corpus, and the story of the death penalty in the modern era of the Supreme Court's Eighth Amendment jurisprudence, have been inextricably intertwined. The legal battle over capital punishment has been fought primarily on the battleground of habeas. Many, if not most, modern habeas restrictions were first developed in an effort to free up the states so that they could more effectively and efficiently carry out the death penalty. The end result of this close and often stormy relationship has been a virtual death spiral of excessive habeas proceduralism. In noncapital cases, habeas litigation is merely a wasteful nuisance. It dissipates scarce resources, produces virtually no benefits, and diminishes the overall reputation of the Great Writ, but it only very rarely leads to the actual reversal of a state criminal conviction or sentence. In capital cases, however, habeas continues to be center stage in a prolonged and bitter struggle that shows no signs of ending any time soon.

CHAPTER EIGHT

The Future of Capital Habeas

W e turn now to the future of habeas corpus in capital cases. Should habeas review be cut back further in capital cases, as we have already proposed for noncapital cases? Or should we preserve, or even expand, habeas review for those who are facing the ultimate punishment? These are exceedingly challenging questions, and they have the gravest of implications for death row inmates, victims' survivors, and society in general.

We begin with the following simple observation: despite the fact that the U.S. Supreme Court and Congress have, for more than fifty years, allowed the unique characteristics of capital cases to shape habeas corpus law and policy in general, there is no inherent reason why habeas should have to apply exactly the same way to capital cases as it does to noncapital cases.[1] Habeas law and policy all too often have been influenced by the misguided belief that habeas is a one-size-fits-all remedy that must be provided in a nominally (even if not effectively) identical manner to all persons convicted of all crimes. Congress halfheartedly attempted to separate capital from noncapital habeas by writing into the Antiterrorism and Effective Death Penalty Act of 1996 (AEDPA) the special opt-in set of habeas rules for capital cases only, but this effort has failed.[2]

In chapter 6 we explained some of the unfortunate consequences of treating state and federal cases alike in habeas. In a similar vein, capital and noncapital cases also require very different habeas approaches. Capital cases today are governed by constitutional rules, namely, the Eighth Amendment's "super due process" and "proportionality" requirements, that are very different from those that generally apply to noncapital cases. But the current rules for reviewing these two very different kinds of cases in habeas do not differ very much at all. The adherence to strict parity in the scope and application of capital and noncapital habeas has led to an unsatisfying and unstable compromise. Noncapital habeas review (but not relief) is too readily granted, squandering time and money and dissipating respect for the writ, while capital habeas review is too frequently constrained.

The lockstep approach to defining the scope and application of habeas corpus to capital and noncapital cases runs contrary to the core concepts of flexibility and prudence that are the historic hallmarks of habeas. Flexibility allows the writ to be used more aggressively by the courts when necessary to address periodic crises, while prudence in extending the writ only as far and as long as it is truly needed conserves both scarce societal resources and its cherished reputation. These twin ideas point the way to a better approach to habeas review in capital cases. The solution starts with decoupling the rules governing the review of capital cases from those in noncapital cases. The habeas remedy must be allowed to adapt to the important differences between the two kinds of cases, differences that are highly relevant to the appropriate scope of habeas review.

The Unique Role of Habeas Review in Capital Cases

Coping with Perpetual Instability

First, as noted in chapter 7, capital cases are different because they involve constitutional rules that, even after more than three decades of Supreme Court jurisprudential and doctrinal development, remain much less settled than most of the rest of constitutional criminal procedure law. Both aspects of Eighth Amendment law—its substantive limits on the scope of the death penalty through proportionality analysis and its super due process procedural rules—are constantly shifting.

This is reflected in the close scrutiny that the Court continues to give to death penalty cases. For many years, observers have predicted that the Court would soon tire of the death penalty and that Eighth Amendment law would thus become relatively more stable and predictable, thereby leading to a rapid increase in the number and pace of executions. Such predictions began soon after *Furman* and *Gregg*. They resurfaced a decade later, in connection with the Court's blockbuster decisions in *Lockhart v. McCree*,[3] upholding the use in capital cases of death-qualified juries from which opponents of capital punishment had been excluded, and *McCleskey v. Kemp*,[4] affirming the constitutionality of the Georgia death penalty in the face of strong empirical evidence that it was handed out more frequently to killers of white victims than to killers of black victims. And they are being heard again today, following the recent decision in *Baze v. Rees*,[5] which rejected claims that the particular drugs used in lethal injections could inflict unconstitutional pain and suffering upon those who are being executed.

Predictions that the Court would extricate itself from the business of reviewing capital cases have proven false.[6] The Court grants review in capital cases at a rate higher than in noncapital criminal cases.[7] It continues to decide anywhere from a handful to more than a dozen new capital cases each year. And every one of those new decisions continues to carry the possibility of making new Eighth Amendment law.

This is especially true because the jurisprudential foundations of the Eighth Amendment remain remarkably weak. Criminal sentencing in the United States has traditionally been left to the discretion of the trial judge, within broad limits set by the governing criminal statute. But in most states, capital sentencing authority was transferred long ago from the judge to the jury. And at the dawn of the modern era of capital punishment, in the early 1970s, the Supreme Court held in *Furman* that the imposition of the death penalty cannot be determined in the unfettered discretion of the jury, because this would create the opportunity for arbitrariness and discrimination to infect the capital sentencing process. At the same time, the Court also held in *Gregg* and *Lockett* that the jury must retain some degree of discretion over the capital sentencing decision in order to do justice to the individual defendant in each particular case.

These two Eighth Amendment principles created obvious tension. In a largely futile effort to resolve this tension, the Court pinned its hopes on the so-called guided-discretion approach to capital sentencing that had been developed by the American Law Institute, the drafters of the Model Penal Code.[8] This approach required the capital sentencing jury to consider statutory lists of aggravating factors that point toward the death penalty and mitigating factors that point the other way. In later cases, the Court complicated matters further by holding that the defendant cannot be limited in terms of mitigating factors but instead can introduce factors that are not on the statutory list. The whole guided-discretion approach has proven to be inherently unstable in application because it has turned out to be impossible to achieve a perfect balance between "guidance" and "discretion." The Court has held that both are constitutionally required: guidance because it contributes to rational decision making, and discretion because it allows for consideration of the moral blameworthiness of each individual defendant. But in practice, every time the Court announces or affirms a new Eighth Amendment legal rule in a capital case, it simultaneously reduces the amount of discretion enjoyed by the capital sentencer. And every time the Court decides in favor of broader discretion, it simultaneously undermines the value of the existing legal rules. Discretion and rules operate at two ends of a single spectrum or continuum; a move in one direction is a move away from the other.

At the end of the day, it becomes impossible to achieve both perfect guidance and perfect discretion. The problem is both inherent and completely intractable, as justices on both sides of the death penalty debate have repeatedly acknowledged.[9]

This perpetual, and irresolvable, jurisprudential debate virtually ensures that the law of the Eighth Amendment will never become truly stable. If the law cannot be built on a firm foundation, then it is doomed to swing back and forth, like a pendulum, from one Court decision to the next. That is the prevailing pattern of Eighth Amendment law. Again, in the typically provocative prose of Justice Scalia:

> Today a petitioner before this Court says that a state sentencing court (1) had unconstitutionally *broad* discretion to sentence him to death instead of imprisonment, *and* (2) had unconstitutionally *narrow* discretion to sentence him to imprisonment instead of death. An observer unacquainted with our death penalty jurisprudence (and in the habit of thinking logically) would probably say these positions cannot both be right. The ultimate choice in capital sentencing, he would point out, is a unitary one—the choice between death and imprisonment. One cannot have discretion whether to select the one yet lack discretion whether to select the other. Our imaginary observer would then be surprised to discover that, under this Court's Eighth Amendment jurisprudence of the past 15 years, petitioner would have a strong chance of winning on *both* of these antagonistic claims, simultaneously. . . . But that just shows that our jurisprudence and logic have long since parted ways.[10]

As if that weren't enough, in recent years, the Court has wavered even on the threshold question of whether the Eighth Amendment should be defined solely in terms of American constitutional norms and values or whether global norms, such as those expressed in European or international human rights law, should be given expression in the Eighth Amendment as well. In *Roper v. Simmons*,[11] Justice Anthony Kennedy, writing for the majority, opined, "It does not lessen our fidelity to the Constitution or our pride in its origins to acknowledge that the express affirmation of certain fundamental rights by other nations and peoples simply underscores the centrality of those same rights within our own heritage of freedom."[12] Four justices, led by Justice Scalia, dissented. This is an additional new source of instability in an area of the law that is already notoriously unstable.

The perpetually unsettled character of Eighth Amendment law means that, much more so than in most other areas of constitutional criminal procedure, habeas courts routinely must deal with changes in the governing law and related issues of possible retroactive application of new Supreme Court decisions. For example, when the Court decided *Atkins v. Virginia*,[13] prohibiting the death penalty for mentally retarded defendants—a substantive Eighth Amendment proportionality ruling with full retroactive application—death row inmates across America filed new petitions seeking relief under this new rule.[14] Habeas has always served as the primary procedural vehicle for vindicating new federal constitutional rights that are retroactively applied. In the Eighth Amendment area, this is a relatively more common occurrence than it is elsewhere in the law. To put it another way, habeas plays a greater role in death penalty cases because, for the most part, habeas is the only way for the Supreme Court's constantly changing views about the Eighth Amendment to be put into meaningful effect.

Oversight of State Judges

A closely related difference between capital and noncapital cases, also potentially relevant to the proper scope of habeas corpus review, is that the Eighth Amendment is one area of constitutional criminal procedure that may still seem relatively strange, even foreign, to many state judges. During the 1960s, state judges sometimes viewed landmark decisions like *Gideon*, *Mapp*, and *Miranda* as alien invaders, disrupting long-established and long-settled state and local practices. Over the decades since, however, the Fourth, Fifth, and Sixth Amendments, and the overarching concepts of Fourteenth Amendment due process and equal protection have become very familiar to state judges, who must deal with those federal constitutional provisions on a daily basis. Today, if a state judge disagrees with a new Supreme Court decision in the area, it is far more likely to reflect a simple difference of opinion about the merits of the issue or the scope of protection, not a wholesale rejection of the Court's authority to render such a decision or of the general supremacy of federal constitutional law.

Eighth Amendment rules are different. Most state judges never have the same day-to-day experience applying the rules that govern capital cases. They have no chance to become truly familiar with those rules. For the most part, and in most jurisdictions, individual state judges deal with death penalty cases only very rarely. When they do, they quickly encounter, often for the one and only time in their judicial careers, the strange notion that the Eighth Amendment imposes special restrictions on both the substantive reach of, and the procedural requirements for imposing, the death penalty.

Eighth Amendment law is, to put it mildly, specialized and complex. Judicial education programs, run by the states or the National Judicial College, seek to prepare judges to handle this special situation, but the programs can only do so much. Until a judge is actually confronted with the harsh realities of a capital trial, it is hard to imagine how difficult it can be. And once the case begins, and the litigation heats up, state judges under pressure may be tempted to revert to the tried-and-true methods that have worked previously in other criminal cases. Of course, this is exactly the wrong way to handle a capital case; the key is for a judge to recognize just how different such a case is from the norm. In the end, the unique challenges of this situation may generate feelings of resentment or even hostility toward the Eighth Amendment law that is largely responsible for making capital cases so hard to handle. The apprehension and aversion state judges may experience when dealing with the ever-changing constitutional rules that govern capital cases are reminiscent of the reactions that prompted the Warren Court's expansive use of habeas review in the 1960s and might justify a similar result today.

Avoiding the Mistaken Execution

Another important feature of capital cases that militates in favor of more expansive habeas corpus review is the special concern over the possibility of a wrongful conviction in such cases, which could lead to the mistaken execution of an innocent person. Over the past two decades, many

Americans, including many judges, have grown increasingly anxious about the risk of such a mistaken execution.[15]

This anxiety is understandable. The death penalty is extreme in its irrevocability; if a mistake is made, no compensation or other remedy can ever come close to making amends. One might even describe a mistaken execution as the ultimate horror. In fact, it was just such a case in England, in the 1950s, that helped to turn the tide of the public policy debate against the death penalty.[16]

Despite recurring claims to the contrary, there is no conclusive proof yet that a mistaken execution has occurred in the United States during the modern era.[17] But the growing number of death row inmates who have been exonerated, some of them on the basis of unassailable DNA evidence, has seriously shaken the faith of many who previously may have believed that the criminal justice system could be trusted never to err in such a high-stakes case.

Indeed, there are good reasons to believe that the risk of error actually may be higher in capital cases than in noncapital cases.[18] The sheer enormity of the interests involved on both sides of a capital case—the life of the defendant and justice for both the murder victim and society at large—puts tremendous pressure on all actors in the state criminal justice system. This pressure starts at the investigative stage of the case, when the police and prosecutor try to determine who is responsible for a brutal, heinous murder. Whenever investigators lack access to a victim's account, as is true in almost all murder cases, they are forced to rely more heavily on statements by witnesses, informants, and the accused himself. All three categories of evidence can carry serious reliability problems. Yet the pressure to solve a murder case may be so intense that these kinds of evidence end up carrying more weight than they should or than they do in investigations of other lower stakes cases with no victim available. And the pressure to find the killer also may increase the likelihood of tunnel vision, the psychological tendency to ignore or discount evidence that undercuts a hypothesis to which one has already committed. Tunnel vision can lead both police and prosecutors to continue down paths that ultimately may result in an erroneous death sentence.[19]

One recent example of the dangers of tunnel vision in a high-profile capital case is the saga of Paul Gregory House, a case we cited previously in chapter 5.[20] House was charged in 1985 in Union County, Tennessee, with the murder of Carolyn Muncey, a young mother who was lured from her home one Saturday night and found dead the next afternoon, down an embankment a short distance away. House was a prime suspect from the start, in part because he was an outsider with a prior record of sex crimes and in part because he lied to the police about his whereabouts on the night of the murder. The key evidence against House at trial consisted of some reddish-brown stains on the jeans he was wearing that night and semen that was found in the body of the victim. The stains turned out to be the victim's blood, and the semen was consistent with House's blood type. House consistently maintained his innocence, but the jury quickly convicted and sentenced House to death.

After trial, House argued that his trial lawyer was constitutionally ineffective for not properly investigating and litigating his innocence[21] and that the local prosecutor violated due process by failing to disclose evidence in his possession that would have helped to exculpate House.[22] Because House's post-trial lawyers had never asserted these innocence-related claims in state court as a basis for overturning House's conviction or death sentence, the federal court was barred from addressing them as "procedurally defaulted." The only way to receive federal review of his ineffective counsel and prosecutorial disclosure claims was to demonstrate actual innocence.

Many years later, in federal habeas corpus, House had that chance. At an evidentiary hearing in 1999, House's new lawyer showed that the blood found on House's jeans likely was splashed there when a vial of the victim's blood kept in the same cardboard box opened up during transport from Tennessee to the Federal Bureau of Investigation crime lab in Washington, DC. The semen in the victim's body turned out to belong not to House but to the victim's husband, who was a known wife beater. And around the time of House's trial, the husband had tearfully confessed to having committed the murder to two female friends, both of whom came forward and attempted to bring the confession to the attention of the local sheriff. Their efforts, however, had been unsuccessful.

In February 2000, the habeas court ultimately decided that, despite this new evidence of innocence, no relief could be granted owing to the procedural default committed by House's previous lawyers in the state courts. In June 2006, the U.S. Supreme Court reversed, ruling that "this is the rare case where—had the jury heard all the conflicting testimony—it is more likely than not that no reasonable juror viewing the record as a whole would lack reasonable doubt." As a result, House was entitled to merits review of his ineffective assistance of counsel and prosecutorial disclosure violations.[23]

Despite this apparent victory in the Supreme Court, House remained on death row. The same local prosecutor who originally put him there doggedly maintained that he was still the murderer and vigorously opposed all efforts to set him free. A year and a half later, the federal district judge to whom the case had been remanded decided that House's constitutional claims were meritorious. Afterward, the prosecutor declared that he would retry House for the Carolyn Muncey murder. House remained in prison until July 2, 2008, when the federal district court finally ordered his release pending the scheduled retrial.

In preparation for the retrial, the prosecutor sent out for independent DNA testing a human hair, presumably belonging to the murderer, that had been found clutched in the lifeless hand of the victim. The test results came back in September 2008 and showed that the hair belonged neither to House nor to the victim's husband but to a third, unidentified male. Even so, the prosecutor continued to argue that House was the murderer—his new theory of the case was that House may have worked together with the unidentified male to commit the crime.

On May 12, 2009, almost twenty-four years after the crime and almost three years after a U.S. Supreme Court ruling that probably "no reasonable juror" would have convicted House on the basis of all of the available evidence, the prosecutor—shortly before an imminent decision by the U.S. Court of Appeals for the Sixth Circuit that might well have ordered him to do so—finally announced that he was dropping all charges against House in the murder of Carolyn Muncey.

Paul Gregory House spent more than twenty years on Tennessee's death row for a heinous crime he apparently did not commit. The local prosecutor's refusal to drop the charges, for almost three years after the Supreme Court's decision in House's favor, almost certainly was influenced by tunnel vision brought on by the fact that House's case was a high-profile capital case in which the prosecutor faced both professional and personal pressures not to concede error. On the professional side, such an admission would have brought strong disapproval from local constituents still outraged by the evil of Carolyn Muncey's murder; on the personal side, it would have meant acknowledging and accepting at least some individual responsibility for a terrible injustice. Indeed, even while asking for the dismissal of all charges against House, the prose-

cutor would admit only that "new evidence, including the forensic ex-
aminations, raises a reasonable doubt that [House] acted alone (and)
whether (his) involvement was as a principal, accomplice, or an accessory
to the crime. . . ." The prosecutor apparently still believes that House is a
guilty man.[24]

The so-called innocence revolution, prompted by cases like that of Paul
Gregory House, has left many Americans wondering whether our courts
can be trusted to carry out the life-and-death task of administering capital punishment in a reliable and accurate manner. And this is the kind
of issue that affects people on both sides of the political divide over capital punishment. As conservative writer George Will once put it, "Con-
servatives, especially, should draw this lesson. . . . Capital punishment,
like the rest of the criminal justice system, is a government program, so
skepticism is in order."[25] Before her retirement from the Supreme Court,
Justice Sandra Day O'Connor expressed similar sentiments. In a speech
before a group of lawyers in Minnesota, she said, "If statistics are any
indication, the system may well be allowing some innocent defendants
to be executed." She added that those who live in Minnesota, where
there is no death penalty, "must breathe a big sigh of relief every day."[26]

Such concerns about executing an innocent man may have led a majority of justices to take a remarkable step in another recent capital case.
As noted in chapter 5, condemned murderer Troy Davis filed an original
habeas petition in the Supreme Court, under Section 2241, alleging his
factual innocence. Rather than dismiss or deny the petition, the Court,
over a dissent by Justices Antonin Scalia and Clarence Thomas, transferred it to the trial court that had imprisoned Davis, ordering that court
to "receive testimony and make findings of fact as to whether evidence
that could not have been obtained at the time of trial clearly establishes
petitioner's innocence."[27] The Supreme Court's rare decision to entertain this claim in an original habeas petition illustrates not only how
concern about the execution of an innocent defendant may be affecting
the justices but also how essential habeas corpus remains to the Court's
ongoing effort to police the constitutionality of the death penalty.

Providing a Vital Forum for Debate

Beyond the special concerns over Eighth Amendment law, and the risk
of a mistaken execution, capital cases are also different simply because

American society continues to be deeply divided over the morality and wisdom of the death penalty. Although those who believe that the death penalty is immoral are a minority in the United States, capital punishment remains one of the most controversial social and political issues of our time. The death penalty serves as a potent symbol, a talisman of respect for law, order, and traditional moral values. Indeed, some would argue that the American public's enduring support for the death penalty is much more about such general issues than it is about the merits of the actual punishment itself. Numerous recent empirical studies that have found that support for the death penalty typically declines to below 50 percent whenever respondents are asked to compare it with the alternative of "true" life imprisonment without any possibility of parole that also includes the possibility of restitution payments to the family of the victim.[28]

Regardless of whether or not public support for capital punishment runs deep or thin, the point is that America remains deeply embroiled in an ongoing social and political crisis surrounding the death penalty. As long as that continues to be so, habeas corpus has a special role to play in this turmoil as it has in other periods of social and political crisis throughout American history: habeas can ensure that arbitrary governmental actions do not trample on the fundamental rights and liberties of individuals.

Habeas Review of Death Sentences Today—
the Difference in Action

Some might argue that the most important reason why the scope and application of habeas corpus should be different in capital cases than in noncapital cases is simply that, as the Supreme Court has repeatedly noted, "death is different."[29] This difference is manifested in many ways. Death is different because capital cases draw the greatest attention from both the media and the public. Death is different because, in such cases, lawyers and judges scrutinize every decision made at both trial and sentencing more carefully than in other cases. Death is different because, in capital cases, there is always not one but at least two lives at issue: the victim's, giving rise to a compelling demand for justice that must be fulfilled, and the defendant's, generating an equally compelling demand for due process and a truthful verdict. And death is different because, as a sanction for crime, it is final and irrevocable.

Others might plausibly argue in response that most, if not all, of these differences are of degree rather than of kind.[30] Even the finality of capital punishment is hardly entirely unique; a prison sentence, although reversible, steals from the wrongly incarcerated defendant time that can never be replaced. The Court already has held that juveniles, who are constitutionally exempted from the death penalty, should now be similarly protected against a sentence of life imprisonment without parole for crimes other than homicide.[31] And there can be little doubt that, if the Court ever were to hold again, as it did in *Furman*, that the death penalty itself is cruel and unusual in violation of the Eighth Amendment, this would surely be followed by the claim that other severe forms of punishment are also unconstitutional. It does not take much imagination to recognize that the death-is-different idea is inherently vulnerable to such slippery slope arguments.

For present purposes, however, there is one clear sense in which it cannot be denied that death is truly different. Habeas today performs a very different role in capital cases than it does in noncapital cases. The writ, it appears, is neither out of reach nor futile for death row inmates. For this reason, habeas actually can make a difference to state police, prosecutors, and judges in capital cases.

The 2007 study of habeas litigation in district courts confirmed this. The study, discussed in earlier chapters in connection with noncapital cases, also examined all 368 habeas cases started by capital petitioners between 2000 and 2002 in the thirteen federal districts with the most capital cases. Table 8.1 presents a comparison of key features of capital and noncapital cases examined in the study.

The most striking difference is the reversal rate. Of the 267 petitioners whose cases were completed in the district court by the end of 2006, 12 percent received relief. By mid-2009, another thirty cases had terminated, including seven more grants, leaving the overall grant rate in the district courts at 13.5 percent (40/297). This grant rate, illustrated in Figure 8.1, is more than thirty-five times that in noncapital cases.[32]

This is not a new development. A study of capital habeas cases prior to AEDPA found that federal courts ordered relief from the death sentence for 40 percent of death row prisoners who applied for such relief.[33] Even now, after the many new restrictions placed on habeas by the

TABLE 8.1. **Litigating Capital and Noncapital Cases Compared**

	Capital cases	Noncapital cases
Petitioners and representation:		
% Cases petitioner without counsel	7.1	92.3
% Cases filed by petitioners who pleaded guilty or nolo	2.7	32.2
Petitions, claims raised:		
Average/median number claims raised per case	28/18	4/3[a]
% Raising claim of ineffective assistance of counsel	81.0	50.4[a]
% Raising a claim of innocence of conviction	10.8	3.9[a]
% Challenging sentence/sentencing proceeding only	5.1	12.9[a]
% Challenging sufficiency of evidence of guilt	25.5	18.9[a]
Litigation:		
% Cases with amended petitions	35.2	11.8
% Answer or motion to dismiss filed by state	82.9	58.2
% Cases including a stay for exhaustion	17.0	2.6
% Cases with discovery ordered	12.5	0.3
% Cases with evidentiary hearing held	9.5	0.4
Average/median number of docket entries	55/44	18/15
Disposition type and reason:		
% Cases dismissed as time barred[b]	4.1	21.7
% Cases dismissed as successive[b]	5.6	6.8
% Cases all claims dismissed as unexhausted[b]	3.4	10.9
% Cases including at least one procedurally defaulted claim[b]	53.3	13.3
% Cases including at least one *Teague*-barred claim[b]	23.9	0.4
% Cases dismissed or denied, without reaching merits	27.7 (64/234)	42.0 (631/1311)[c]
% Granted relief on any claim[b]	12.4 (33/267)	0.35 (7/1986)
% Of grants on sentence only	69.7	0.0

[a] Of 1,521 noncapital cases with claims information available (63.8 percent of the 2,384 cases in sample).

[b] Of nontransferred, terminated cases (267 capital cases, 1,986 noncapital cases).

[c] Of the 1,979 cases that had terminated without grant or transfer, 1,311 had claims information.

Court and Congress, capital habeas courts continue to grant relief regularly. See figure 8.1.

In addition, the results of the study confirm that federal habeas courts are most likely to disrupt state capital convictions and sentences for exactly those reasons that set capital cases apart from noncapital cases. The most likely grounds for capital habeas reversals are Eighth Amendment and other federal constitutional rules that are unique to capital cases—federal judges, in other words, do not seem to be simply applying the same constitutional rules differently in order to provide capital defendants more protection than noncapital defendants.

Three specific categories of claims were associated with a higher likelihood of capital habeas relief. First were claims invoking new and retroactive interpretations of the Eighth Amendment—for example, claims

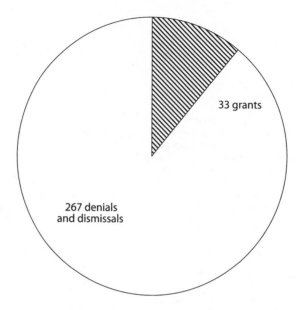

FIGURE 8.1. 2007 Study, Capital Prisoner Petition Terminations

that the petitioner was legally ineligible to receive a death sentence because, when he committed the crime, he was either a juvenile or mentally retarded.[34] Second were claims that the petitioner received ineffective assistance of counsel during the sentencing phase of the capital
trial.[35] These two kinds of rules are among those the Supreme Court has
frequently modified in capital cases in recent years, forcing lower courts
to repeatedly change course in order to implement the steady stream of
new Court decisions.[36] The pattern of grants did not change in the period between the time the study was concluded and this writing. Of the
additional seven capital cases that ordered relief between 2006 and mid-
2009, four involved a violation of a rule unique to capital sentencing.[37]
Finally, and interestingly, even though no capital habeas petitioner in the
study sample received habeas relief on a claim of actual innocence based
on newly discovered evidence, the mere presence of such a claim was
correlated with a higher likelihood of habeas relief on another claim.[38]
This suggests that federal judges might be considering the risk of executing an innocent defendant when evaluating whether capital sentences
comply with federal law.

These three features that are associated with habeas relief in the capital cases examined in the study—legal ineligibility for the death pen-

alty, ineffective assistance of counsel at capital sentencing, and the risk of a mistaken execution—are all features that are present only in capital cases. The much higher success rate in capital habeas than in noncapital habeas, together with the specific reasons why capital habeas petitions tend to succeed, both indicate that, at least in the view of federal habeas courts, there is a special need for habeas review in capital cases that is not present in noncapital cases.

Improving Habeas Review of Capital Cases

For all of the above reasons, federal habeas corpus review of state capital cases should not be substantially restricted. Given that most of these reasons would also apply to collateral review under Section 2255 of the relatively rare death sentences imposed for federal crimes, the same analysis should also prevail there. The vicissitudes of modern Eighth Amendment law dominate capital proceedings, whether they take place in federal court or state court. Accordingly, the two collateral remedies—for state and federal capital cases, respectively—should be structured and applied in the same general way.

The results of capital habeas litigation today essentially speak for themselves. The rate of habeas relief for problems unique to capital cases demonstrates that the federal habeas courts perceive a continuing need for broad habeas jurisdiction in capital cases. Habeas courts can no longer hope to correct constitutional errors on a case-by-case basis for the millions of state noncapital prisoners, even if those courts were to receive a significant infusion of new public resources. The provision of competent counsel to assist petitioners, vital for this complicated litigation, would be hopelessly impractical, not to mention politically suicidal, across the vast range of noncapital criminal cases. Because of the much smaller number of capital cases, however, courts can continue to provide capital habeas petitioners with counsel and can devote significant judicial time and energy to the review of their constitutional claims.

Preserving broad habeas review of capital cases does not mean, however, that we cannot make improvements to the rules and procedures that apply to capital habeas today. Reform of capital habeas should be designed primarily to facilitate the unique functions it performs in such cases: interpreting and applying Eighth Amendment law and guarding against the execution of an innocent person.

For example, as we explained in chapter 5, the Supreme Court has yet to define or explain the constitutional standards for factual innocence as a stand-alone claim that might warrant a habeas reversal even in the absence of any other constitutional violation.[39] The rise of DNA evidence in the 1990s has permanently changed the terms of the death penalty debate outside of the courts. The study findings suggest that judicial concerns about the risk of executing an innocent person might be influencing district court decisions in capital habeas cases. But this concern has yet to be reflected adequately in habeas law. And even if the Court decides not to recognize the bare-innocence claim as a general matter of constitutional due process, the Court could nevertheless recognize the claim within the narrower context of capital cases under the Eighth Amendment.

Additionally, continuing efforts must be made to increase the efficiency of habeas review in these cases. In capital cases, as recent studies have shown, habeas litigation too often drags on for years, even decades.[40] One important reason is that, unlike most noncapital prisoners seeking release from custody, most death row inmates have no inherent incentive to try to speed up the pace of habeas litigation. Delay is almost always preferable to the alternative, which is timely enforcement of the death sentence. The changes adopted by Congress in 1996 to streamline habeas review have yet to succeed and are unlikely to do so anytime soon.

Yet improvements are possible. The 2007 study confirms that some courts are much, much slower than other courts in resolving the same sorts of claims, holding all else constant.[41] For example, cases resolving petitions filed by Pennsylvania and Arizona death row inmates take much longer than those filed by Texas inmates. In California and Nevada district courts, the vast majority of capital cases filed in 2000, 2001, or 2002 were still pending as of mid-2009.[42] The constitutional rules governing these capital cases do not differ from district to district; but local legal culture, procedural rules, and litigation expectations do. So does the speed with which the states respond to petitions, provide access to records, and provide counsel. The federal courts should strive to adopt more uniform and efficient procedures in capital habeas cases, no matter where they are filed, and help to diagnose the causes of unusually long or and repetitive delays.

The 2007 study also found that in many districts, much of the time that elapses before the final disposition of a capital habeas petition results from proceedings in the state courts. The combination of the AEDPA filing deadline, the longstanding rule that petitioners must first attempt to raise new claims in state court before a federal court can consider them, and the ban on successive petitions has created a new source of delay—the stay. Petitioners can only file for habeas once but may have to do so before some of their claims have made it through the state courts. As a result, district courts are granting stays in federal habeas cases while the petitioners finish exhausting their new claims in the state courts. In the study sample, these stays often added years to the time it takes federal courts to resolve petitions.[43] Eleven of the fourteen capital cases from the study that had been filed in Nevada and pending at the end of 2006, for example, were still stayed for state proceedings in mid-2009. Some reduction in delay may follow if more courts heeded the Court's warning that these stays should not be routinely granted but should be permitted only when there is some likelihood of relief, and then only for a reasonable time.[44]

A more effective response would be federal initiatives to help state courts improve their processing of capital cases. Efforts to assist states to provide skilled state postconviction counsel and reduce delay in their own postconviction proceedings would, in the long term, conserve federal resources used in administering and monitoring these cases while they are stayed for state proceedings. Finally, although understandable given the constantly changing rules under the Eighth Amendment, stays to await the decisions of other federal courts should also be discouraged.[45]

Another source of delay that could use a fresh look is litigation unrelated to the merits of the petitioner's constitutional claims. The statute of limitations for filing a petition is litigated in many of these cases, but only 4 percent of all terminated cases included any claim rejected on this basis, and those cases actually took longer to resolve than cases that had no claims dismissed as filed too late.[46] State procedural default was the basis for rejecting a claim in just over half of the terminated cases, but this defense too appears to contribute to rather than reduce delay. Cases in the study with defaulted claims took 30–57 percent longer than cases without such claims, holding all else constant.[47] At the very least, in light of these findings, it would seem to make sense to permit federal judges to avoid the complicated analyses of procedural default and filing deadlines and simply deny claims after consideration on the merits, as they are able to do with claims that have yet to be exhausted in state court.

In addition, at least in capital cases, the Supreme Court should consider loosening the restraints of the procedural default doctrine, which often prevent habeas courts from addressing alleged constitutional errors on their merits simply because the petitioner's trial or appellate lawyer made a negligent mistake in failing to press the issue properly in the state courts.[48]

Finally, the 2007 study found that the total number of claims filed in a habeas petition had a significant impact on the likelihood that these cases—all filed between 2000 and 2002—were resolved by the end of 2006. Most petitions included fewer than twenty claims, but 5 percent raised more than eighty-eight separate claims. Every ten additional claims made termination 20 percent less likely.[49] Arbitrarily capping the number of claims by statute would be unrealistic and might create even more worthless litigation over whether certain kinds of claims should be counted separately or together. But reasonable page limits for habeas pleadings in capital cases might be a reasonable proxy.

These recommendations are quite different from our proposals for restricting habeas review of state noncapital cases. But they are carefully tailored to the specific kinds of review that are needed in these particular cases. In noncapital cases, the need for habeas courts to oversee the state courts' interpretation of new and ever-changing federal law has long passed. In capital cases, it has not. Moreover, capital cases are relatively small in number; involve uniquely heightened concerns about substantive justice, including the possible execution of an innocent person; and remain the subject of intense societal debate. Until these conditions that currently continue to justify relatively aggressive federal habeas review of capital cases have receded, the broad application of the writ in these special cases remains entirely appropriate.

CHAPTER NINE

Sentence-Administration Claims: Square Peg in a Round Hole

S o far, we have argued that the venerable role of habeas corpus as protection against unjust detention without conviction remains vital today and that it should be fully preserved and strengthened. We have also maintained that although the writ was once an important means of encouraging institutional and structural reform of judicial review of criminal cases in the state courts, it is no longer needed to perform that role and cannot effectively remedy constitutional violations on a case-by-case basis. We have distinguished the review of federal criminal cases and have argued that the statutory substitute for habeas, Section 2255, must remain available for convicted federal prisoners, even though habeas for state prisoners should be contracted. And we have supported the continued broad use of federal habeas review in capital cases, because of the many reasons—especially the relative instability of Eighth Amendment law and concerns about the risk of mistaken executions—that lead federal habeas courts to continue to grant the writ in capital cases at exceptionally high rates.

In this chapter we turn to an entirely different use of habeas, one that has burst onto the scene only in the past few decades: review of the administration of state prison sentences by prison and parole officials. This corner of the habeas universe has become surprisingly large and problematic, but it has been entirely ignored by habeas policy makers. While no one was paying attention, federal habeas courts have been quietly transformed into review boards for prison and parole officials, evaluating actions that have nothing to do with whether a prison inmate's conviction or sentence violated the Constitution. We believe that the problems posed in these cases are intolerable and that the writ is being squandered by its routine application to these cases. We offer three proposals for reform.[1]

Sentence-Administration Claims and Habeas Today

The 2007 study exposed a startling statistic: in more than one of every six habeas cases (17.8 percent) filed in 2003 and 2004 by state prisoners serving noncapital sentences, the prisoner did not challenge the constitutionality of his convictions or sentence. Instead, he claimed that state officials failed to comply with due process in deciding not to release him sooner.[2] These unique habeas claims consist of constitutional challenges to a number of routine administrative decisions, primarily decisions revoking good-time credits following prison disciplinary proceedings and decisions denying, deferring, or administering release on parole.

These claims make up an even higher proportion of all habeas filings in the states with the largest prison populations. For example, an estimated 22 percent of all noncapital habeas petitions in California and Florida raised this type of claim, and about a third of all petitions filed in Texas (35 percent) and Pennsylvania (32 percent) did so. In Indiana, the study found that a clear majority (61 percent) of all habeas petitions contested the actions of prison or parole administrators and not criminal judgments.[3]

Such claims compete for limited judicial attention with all other habeas claims, including many that might reasonably be viewed as far more compelling. Nationwide, the study revealed, more habeas petitions are filed raising a sentence-administration claim than are filed challenging the prisoner's conviction or sentence on the basis of lost, suppressed, undisclosed, or false evidence (13 percent of all noncapital habeas cases) or on the basis of an invalid guilty plea, including those caused by ineffective assistance of counsel during the plea process (14.8 percent of all noncapital habeas cases).[4]

Not only are these claims voluminous, they are almost entirely pointless. The likelihood that any prisoner will succeed with a sentence-administration claim is exceedingly remote. The 2007 study, which examined 2,384 randomly selected habeas filings by state prisoners serving noncapital sentences (at least 327 of which challenged a sentence-administration decision) did not find a *single case* in which habeas relief was granted on a sentence-administration claim.[5] This suggests a rate of relief that is at least as low, and perhaps even lower, than the miniscule success rate of 0.35 percent for challenges to noncapital state judgments, as examined in chapter 4.

The Growth of Habeas Oversight of State Administrative Decisions

How did this happen? How was the Great Writ converted into a mechanism for repetitive yet meaningless review of the day-to-day decisions of state prison and parole officials? The answers to these questions lie in a series of facially unrelated and seemingly benign developments that nevertheless combined to produce a perfect storm of misguided policy.

Expanding Constitutional Rights

The first step was the Supreme Court's decision to expand the rights of state prison inmates under the Due Process Clause of the Fourteenth Amendment. Due process is the foundation for most of the procedural rights enjoyed by defendants at trial and at sentencing, but historically it had little or no application to the discretionary decisions made by parole or prison officials that affected a prison inmate's opportunity to obtain early release from prison. Any release from custody that might be granted before the expiration of a lawfully imposed sentence was a matter of grace and not a legal entitlement. Since the inmate had no legal right to be released early, a decision to deny or delay such release could not result in a constitutionally significant deprivation.[6]

In the 1970s, however, the Supreme Court began to expand the application of the Due Process Clause to decisions by state officials. The Court first held that state laws conferring various benefits—welfare benefits and unemployment compensation, for example—created a legal entitlement to those benefits for those who received them. Any decision to take away such benefits, the Court decided, must comply with due process.[7] Even though the state had no obligation to provide such benefits in the first place and chose to do so entirely as a matter of legislative grace, the state's decision to provide the benefits was held to create a so-called new property right in those benefits.[8] This was enough to trigger the Due Process Clause. To comply, the state had to provide notice to the affected person and an opportunity for a hearing before terminating such benefits.

Relying on these "new property right" cases, the Supreme Court in 1972 held that the early release of a prison inmate on parole gives rise to a liberty interest worthy of protection under the Due Process Clause.[9] As a result, a state parole board could no longer revoke an inmate's parole release without providing fair notice to the inmate, a statement of reasons for the decision, "some" evidence supporting the decision, and an opportunity (such as a hearing) to rebut that evidence.[10]

The Court later extended the same rule to corrections decisions that had the effect of delaying a prisoner's release past a presumptive release date established by state law. The Court initially held that a decision by prison officials to revoke an inmate's earned good-time credits and delay his presumptive release date must also meet due process standards.[11] Then, in 1979, the Court applied the Due Process Clause to a decision to deny release on parole, when Nebraska's law provided that an inmate "shall" be released on parole "unless" one of four conditions (such as a "substantial risk" that the inmate would not conform to the conditions of parole) was present.[12] This scheme, the Court agreed, created a constitutionally protected liberty interest in release, even though the law did not grant the inmate an absolute right to actual release if the authorities found one of the conditions for continued confinement.[13] The denial of parole under such a law, the Court concluded, must comply with due process requirements, but those requirements did not apply to parole decisions in states whose laws did not create a similar presumption in favor of early release.[14]

As a result of these rulings, thousands of state prison inmates who previously could protest only those prison conditions that violated equal protection, the First Amendment, or the Eighth Amendment's prohibition against cruel and unusual punishments suddenly acquired a new federal cause of action. The Court granted to them the new right to bring a due process challenge each and every time they had their parole revoked, were disciplined and lost good-time credits, or were denied presumptive release on parole.

Shifting to the Habeas Forum

The second step that led to the large number of habeas cases challenging these administrative decisions was the Court's determination, made gradually over an extended period of more than twenty years, that the proper federal forum for these challenges is federal habeas and not a lawsuit under 42 U.S.C. § 1983—the federal civil rights statute, enacted after the Civil War, that allows persons to sue government officials who have violated their federal constitutional rights. This development began in 1973, in a case in which prison inmates filed a Section 1983 lawsuit challenging the revocation of their good-time credits.[15] The Court explained that while Section 1983 could be used to raise many different kinds of constitutional claims, including challenges to conditions of confinement in prison, habeas was the appropriate forum for the inmates' claims because the claims went to the validity of their custody and if successful would result in their release.[16]

For a time, the Court appeared to require that a prisoner use habeas only if he sought a remedy for the alleged deprivation of due process that would speed up his release, such as the restoration of lost good-time credits. Other potential remedies, such as damages, could still be the subject of a Section 1983 lawsuit.[17] But in the 1990s, the Court ruled that any time an inmate seeks a decision from a federal court that would necessarily undermine the legality of a challenged state action affecting the timing of release, then the inmate must file his claim in habeas instead of through 42 U.S.C. § 1983—even if the inmate does not actually seek earlier release and requests only a damages remedy.[18]

Shifts in State Sentencing Policy

The third step leading to the large number of sentence-administration claims filed in habeas today was the explosion in the number of state prisoners who became eligible to raise the federal due process rights first recognized by the Supreme Court in the 1970s. Forty years ago, when the Supreme Court first recognized the due process implications of legal entitlements to early release from prison, only a few states had laws creating such entitlements.[19] Parole denials and revocation of good-time credits in those few "presumptive release" states triggered the new federal due process rights; but in all other states, such decisions remained free from constitutional oversight, because prisoners enjoyed neither a legal right nor a legally cognizable expectation of early release that could be protected by due process.

In the 1980s and 1990s, state sentencing policy was transformed. Dramatic increases in crime in the 1970s, combined with a dramatic loss of confidence in the predictive and therapeutic value of psychology, led to a collapse in the traditional rehabilitative ideal in criminal sentencing.[20] Instead, the focus of state penal policy shifted to retribution—the belief that a person's punishment should be based on what he deserves, rather than on some vague notion of when he has been "cured" enough to be released back into society. In addition, societal concerns about the perceived tendencies of liberal judges and corrupt or ill-informed parole boards to go easy on criminals led to a call for truth in sentencing, emphasizing fixed sentences to be determined at the time of the original sentencing hearing.[21] Finally, criminal justice experts sought to reduce disparate treatment of similarly situated offenders and to use their expertise to help decide the appropriate punishment for each crime and criminal.[22]

These forces combined to produce a seismic shift from traditional sentencing, in which a judge chooses an initial indeterminate sentence from a wide range of statutory options and a parole board decides on the prisoner's ultimate release, to determinate sentencing, in which the prisoner is told on the day of his sentencing in court exactly how much time he will have to serve in prison. New sentencing statutes abolished discretionary parole release, substituting instead legal rules that created presumptive release dates.[23]

Lost in this effort to reform sentencing law was the fact that every prisoner sentenced under these new mandatory-release systems would automatically gain a liberty interest in release protected by the Due Process Clause. As a result, every prisoner sentenced under this sort of statutory scheme could pursue federal habeas relief after each and every prison disciplinary and parole proceeding that delayed his release by alleging that the proceeding failed to comply with federal due process requirements.

Although most states have retained discretionary release for at least some offenders, by the end of 2002, only sixteen states retained full discretionary authority for their parole boards to release all inmates.[24] In these sixteen states, inmates whose parole is denied or good time revoked do not have the ability to file due process challenges to these decisions in habeas. However, of the seven states with the largest prison populations in the country—California, Texas, Florida, New York, Michigan, Ohio, and Illinois—all but one of them now use mandatory-release schemes for at least some offenders.[25] Prisoners subject to mandatory release in these states, and in other states as well, now routinely, and repeatedly, challenge their disciplinary hearings and parole denials in federal court by filing petitions for habeas relief.

Prison Populations Transformed

The fourth step leading to the current role of habeas courts as overseers of state corrections and parole decisions was the shift in state prison populations in the 1980s and 1990s. After states replaced discretionary parole release and assessments of likely recidivism with mandatory release, parole revocation rates rose sharply. A growing proportion of those who were admitted to state prisons in the 1980s and 1990s were "violators," convicted felons who were returned to prison after their release on parole had been revoked for new crimes or for failure to comply with other conditions of release. By 1998, the category of "violators" grew to more than a third of all state prison admissions, double the proportion in 1980.[26]

Violators, by definition, are prisoners who already have served a portion of their prison sentence prior to being released. By the time they are returned to prison for violating the terms of their release, they have already had their one (and, in most cases, their only) opportunity to file a federal habeas petition to challenge their original state criminal proceedings. After readmission to prison, violators are therefore far less likely than new prison admittees to file a collateral attack on their original conviction and sentence. Except in the rarest of situations, any second challenge to the same state judgment would be dismissed quickly by the habeas court without review on the merits.

But throughout the remainder of a violator's custody, he can continue to attack the constitutionality of each and every decision made by state prison and parole authorities that affects the exact timing of his release. In 1986, for example, one report found that 53 percent of state prison inmates were charged with a violation during their current sentence; 94 percent of those were found guilty, and 12 percent lost good-time credits.[27] An increase in the proportion of prisoners who are returned to prison after an initial release therefore produces a corresponding increase in the percentage of federal habeas petitions that attack sentence-administration decisions rather than criminal judgments.

In addition, state prisoners are locked up longer these days than they used to be. From 1990 to 2004, the average time a state prisoner remained in custody increased.[28] Because decisions affecting the exact timing of release occur repeatedly throughout a prisoner's stay, longer periods of incarceration inevitably produce more administrative decisions for prisoners to challenge. Finally, state prison populations exploded in absolute terms over the same period, jumping from 681,000 in 1989 to more than 1,400,000 in 2006.[29]

Through this strange confluence of Supreme Court rulings with unanticipated consequences and substantial changes in state penal policies, the federal courts are today routinely asked to oversee prison disciplinary and parole decisions for the nation's growing prison population.

The Mismatched Remedy

Had Congress clearly understood these forces and their impact on habeas, it could have addressed the problem when it modified the habeas statute in the Antiterrorism and Effective Death Penalty Act of 1996 (AEDPA). But that did not happen. At the time that AEDPA was drafted, the Supreme Court had yet to announce definitively that most challenges to disciplinary and parole proceedings must be filed as habeas cases rather than in Section 1983 actions. Moreover, at the time, few, if any, legislators anticipated the full impact of the policy shift toward mandatory-release systems on constitutional challenges to prison disciplinary proceedings.[30] In the years leading up to the passage of AEDPA, there is no indication in the legislative history that Congressional lawmakers ever anticipated the application of the new federal habeas provisions to constitutional attacks by noncapital state prisoners on administrative decisions that affected the timing of their release from prison.

In shaping modern habeas law and policy, Congress and the federal courts consistently have assumed that the purpose of the primary federal habeas statute applicable to state prisoners, 28 U.S.C. § 2254, is to provide a forum for the prisoner to collaterally attack his conviction or sentence by alleging a constitutional error in the judicial process that led to his incarceration. Habeas is considered a collateral remedy precisely because it allows for reexamination of a state court judgment that already has been the subject of judicial review on direct appeal and in state postconviction proceedings.

This fundamental assumption has led to the development of rules of habeas procedure that are tailored to the collateral review context.

The rules do not fit well at all when applied to sentence-administration claims. Some states do not even provide their own judicial review of the administrative decisions of prison or parole authorities, so that federal judges evaluating a habeas claim must review the administrative decision directly. And they must do so under habeas rules that were never designed for such cases and do not make sense when applied to them.

The upshot is that applying the current federal habeas statute to these sentence-administration claims is like trying to fit square pegs into round holes. Congress passed a statute designed for reviewing state court criminal judgments, but federal habeas courts are forced to use it, day after day, to review administrative actions by state corrections officials. The problem is not only that the provisions in the statute are difficult to apply to these cases. In practice, some of the limitations that were designed to speed up habeas challenges to convictions and sentences have actually backfired in sentence-administration cases.

Take the statute of limitations, one of the most important new restrictions in AEDPA, which was designed to ensure that federal courts grant relief only to those state prisoners—and particularly only those death row inmates—who speed their way to federal court after completing their challenges in state court. Some judges do not apply this restriction to administrative challenges, and the ones who do cannot agree about when the limitations period begins to run or when it must be tolled.

The provision is perplexing in this context, in part because the reasons to insist that an inmate challenge his state judgment promptly do not support a similar filing deadline for challenges to administrative decisions about the timing of his release. When a prisoner attacks his conviction or sentence, the filing deadline protects the state against the loss of the proof it might need for retrial or resentencing if the writ is granted and promotes finality of criminal judgments so that all concerned know at some point that the conviction and sentence will stick. These reasons for adopting a habeas filing deadline have nothing to do with the administration of criminal judgments that are already final. No matter how long a prisoner delays in raising a claim that he should be released earlier than the state says, the validity and finality of the original conviction and sentence are never in jeopardy. A delayed challenge to an administrative decision affecting the timing of release from a lawfully imposed prison term never risks loss of evidence needed for relitigation of guilt or sentence. If an administrative decision affecting the timing of release is flawed, habeas relief would, at most, require a new administrative hearing and might require merely changes to the record. More fundamentally, prisoners hardly need encouragement to object promptly to decisions denying or delaying release.

Not surprisingly, the litigation needed to sort all of this out in sentence-administration challenges is so time-consuming that the statute of limitations provision fails even as a measure to promote efficiency. The application of the present statute of limitations provision to these claims may very well have increased litigation costs for the states and the federal courts, instead of reducing them. Among all noncapital habeas cases examined in the 2007 study, those dismissed as filed too late tend to be dismissed more quickly than others, suggesting that the statute of limitations at least saves time for the federal courts and presumably for the state's attorneys who must defend these cases.[31] But in cases that raise sentence-administration challenges, the application of the statute of limitations seems to have the opposite effect. Cases with challenges to sentence-administration decisions that were dismissed as time barred took longer, on average, to complete in district court than those that were not dismissed as time barred.[32] Deciding whether an inmate received due process at his hearing is apparently far easier than resolving whether his petition raising such a claim was filed too late.

The bar against successive petitions also creates headaches in these cases.[33] The exceptions to the successive petition bar, in particular, make little sense in this context. The first exception is for claims that rely on "a new rule of constitutional law, made retroactive to cases on collateral review by the Supreme Court." As we discussed in chapter 5, this language has been interpreted narrowly to include only new expansions of the Eighth Amendment's cruel and unusual punishments clause and would likely never encompass the procedural due process rules regulating the executive decisions made in enforcing an otherwise lawful prison sentence. The second exception is for petitioners who can show that "no reasonable fact-finder would have found the applicant guilty of the underlying offense" had the alleged error not occurred. But a prisoner raising a sentence-administration claim is not even challenging his underlying conviction.

Exhaustion and procedural default rules are also difficult to apply in this context. Not only must a court determine which administrative remedies, if any, must be pursued in addition to judicial remedies, but the courts are only just now working out the details of when a prisoner's failure to comply with these administrative remedies will be excused. For example, the "fundamental miscarriage of justice" exception to the procedural default doctrine has no meaning in such cases, since it requires a showing that the challenged action led to the conviction of an innocent person. No matter what prison and parole officials may do, their actions take place after the underlying conviction and thus cannot possibly affect the accuracy of that conviction one way or the other.

All of this procedural litigation, over whether a federal court may even reach the merits of a prisoner's claim that a disciplinary hearing or parole proceeding violated the requirements of due process, is quite far afield from the work the Great Writ was supposed to do. Federal courts should not be wasting their time trying to apply the habeas statute to a situation it was never meant to address. Nor should they be second-guessing whether state officials should have released a prisoner before the expiration of his validly imposed sentence, every time the prisoner faces disciplinary action in prison or comes up for parole.

Three Solutions

Consider again one of the most important functions performed by the writ in our criminal justice system—to provide those in custody with some form of judicial review of allegations that they are being held in violation of federal law when no such review is otherwise available. This suggests that whatever solution we may devise for these sentence-administration decisions, that solution should provide for adequate review of constitutional claims not subject to scrutiny by any other judge. This would be the case in those states that do not grant their state courts jurisdiction to hear certain sentence-administration claims. Just as collateral review under Section 2255 should remain available for claims that convicted federal prisoners cannot raise on appeal, and just as habeas review under Section 2241 should be safeguarded for cases of executive detention without conviction, claims from state prisoners who were denied release at the expiration of their sentence, in violation of the Constitution, should be considered by federal courts when those claims have no other judicial audience.

But these "first bite at the apple" cases are concentrated in a few states that have refused to grant their state courts jurisdiction over these claims. The vast majority of these challenges, on the other hand, are "second bite at the apple" cases, where the federal habeas petition represents the prisoner's second chance to litigate a claim of unconstitutional delay in release, following an earlier opportunity to object to that decision in state court.

One interim solution to the problems created by litigating these cases in federal habeas, as they are now, would be to move the claims from Section 2254 to a different remedial scheme that is not as ill fitting. It would be a slight improvement to require prisoners to file these claims under 28 U.S.C. § 2241, the general federal habeas statute that is used for challenges to detention without conviction and that is not encumbered by the 1996 act's amendments. This would help to solve the problem of square pegs and round holes, but it would still leave all of this routine prisoner litigation within the scope of traditional habeas review.

A somewhat better solution would be to remove these claims from habeas review and create a tailored statutory substitute, such as a modified version of the Prison Litigation Reform Act or a new federal statute specifically designed to deal with allegations that prison and parole officials are continuing to hold an inmate in custody in violation of the Constitution. Moving these claims from traditional habeas to another, substitute federal judicial forum would allow for the development of new procedural rules suited to such cases, just as the adoption of Section 2255 permitted Congress to tailor-make the procedural rules for challenges to convictions and sentences filed by federal prisoners. For example, the new statute could include measures designed to deter the filing of frivolous claims, measures that might be inappropriate if applied to prisoners challenging the legality of their convictions and sentences.

Perhaps the most far-reaching solution to the problems caused by using habeas to review the endless volume of overwhelmingly meritless challenges to disciplinary and parole decisions would be to rethink the substantive law that rendered these decisions subject to case-by-case constitutional oversight in the first place. Litigation about the constitutionality of the procedures used in prison and parole hearings originated with two key decisions: the decision by individual states to withdraw discretion from parole boards and substitute rigid rules governing release, and the decision of the Supreme Court to protect the resulting entitlement to early release through constitutionally based due process rights. States have no control over the Court's interpretation of the Constitution, but they do control their own sentencing policy.

We suggest that the states should take off their blinders and consider the full costs of adopting mandatory-release statutes as they continue to reform their sentencing statutes. Prisoners whose good-time credits entitle them to early release will file constitutional claims attacking administrative decisions, first in state court, then in federal court, and states' attorneys will be called upon to defend all of these cases. Prisoners whose release is determined by the discretion of a parole board, by contrast, have no such constitutional claims to litigate. With the shift away from discretionary release decisions to predetermined release dates, the states essentially opened the floodgates to wasteful habeas litigation.

Eliminating such litigation over early release decisions is, of course, only one of several considerations that states must weigh in adopting sentencing policy. States will want to consider whether prison growth and its attendant burdens can be more effectively managed through mandatory or discretionary release, for example, a question whose answer may differ from state to state.[34] States should also consider carefully whether constraints other than discretionary release might be available to check legislators' tendencies to adopt ever more severe sentences[35] and whether parole release decision making could be improved, rather than abandoned, by combining newer research-based parole guidelines designed to reduce the risk of recidivism with institutional reforms to insulate the relevant agency from political influence.[36] States ignore at their peril any of these factors when choosing sentencing policy, including the costs of expanded habeas litigation.

*   *   *

Insisting that state prisoners challenge prison administrative decisions under a federal habeas statute that was designed for reviewing the constitutionality of convictions and sentences is a mistake. A federal statutory substitute for habeas review, tailored to these unique cases, is overdue. A careful legislative solution could address the specific problems presented by decisions affecting the early release of convicted prisoners, just as statutes providing judicial review of routine pretrial detention and civil commitment decisions essentially replaced habeas challenges in those contexts. The more radical approach of rethinking state mandatory prison release systems could entirely eliminate thousands of habeas cases in which prisoners claim they should have been released sooner but were not because of some constitutional flaw in a decision made by a prison or parole official.

Either kind of response—a new federal statutory substitute for habeas

review or a return by the states to discretionary release—would reduce
the strain these cases currently place on both the federal courts and financially strapped state governments. More importantly, these steps
would conserve the scarce resources of federal habeas for the cases for
which the writ really matters—shifting those resources away from the
early release of prisoners who do not even contest the legality of their
criminal convictions and sentences, and who almost never prevail anyway, and reserving them instead for cases involving arbitrary imprisonment without any conviction at all, wrongful convictions, and death
sentences.

CHAPTER TEN

Habeas for the Twenty-First Century

We have attempted in this book to present a new perspective on the ancient habeas corpus remedy, one which is based not only in the historical development and application of habeas but also on the latest empirical information about its contemporary use by federal district judges. By considering both the use of habeas corpus in all of its various forms over the last two centuries and the extraordinary findings revealed by new data, we have exposed striking patterns that are not easily seen when the writ is viewed only in a single context or at a single moment in time. These same patterns point the way forward to sound habeas policy for the twenty-first century and beyond.

First and foremost, habeas must always remain a flexible judicial remedy, adaptable to enforce the rule of law and protect individual liberty whenever either detention practices or detention law shifts significantly, as each is apt to do periodically, especially during times of serious political or social crisis. This flexibility allows the Supreme Court to press habeas into service as a stopgap, providing judicial review for novel detention schemes until alternative review mechanisms become available, and helping to shape the contours of those mechanisms through individual habeas decisions. Flexibility also permits the Court to use habeas to respond to bold assertions of power by the political branches of the federal government or by the states that threaten the careful balance of powers our Constitution protects.

Second, these central functions of habeas review are intrinsically dynamic and temporary. Habeas review is misused if it continues to be invoked routinely even after the appearance of adequate alternative judicial review mechanisms or after the passing of the particular crisis that necessitated its intervention. Whenever such misuse occurs, habeas risks losing its special status as an exceptional remedy requiring immediate obedience by the executive and a systematic response from the legislature and transforms instead into a burdensome and even despised source of wasteful litigation—a process to be streamlined, routinized, and ultimately, weakened. In order to preserve both its flexibility and its moral authority, habeas must always be considered a remedy of last resort, to be used only so long as is absolutely necessary. The scope of habeas, in other words, must never become a one-way ratchet that expands but never contracts.

Whenever a particular detention scheme is used repeatedly and has become entrenched, case-by-case habeas review of the legality of such detentions should be replaced by alternative judicial review mechanisms that are better suited to address the specific issues raised by the particular context. The adequacy of these substitute mechanisms for enforcing federal law remains subject to review by the Supreme Court through the Suspension Clause, however, leaving the Court with the last word on whether broad habeas review is truly no longer necessary.

This historical pattern is apparent in the development of such alternative judicial review options for pretrial detention and civil commitment decisions. The same dynamic is also familiar in the very context in which habeas corpus originally began, namely, executive detention. There, as we pointed out in chapter 2, confrontations between the political branches and the Supreme Court have recurred regularly over the centuries. In repeated rounds of legislative experimentation and judicial rejection, habeas has been used to curb understandably aggressive responses by Congress and the president to each new periodic threat to public safety. Over time, the Court's habeas decisions have provided guideposts for fair detention and judicial review policies, which in turn have allowed the use of habeas to recede.

It is now time to take account of another fundamental shift affecting the proper scope of habeas: the diminished need for federal judicial review in state criminal cases. The Supreme Court expanded habeas corpus in the 1950s and 1960s to allow federal judges to announce and enforce new constitutional rules of criminal procedure for state courts and to stimulate meaningful institutional and attitudinal reforms of judicial review in the states. These institutional goals have now, for the most part, been achieved. At least in noncapital cases, the current elaborate habeas structure should now be dismantled, and habeas review should be returned to its traditionally more limited scope.

Admittedly, this use of habeas corpus to announce, and then to enforce, federal constitutional rules for state criminal justice is a relatively recent adaptation that commenced in earnest less than fifty years ago. Reasonable people, particularly those who lived through the turbulent political and social crisis that first prompted this use, may resist our claim that the serious federalism conflict that originally provoked the Warren Court into action has indeed passed. But whatever one might think about that claim, the stark statistical picture revealed by the research presented in chapter 4 is impossible to ignore. Habeas today is, in fact, utterly worthless to the vast majority of state criminal defendants. Relief comes far too little and far too late to make any difference. Except in the narrow categories of special situations we identify in chapter 5, as well as in the capital cases we discuss in chapters 7 and 8, habeas review can no longer contribute meaningfully to the enforcement of federal constitutional law in state criminal cases. Habeas cannot correct errors in the vast majority of individual cases, nor can it prompt needed systematic changes in state defense representation systems. Routine habeas review of state criminal cases not only wastes scarce resources, it prevents those resources from being deployed more effectively to address persistent deficiencies in state defense services, deficiencies that habeas has no reasonable chance of correcting or deterring.

We have proposed a narrowly tailored statutory scheme for the habeas review of state noncapital criminal cases that responds to this fundamental change in institutional circumstances. The federal habeas review that we outline in chapter 5 would supplement the judicial review that state prisoners already receive from their now transformed state courts, which today routinely apply, rather than defy, federal criminal procedure law. Under our proposal, federal habeas review of noncapital cases would be preserved only for constitutional claims that require retroactive application of a new constitutional rule or that are accompanied by a strong showing of innocence. The constitutional adequacy of this curtailed review can be carefully monitored by the Supreme Court using the Suspension Clause—a seemingly novel recommendation, but well grounded both in the Court's recent precedents and in the larger patterns of habeas history that we identify in this book. As for the ongoing challenge of assisting the states to comply with the Constitution's commands for criminal justice, we suggest that Congress should shift its focus from ineffectual habeas litigation at the back end to the vigorous encouragement of meaningful state reforms in defense services at the front end.

Our fresh look at the writ has also prompted us to suggest several other reforms, albeit relatively less dramatic than our proposal for the review of state criminal judgments. In chapter 6, we argued that Congress should decouple habeas review of state criminal judgments from the collateral review of federal criminal judgments. The availability of Section 2255, the current statutory substitute for habeas review of federal criminal convictions, should remain more extensive than habeas review of state criminal judgments because Section 2255 provides the first and only bite at the apple of judicial review for federal claims that could not be raised on direct appeal. These claims include retroactive applications of new interpretations of substantive federal law, as well as claims based on facts outside of the record—such as ineffective assistance of counsel and prosecutorial suppression of exculpatory evidence, newly discovered evidence of innocence, and challenges to sentences based on subsequently vacated or uncounselled prior convictions.

In chapters 7 and 8, we explained why federal habeas review of capital cases should be preserved in a much more robust form than habeas review of noncapital cases. Because of its many inherent contradictions, the Eighth Amendment law that is virtually unique to capital cases remains in constant motion and will likely remain so forever. So long as the Court continues to announce new constitutional rules under the cruel and unusual punishments clause of the Eighth Amendment, it will continue to need the help of the lower federal courts to refine, apply, and enforce this shifting doctrine—just as the Warren Court did when it first announced its new due process rules for state criminal cases during the "criminal procedure revolution" nearly fifty years ago. In capital cases, in other words, the revolution is far from over. And so long as a significant portion of the judiciary and the American public remains deeply troubled about the possibility of mistakenly executing an innocent person, habeas review provides a badly needed forum for the presentation of new and compelling evidence of innocence. The latest empirical research suggests that the lower federal courts currently serve exactly these core functions in their habeas review of capital cases. The goal for capital habeas should be to enable these courts to do so more effectively and efficiently.

Finally, in chapter 9, we exposed, through new empirical findings, the startlingly large volume of habeas corpus petitions that challenge not a prisoner's underlying conviction or sentence but instead an administrative decision affecting the prisoner's opportunity for early release. A statutory substitute for habeas review, specifically tailored to these unique cases, is long overdue. It would reduce the strain these cases currently place on the personnel and resources of the federal courts and on financially strapped state governments. And it would help to conserve scarce resources for those cases where the writ really matters most.

Popular perceptions of habeas corpus have for too long been distorted by the immense volume of meritless petitions filed by state and federal prisoners serving noncapital sentences. The bigger picture of habeas, both historically and functionally, extends well beyond these cases. The Framers had good reason to believe that habeas corpus was a vital component of the new, balanced system of government they sought to create and would help to protect against the kinds of tyranny they sought to abolish forever. Examining habeas corpus within this larger historical and theoretical framework should help to broaden the contemporary conversation about habeas reform and point the way to a better future for the Great Writ.

Notes

Chapter One

1. For a detailed account of the Lakhdar Boumediene case, see Edward Cody, "Ex-Detainee Describes Struggle for Exoneration," *Washington Post*, May 26, 2009, http://www.washingtonpost.com/wp-dyn/content/article/2009/05/25/AR2009052502263.html; Jake Tapper, Karen Travers, and Stephanie Z. Smith, "Recently Released Gitmo Detainee Talks to ABC News," *ABC News*, June 8, 2009, http://abcnews.go.com/Politics/story?id=7778310&page=1.

2. This allegation appears in Boumediene's interviews with both the *Washington Post* and *ABC News*. The *Post* acknowledges, however, that "Boumediene's version of events is impossible to verify independently." See Cody, "Ex-Detainee Describes Struggle."

3. *Boumediene v. Bush*, 476 F.3d 981 (D.C. Cir. 2007).

4. *Boumediene v. Bush*, 128 S. Ct. 2229 (2008). The case is discussed further in chapters 2 and 5.

5. *Boumediene v. Bush*, 579 F.Supp.2d 191, 197 (D.D.C. 2008).

6. See Cody, "Ex-Detainee Describes Struggle."

7. See Tapper, Travers, and Smith, "Recently Released Gitmo Detainee Talks."

8. See *Boumediene*, 128 S. Ct. at 2245 ("by the 1600's, the writ was deemed less an instrument of the King's power and more a restraint upon it"); *Fay v. Noia*, 372 U.S. 391, 399–402 (1963); Paul D. Halliday, *Habeas Corpus: From England to Empire* (Cambridge, MA: Belknap Press of Harvard University Press, 2010), 11–18, 29.

9. U.S. Constitution, art. I, § 9, cl. 2.

10. For a general discussion of the federalism crisis after the Civil War, and its effect on habeas jurisdiction, see Jordan Steiker, "Incorporating the Suspension Clause: Is There a Constitutional Right to Federal Habeas Corpus for State Prisoners?," *Michigan Law Review* 92 (1994): 862.

11. See Joseph L. Hoffmann and William J. Stuntz, "Habeas after the Revolution," *Supreme Court Review* 1993 (1994): 65.

12. 3 William Blackstone, *Commentaries on the Laws of England* (Am. ed. 1832), *129–31; Dallin H. Oaks, "Habeas Corpus in the States—1776–1865," *University of Chicago Law Review* 32 (1964–1965): 243.

13. *Black's Law Dictionary*, 6th ed. (St. Paul, MN: West Publishing Co., 1990), 709.

14. For more on the history of the writ generally, see Halliday, *Habeas Corpus*; William F. Duker, *A Constitutional History of Habeas Corpus* (Westport, CT: Greenwood Press, 1980); and Stephen I. Vladeck, "The New Habeas Revisionism," *Harvard Law Review* 124 (forthcoming 2011).

15. 3 Blackstone, *Commentaries*, *129.

16. Oaks, "Habeas Corpus in the States," 243–44.

17. For a general discussion of this procedure, known as an order to "show cause," see Mark D. Falkoff, "Back to Basics: Habeas Corpus Procedures and Long-Term Executive Detention," *Denver University Law Review* 86 (2009): 961, 974–75.

18. Oaks, "Legal History in the High Court," 460.

19. Blackstone reports the first recorded use of habeas corpus "in the thirty-third year of Edward I." *Secretary of State for Home Affairs v. O'Brien*, [1923] A.C. 603, 609 (H. L.), as quoted in *Fay*, 372 U.S. at 400. Paul Halliday dates the use of the *ad sujiciendum* writ somewhat later, arguing that generally the medieval writs displayed no "impulse to make a vigorous review of the circumstances underlying an imprisonment order," but notes that by the latter part of the fifteenth century judges were using the writ in this way. Halliday, *Habeas Corpus*, 16–18, 29–30.

20. Halliday, *Habeas Corpus*, 29, 80–83, 117–33, 154–55, 323–24, 331; Dallin H. Oaks, "Legal History in the High Court: Habeas Corpus," *Michigan Law Review* 64 (1966): 459–60.

21. Oaks, "Legal History in the High Court," 460; Halliday, *Habeas Corpus*, 220–26.

22. Halliday, *Habeas Corpus*, 237–46. This last issue addressed in the 1679 act remains as current as today's headlines. In May 2010, the D.C. Circuit ruled that *Boumediene* did not apply to alleged "enemy combatants" held at the Bagram Air Force Base in Afghanistan, but declined to determine whether the U.S. government could avoid the reach of habeas courts by transporting such prisoners there. See *al-Maqaleh v. Gates*, 605 F.3d 84, 98 (D.C. Cir. 2010).

23. Halliday, *Habeas Corpus*, 7, 308.

24. Ibid., 253.

25. Joseph L. Hoffmann and Nancy J. King, "Rethinking the Federal Role in State Criminal Justice," *New York University Law Review* 89 (2009): 791, 841–42;

1 Donald E. Wilkes, Jr., *State Postconviction Remedies and Relief Handbook with Forms* (St. Paul, MN: Thomson/West 2007), 29–45. We discuss the development of state postconviction review of constitutional claims in chapters 3–5.

26. *Ex parte Bollman*, 8 U.S. 75, 93–94 (1807).

27. Alexander Hamilton, "Federalist, Number 84," in Clinton Rossiter, ed., *The Federalist Papers* (New York: Penguin Putnam, 1999).

28. Alexander Hamilton, "Federalist, Number 83," in Rossiter, *The Federalist Papers*.

29. U.S. Constitution, art. I, § 9, cl. 2.

30. Halliday, *Habeas Corpus*, 250–53.

31. Several scholars have advanced the alternative explanation that the Framers added the clause to prevent Congress from removing state judicial authority to free those held in federal custody. See Duker, *A Constitutional History of Habeas Corpus*, 126–81. Additional authorities are collected in Todd E. Pettys, "State Habeas Relief for Federal Extrajudicial Detainees," *Minnesota Law Review* 92 (2007): 265, 309–10. The Supreme Court, however, has held that state courts have no such authority. *Tarble's Case*, 80 U.S. 397, 411–12 (1872).

32. Act of September 24, 1789, ch. 20, § 14, 1 Stat. 81–82.

33. *Boumediene*, 128 S. Ct. at 2248. See also Daniel J. Meltzer, "Habeas Corpus, Suspension, and Guantánamo: The Boumediene Decision," *Supreme Court Review* 2008 (2008): 1, 15 n. 62; sources in notes 34 and 35.

34. For example, *Ex parte Yerger*, 75 U.S. 85, 101 (1868) ("As limited by the act of 1789, [habeas jurisdiction] did not extend to cases of imprisonment after conviction, under sentences of competent tribunals. . . ."); *Ex parte Dorr*, 44 U.S. 103, 105 (1845) ("Neither this nor any other court of the United States, or judge thereof, can issue a habeas corpus to bring up a prisoner, who is in custody under a sentence or execution of a state court, for any other purpose than to be used as a witness."); Rex A. Collings, Jr., "Habeas Corpus for Convicts—Constitutional Right or Legislative Grace?," *California Law Review* 40 (1952): 335, 345 (concluding that "under our constitution, at least as it was understood in 1789, there was no right on the part of convicted prisoners to the privilege of habeas corpus").

35. This account of habeas history has been adopted by the United States Supreme Court. See, for example, *Felker v. Turpin*, 518 U.S. 651, 663 (1996) (stating, "the first Congress made the writ of habeas corpus available only to prisoners confined under the authority of the United States, not under state authority"); *Ex parte Yerger*, 75 U.S. at 101–102:

> As limited by the act of 1789, [habeas jurisdiction] did not extend to cases of imprisonment after conviction, under sentences of competent tribunals; nor to prisoners in jail, unless in custody under or by color of the authority of the United States, or

committed for trial before some court of the United States, or
required to be brought into court to testify. But this limitation
has been gradually narrowed, and the benefits of the writ have
been extended, first in 1833, to prisoners confined under any authority, whether State or National, for any act done or omitted
in pursuance of a law of the United States, or of any order, process, or decree of any judge of court of the United States; then in
1842 to prisoners being subjects or citizens of foreign States, in
custody under National or State authority for acts done or omitted by or under color of foreign authority, and alleged to be valid
under the law of nations; and finally, in 1867, to all cases where
any person may be restrained of liberty in violation of the Constitution, or of any treaty or law of the United States. (citations
omitted)

Nevertheless, some scholars have questioned this assessment of the extent of
habeas review available under both the 1789 act and the common law that preceded that act. See Eric M. Freedman, *Habeas Corpus: Rethinking the Great Writ
of Liberty* (New York: New York University Press, 2001) (collecting authority to
support thesis that federal judges retained power to issue the writ to free state-
convicted prisoners under the 1789 act). See also 1 Randy Hertz and James S.
Liebman, *Federal Habeas Corpus Practice and Procedure*, 5th ed. (Newark, NJ:
Matthew Bender, 2005), 39, 46–49 (stating that the 1789 act "did not limit habeas
corpus review either to jurisdictional claims or to claims attacking pretrial as opposed to postconviction detention" but instead "used habeas corpus as a substitute for the Court's direct review of nationally important questions when the
latter review was not meaningfully available to incarcerated individuals"). Compare also *Fay v. Noia*, 372 U.S. 391, 405 (1963) (stating, "at the time that the Suspension Clause was written into our Federal Constitution and the first Judiciary
Act was passed conferring habeas corpus jurisdiction upon the federal judiciary,
there was respectable common-law authority for the proposition that habeas was
available to remedy any kind of governmental restraint contrary to fundamental law") and ibid., 409 (stating that the "Judiciary Act did not extend federal habeas to prisoners in state custody").

This ongoing debate about the state of the law 220 years ago is fueled by the
Court's assumption, voiced in several different decisions, that "'at the absolute
minimum,' the Suspension Clause protects the writ 'as it existed in 1789.'" *INS
v. St. Cyr*, 533 U.S. at 301 (quoting *Felker v. Turpin*, 518 U.S. 651, 663–64 (1996)).
The view that the Suspension Clause protects *only* the writ as it existed when the
Constitution was written appears to be the view of Justices Scalia, Thomas, Alito, and Chief Justice Roberts. See *Boumediene*, 128 S. Ct. at 2297 ("The writ as
preserved in the Constitution could not possibly extend farther than the com-

mon law provided when that Clause was written.") (Scalia, J., dissenting, joined by the Chief Justice, and Justices Thomas and Alito); ibid., n. 2 ("The [majority] opinion seeks to avoid this straightforward conclusion by saying that the Court has been 'careful not to foreclose the possibility that the protections of the Suspension Clause have expanded along with post-1789 developments that define the present scope of the writ.' . . . But not foreclosing the possibility that they have expanded is not the same as demonstrating (or at least holding without demonstration, which seems to suffice for today's majority) that they have expanded."); ibid., 2303 ("The nature of the writ of habeas corpus that cannot be suspended must be defined by the common-law writ that was available at the time of the founding.").

We discuss the scope of the Suspension Clause later in this volume and maintain that the clause does guarantee some federal judicial review for those convicted in state courts. But our argument does not turn on whether or not federal courts held that authority in 1789. We reject a reading of the Suspension Clause that would so limit its scope and instead argue that even if the clause initially protected only federal prisoners, the Fourteenth Amendment extended its reach to those in state custody.

36. Force Act of March 2, 1833, ch. 57, § 7, 4 Stat. 634–35, discussed in *Fay*, 372 U.S. at 401 n. 9.

37. Act of August 29, 1842, ch. 257, 5 Stat. 539–40, discussed in *Fay*, 372 U.S. at 401 n. 9. See also *Felker*, 518 U.S. at 659–60 (stating, "Before the Act of 1867, the only instances in which a federal court could issue the writ to produce a state prisoner were if the prisoner was 'necessary to be brought into court to testify,' Act of Sept. 24, 1789, ch. 20, § 14, 1 Stat. 82, was 'committed . . . for any act done . . . in pursuance of a law of the United States,' Act of Mar. 2, 1833, ch. 57, § 7, 4 Stat. 634–35, or was a 'subjec[t] or citize[n] of a foreign State, and domiciled therein,' and held under state law, Act of Aug. 29, 1842, ch. 257, 5 Stat. 539–40.").

38. John E. Nowak, "Federalism and the Civil War Amendments," *Ohio Northern University Law Review* 23 (1997): 1209, 1214.

39. Act of February 5, 1867, ch. 28, § 1, 14 Stat. 385–86.

40. Hoffmann and Stuntz, "Habeas after the Revolution," 65.

41. *Fay*, 372 U.S. at 401 n. 9.

42. These statutory changes were preceded by a 1947 report detailing some of the reasons for the changes. See *Report of the Judicial Conference of Senior Circuit Judges September 1947, Annual Report of the Director of the Administrative Office of the United States Courts* (Washington, DC: Government Printing Office, 1947), 17.

43. See, for example, *Mapp v. Ohio*, 368 U.S. 871 (1961) (right to exclusion of evidence seized in violation of Fourth Amendment); *Gideon v. Wainwright*, 372 U.S. 335 (1963) (right to appointed counsel for indigent defendants); *Miranda v.*

Arizona, 384 U.S. 436 (1966) (right to receive warnings prior to custodial police interrogations).

44. We discuss these Warren Court developments in greater detail in chapter 3.

45. We discuss capital habeas in chapters 7 and 8.

46. *Boumediene*, 128 S. Ct. at 2247.

47. *Fay*, 372 U.S. at 401.

48. *Wainwright v. Sykes*, 433 U.S. 72, 81 (1977).

49. *Brown v. Allen*, 344 U.S. 443, 536 (1953) (Jackson, J., concurring in the result).

50. Ibid., 537.

51. See *State v. Graham*, 244 Kan. 194, 768 P.2d 259 (1989) (affirming conviction and sentence); *Graham v. State*, 820 P.2d 419; 1991 Kan. App. LEXIS 947 (1991) (upholding denial of motion to vacate sentence). In the 1987 case, the trial judge originally sentenced Graham to fifteen years to life based on two prior drug felonies, one in Arkansas and one in Kansas, as well as a number of misdemeanors. The Arkansas conviction was later overturned because Graham had pleaded guilty without the assistance of counsel. The Kansas Supreme Court, on a state postconviction motion filed by Graham, therefore ordered the trial judge to reconsider the original sentence. *Graham v. State*, 263 Kan. 742, 952 P.2d 1266 (1998). The trial judge did so, but because Graham was not addicted to drugs and thus could not benefit from any drug treatment programs, because he blamed everyone else for his problems, and because he manifested an antisocial personality with no hope of rehabilitation, the trial judge reimposed the same sentence of fifteen years to life. The resentencing was affirmed. *State v. Graham*, 72 Kan. 2, 30 P.3d 310 (2001).

52. See Fed. R. Evid. 404(b) (providing, "Evidence of other crimes, wrongs, or acts is not admissible to prove the character of a person in order to show action in conformity therewith. It may, however, be admissible for other purposes, such as proof of motive, opportunity, intent, preparation, plan, *knowledge*, identity, or *absence of mistake or accident*. . . .") (emphasis added).

53. For a full account of Graham's federal habeas litigation, see *Graham v. Attorney General of Kansas*, 231 Fed.Appx. 790; 2007 U.S. App. LEXIS 8718 (10th Cir. 2007) (unpublished opinion denying certificate of appealability); *Graham v. McKune*, 2006 U.S. Dist. LEXIS 92429 (D. Kan. Dec. 15, 2006) (denying habeas petition).

54. *Fay*, 372 U.S. at 399.

55. *Schneckloth v. Bustamonte*, 412 U.S. 218, 275 (1973) (Powell, J., concurring).

56. For a leading article on the subject of federal courts and their discretion to decline the exercise of jurisdiction, see David L. Shapiro, "Jurisdiction and Discretion," *New York University Law Review* 60 (1985): 543.

57. Nancy J. King, Fred L. Cheesman II, and Brian J. Ostrom, *Final Technical Report: Habeas Litigation in U.S. District Courts* (2007), hereinafter King et al., "Habeas Study," available at http://www.ncjrs.gov/pdffiles1/nij/grants/219559 .pdf. The study was funded by Vanderbilt University Law School and the National Institute of Justice.

58. *Boumediene*, 128 S. Ct. at 2246.

Chapter Two

1. *Rumsfeld v. Padilla*, 542 U.S. 426, 441 (2004).

2. *Boumediene v. Bush*, 128 S. Ct. 2229, 2247 (2008) (quoting Alexander Hamilton, who in turn quoted Blackstone).

3. See chapter 1, at notes 34 and 35 (noting that this is the prevailing but not universal interpretation of the 1789 act and of the scope of the common law writ at the time).

4. *INS v. St. Cyr*, 533 U.S. 289, 301 (2001).

5. U.S. Constitution, art. I, § 9, cl. 2.

6. *Boumediene*, 128 S. Ct. at 2236.

7. *Boumediene*, 128 S. Ct. at 2245–47. See also *The Continental Journal, and Weekly Advertiser*, March 5, 1778, 3, quoted in Paul D. Halliday and G. Edward White, "The Suspension Clause: English Text, Imperial Contexts, and American Implications," *Virginia Law Review* 94 (2008): 575, 649. There the authors note, "None other than General Washington, in his manifesto of September 1777, noted among other wrongs against North Americans that 'arbitrary imprisonment has received the sanction of British laws by the suspension of the Habeas Corpus Act.'"

8. *Boumediene*, 128 S. Ct. at 2269.

9. *United States v. More*, 7 U.S. 159 (1805) (criminal judgments not subject to writ of error).

10. *Ex parte Burford*, 7 U.S. 448, 450–53 (1806) (emphasis deleted).

11. *United States v. Hamilton*, 3 U.S. 17 (1795). See also *United States v. Villato*, 2 Dall. 370, 373 (C.C. Pa. 1797) (releasing Spanish citizen detained on charge of treason).

12. *Ex parte Bollman*, 8 U.S. 75 (1807). See Eric M. Freedman, *Habeas Corpus: Rethinking the Great Writ of Liberty* (New York: New York University Press, 2003).

13. During part of this period, see text at note 100, the Supreme Court had no authority to hear appeals from habeas cases. *Ex parte Mirzan*, 119 U.S. 584 (1887). Even after jurisdiction was restored, the Court declined to grant relief in several cases challenging pretrial detention including *In re Lancaster*, 137 U.S. 393, 395 (1890), and *Johnson v. Hoy*, 227 U.S. 245 (1913).

14. *Stack v. Boyle*, 342 U.S. 1 (1951).

15. The general requirement that appellate review must be exhausted before seeking a writ, had, by then, been well established in an earlier habeas case from a pretrial detainee. *Ex parte Royall*, 117 U.S. 241 (1886).

16. *Stack*, 342 U.S. at 5–6.

17. David Rossman, "'Were There No Appeal': The History of Review in American Criminal Courts," *Journal of Criminal Law and Criminology* 81 (1990): 518, 564–65; Lester Bernhardt Orfield, *Criminal Appeals in America* (Boston: Little, Brown & Co. 1939), 91–93, 244–50.

18. See Bail Reform Act of 1966, June 22, 1966, Public Law 89-465, § 3147, 80 Stat. 214. Since 1966, constitutional challenges to pretrial detention in federal cases have been raised using appeal rather than habeas. The most prominent example is the Court's decision in *Salerno v. United States*, 481 U.S. 739 (1987). The Court in *Salerno* upheld as constitutional the innovation in the Bail Reform Act of 1984 that authorized federal judges to deny pretrial release not only to defendants who were flight risks but also to defendants they deemed dangerous.

19. Act of September 7, 1949, ch. 535, 63 Stat. 686, discussed in *United States v. Comstock*, 130 S. Ct. 1949, 1960 (2010).

20. *Greenwood v. United States*, 350 U.S. 366, 375 (1956).

21. See Helene R. Banks, "Immediate Appeal of Pretrial Commitment Orders: 'It's Now or Never,'" *Fordham Law Review* 55 (1987): 785, 808 n. 71; "Due Process for All: Constitutional Standards for Involuntary Civil Commitment and Release," *University of Chicago Law Review* 34 (1967): 633.

22. *Lynch v. Overholser*, 369 U.S. 705 (1962).

23. See The Insanity Defense Reform Act of 1984, October 12, 1984, Public Law 98-473, 98 Stat. 2057, codified at 18 U.S.C. §§ 4241–47.

24. See *Foucha v. Louisiana*, 504 U.S. 71, 81–82 (1992); *Addington v. Texas*, 441 U.S. 418 (1979).

25. Monica Davey and Abby Goodnough, "Doubts Rise as States Hold Sex Offenders after Prison," *New York Times*, March 4, 2007, http://www.nytimes.com/2007/03/04/us/04civil.html; John Q. LaFond, "The Future of Involuntary Civil Commitment in the U.S.A. After *Kansas v. Hendricks*," *Behavioral Sciences and the Law* 18 (2000): 153; W. Lawrence Fitch, "Sexual Offender Commitment in the United States," *Annals of the New York Academy of Sciences* 989 (2003): 489 (reporting 2,478 individuals confined under these laws as of 2002 in fifteen states).

26. *Seling v. Young*, 531 U.S. 250 (2001); *Kansas v. Hendricks*, 521 U.S. 346 (1997); *Kansas v. Crane*, 534 U.S. 407 (2002).

27. Adam Walsh Child Protection and Safety Act of 2006, July 27, 2006, Public Law 109-248, 120 Stat. 587, codified at 18 U.S.C. §§ 4247–48.

28. Congress included an express provision in the act anticipating habeas challenges. See 18 U.S.C. § 4247(g) (entitled "Habeas Corpus Unimpaired," and

providing that "nothing precludes a person who is committed under in the act "from establishing by writ of habeas corpus the illegality of his detention"). In *Comstock*, the Supreme Court upheld the constitutionality of the statute under the Necessary and Proper Clause but did not reach other constitutional challenges to the statute, such as objections to the burden of proof. See *Timms v. Johns*, 700 F. Supp. 2d 764 (E.D.N.C. 2010) (granting writ).

29. Halliday and White, "The Suspension Clause," 692 (quoting the argument of Robert Goodloe Harper).

30. *In re Low Yam Chow*, 13 F. 605, 615 (D. Ca. 1882) (also known as the "Chinese Merchant's Case"). For a summary of the use of habeas in immigration cases through the 1950s, see Gerald L. Neuman, "Habeas Corpus, Executive Detention, and the Removal of Aliens," *Columbia Law Review* 98 (1998): 961, 1004–20.

31. *Chae Chan Ping v. United States*, 130 U.S. 581, 595 (1889) (also known as the "Chinese Exclusion Case").

32. Act of May 6, 1882, ch. 126, §§ 1–15, 22 Stat. 58.

33. Christian G. Fritz, "A Nineteenth Century 'Habeas Corpus Mill': The Chinese before the Federal Courts in California," *American Journal of Legal History* 32 (1988): 347–72.

34. Judge Hoffman personally heard over seven thousand petitions between June 27, 1882, and December 1, 1890. Fritz, "Habeas Corpus Mill," 348. Hoffman insisted that each detainee had a right to present any evidence, written or oral. He wrote at one point that "[f]or five or six weeks, even with night sessions, I have been unable to make any great impression on them. All ordinary business, public and private, of the court is necessarily suspended, or if resumed, these passengers, many of whom may be entitled to their discharge, are left either in custody or on bail awaiting the determination of their cases." Ibid., 359.

35. Chinese Immigration Act of July 5, 1884, ch. 220, 23 Stat. 115–18.

36. *In re Chew Heong*, 21 F. 791, 808 (C. C. Cal. 1884) (denying writ), *rev'd by Chew Heong v. United States*, 112 U.S. 536 (1884) (granting writ). See also *Chin Yow v. United States*, 208 U.S. 8 (1908) (granting writ).

37. Edward Prince Hutchinson, *Legislative History of American Immigration Policy, 1798–1965* (Philadelphia, PA: University of Pennsylvania Press 1981), 626–27.

38. Act of September 13, 1888, ch. 1015, 25 Stat. 476, §§ 6, 7, amended, Act of October 1, 1888, ch. 1064, 25 Stat. 504.

39. *Chae Chan Ping*, 130 U.S. at 581.

40. Fritz, "Habeas Corpus Mill," 359–71.

41. A similar saga played out in cases of Japanese laborers, ending in the Supreme Court rejecting the argument of the president that aliens detained for deportation were barred by statute from seeking habeas relief in federal court. See

The Japanese Immigrant Case, 189 U.S. 86, 100–101 (1903) (barring any executive officer to cause an alien "to be taken into custody and deported without giving him all opportunity to be heard upon the questions involving his right to be and remain in the United States. No such arbitrary power can exist where the principles involved in due process of law are recognized.").

42. Immigration Act of March 3, 1903, ch. 1012, 32 Stat. 1213–22; Hutchinson, "American Immigration Policy," 424.

43. See Federal Bureau of Investigation, "FBI History: The Nation Calls 1908–1923," http://www.fbi.gov/fbihistorybook.htm.

44. Federal Bureau of Investigation, "FBI History, 'Black Tom' Bombing Propels Bureau into National Security Arena," http://www.fbi.gov/fbihistory book.htm. The "Black Tom" explosion was named for the Black Tom rail yard in which the explosives were stored in railroad cars.

45. Anarchist Exclusion Act of October 16, 1918, ch. 186, 40 Stat. 1012, as amended by Act of June 5, 1920, ch. 251, 41 Stat. 1008.

46. Paul Avrich, *Sacco and Vanzetti: The Anarchist Background* (Princeton, NJ: Princeton University Press, 1991); Robert K. Murray, *Red Scare: A Study in National Hysteria, 1919–1920* (Minneapolis: University of Minnesota Press, 1955), 70, 78–79, 251. More than five hundred of those detained were deported.

47. See, for example, *Minotto v. Bradley*, 252 F. 600 (N.D. Ill. 1918) (granting review, but ultimately finding that petitioner was an German alien enemy within the terms of the statute).

48. *Kessler v. Strecker*, 307 U.S. 22 (1939).

49. See *Bridges v. Wixon*, 326 U.S. 135, 149 (1945).

50. See William F. Harvey, "28 U.S.C. 2255: From Habeas Corpus to Coram Nobis," *Washburn Law Journal* 1 (1960–62): 381, 391; William H. Speck, "Statistics on Federal Habeas Corpus," *Ohio State Law Journal* 10 (1949): 338, 341.

51. *Ludecke v. Watkins*, 335 U.S. 160, 175 (1948).

52. Immigration and Nationality Act, June 27, 1952, Public Law 82–414, 66 Stat. 163, codified at 8 U.S.C. § 1101 et seq.

53. See *Heikkila v. Barber*, 345 U.S. 229, 234–35 (1953).

54. *Carlson v. Landon*, 342 U.S. 524 (1952).

55. *Harisiades v. Shaughnessy*, 342 U.S. 580, 590 (1952).

56. Congressional Research Service, "Immigration-Related Detention: Current Legislative Issues," (January 30, 2008), 8, http://www.shusterman.com/pdf/detention-crs108.pdf.

57. Mario Antonio Rivera, *Decision and Structure, U.S. Refugee Policy in the Mariel Crisis* (Lanham, MD: University Press of America, 1991), Introduction, 140.

58. See United States Department of Justice, Federal Bureau of Prisons, Oversight Committee, "Report to the Attorney General on the Disturbances

at the Federal Detention Center, Oakdale, Louisiana and the U.S. Penitentiary, Atlanta Georgia (February 1, 1988), in Subcommittee on Courts, Civil Liberties, and the Administration of Justice of the Committee on the Judiciary House of Representatives, *Hearing on Mariel Cuban Detainees: Events Preceding and Following the November 1987 Riots*, 100th Congress, 2d Sess., February 4, 1988, 265, 292–93; "Testimony of Cary Copeland, Deputy Associate Attorney General; accompanied by George C. Calhoun, coordinator, Cuban Parole and Repatriation Program Office of Associate Attorney General; Craig Raysford, Associate General Counsel, Immigration and Naturalization Service; and Foustino Pino, Assistant Director for Administration, Community Relations Service," in Subcommittee on Immigration, Refugees, and International Law of the Committee on the Judiciary House of Representatives, *Hearing on HR 4330 and HR 4349 Mariel Cuban Detainees*, 100th Congress, 2d Sess., July 6, 1988, 22–23.

59. "Testimony of Hon. Marvin Shoob, U.S. District Judge for the Northern District of Georgia," Subcommittee on Courts, Civil Liberties, and the Administration of Justice of the Committee on the Judiciary House of Representatives, *Hearing on Mariel Cuban Detainees*, 160.

60. Ibid., 122.

61. "Marvin H. Shoob," in *The Almanac of the Federal Judiciary* (Frederick, MD: Aspen, 1995), also available at 2010 WL 2138805. Shoob had been appointed to the bench by the president whose policies he lambasted. Mark Curriden, "Judge Shoob's Law: Be Fair, Be Frank," *Atlanta Journal Constitution*, September 9, 1992, A2, A9.

62. R. Robin McDonald, "Judge Recalls Role of Habeas in Earlier Crisis," *Fulton County Daily Report*, October 31, 2006; Mark S. Hamm, *The Abandoned Ones, The Imprisonment and Uprising of the Mariel Boat People* (Boston, MA.: Northeastern University Press, 1995), 72.

63. *Fernandez-Roque v. Smith*, 734 F.2d 576 (11th Cir. 1984); *Fernandez-Roque v. Smith*, 622 F. Supp. 887 (N.D. Ga. 1985).

64. Letter from Congressman John Lewis, Subcommittee on Courts, Civil Liberties, and the Administration of Justice of the Committee on the Judiciary House of Representatives, *Hearing on Mariel Cuban Detainees: Events Preceding and Following the November 1987 Riots*, 100th Congress, 2d Sess., February 4, 1988, 6–7; Hamm, *The Abandoned Ones*, 89.

65. "Statement of Cary H. Copeland, Deputy Associate Attorney General," in Subcommittee on Immigration, Refugees and International Law, Committee on the Judiciary U.S. House of Representatives, *Hearing Regarding the Mariel Cuban Program and Related Legislation*, 100th Congress, 2d Sess. July 6, 1988, 28.

66. Antiterrorism and Effective Death Penalty Act of 1996, April 24, 1996, Public Law 104-132, 110 Stat. 1214; Illegal Immigration Reform and Immigrant

Responsibility Act of 1996, September 30, 1996, Public Law 104-208, 110 Stat. 3009–546.

67. Mark Dow, *American Gulag: Inside US Immigration Prisons* (Berkeley, CA: University of California Press, 2004), 31, 193, 279.

68. See Gerald L. Neuman, "Jurisdiction and the Rule of Law after the 1996 Immigration Act," *Harvard Law Review* 113 (2000): 1977–80.

69. *St. Cyr*, 533 U.S. at 289, 301, 305.

70. *Zadvydas v. Davis*, 533 U.S. 678, 682, 690 (2001).

71. *Clark v. Martinez*, 543 U.S. 371 (2005). By November 2003, the number was 1,100. Dow, *American Gulag*, 279, 296, 370.

72. See Kelsey E. Papst, "Protecting the Voiceless: Ensuring ICE's Compliance with Standards that Protect Immigration Detainees," *McGeorge Law Review* 40 (2009): 263–64; "Federal Courts Snapshot: Defendants Charged with Terrorism in the Federal Courts," *Third Branch* 38, no. 6 (June 2006), http://www.uscourts.gov/ttb/06–06/snapshot/index.html. In 2010, the Supreme Court rebuffed efforts to invalidate one of these statutes, 18 U.S.C. § 2339B(a)(1), which made it a crime to "knowingly provid[e] material support or resources to a foreign terrorist organization." *Holder v. Humanitarian Law Project,* 130 S. Ct. 2705 (2010).

73. Ricardo J. Bascuas, "The Unconstitutionality of 'Hold Until Cleared': Reexamining Material Witness Detentions in the Wake of the September 11th Dragnet," *Vanderbilt Law Review* 58 (2005): 686, 692, 698; Adam Liptak, "Threats and Responses: The Detainees; for Post-9/11 Material Witnesses, It Is a Terror of a Different Kind," *New York Times*, August 19, 2004, http://www.nytimes.com/2004/08/19/us/threats-responses-detainees-for-post-9-11-material-witness-it-terror-different.html; *United States v. Awadallah*, 349 F.3d 42, 47 (2d Cir. 2003); *al-Kidd v. Ashcroft*, 580 F.3d 949 (9th Cir. 2010) (allowing al-Kidd to sue the attorney general for illegal detention under the material witness statute, and detailing the allegations regarding that detention), review granted, 2010 WL 2812283 (October 18, 2010).

74. The Department of Homeland Security Act of 2002, November 25, 2002, Public Law 107-296, 116 Stat. 2135, codified at 6 U.S.C. §§ 101 et seq.

75. The USA Patriot Act of 2001, October 26, 2001, Public Law 107-56, § 412, 115 Stat. 272, codified at 8 U.S.C. § 1226a.

76. Office of the Inspector General, U.S. Department of Justice, "The September 11 Detainees: A Review of the Treatment of Aliens Held on Immigration Charges in Connection with the Investigation of the September 11 Attacks," 2, 188 (June 2003), http://www.usdoj.gov/oig/special/0306/index.htm.

77. Dow, *American Gulag*, 26.

78. Office of the Inspector General, "The September 11 Detainees," 70, 186–87.

79. *Demore v. Kim*, 538 U.S. 510 (2003) (interpreting IIRIRA to not clearly cut off habeas review, thus avoiding Suspension Clause issue).

80. See Michael Chertoff, Secretary U.S. Department of Homeland Security, Statement, Senate Committee on the Judiciary, *Hearing on Comprehensive Immigration Reform*, 110th Cong., 1st Sess. (February 28, 2007), 122, 123–24.

81. See Louis Reedt and Jessica Widico-Stroop, United States Sentencing Commission, "Changing Face of Federal Criminal Sentencing" (2009, 2), http://www.ussc.gov/general/20081230_Changing_Face_Fed_Sent.pdf; Courtney Semisch, United States Sentencing Commission, "Alternative Sentencing in the Federal Criminal Justice System" (2009, 4, nn. 29–30), http://www.ussc.gov/general/20090206_Alternatives.pdf .

82. See Government Accountability Office, "Alien Detention Standards: Telephone Access Problems Were Pervasive at Detention Facilities; Other Deficiencies Did Not Show a Pattern of Noncompliance," Report No. GAO-07-875 (July 2007): i, 1, http://www.gao.gov/new.items/d07875.pdf ; Representative Zoe Lofgren, "Opening Statement," House Committee on the Judiciary, Subcommittee on Immigration, Citizenship, Refugees, Border Security, and International Law, *Hearing on Detention and Removal: Immigration Detainee Medical Care*, 110th Cong., 1st Sess., October 4, 2007, 119 (reporting that less than one hundred thousand detainees were held in 2001, compared with approximately three hundred thousand in 2006). In 2008 nearly 359,000 people were removed under immigration laws, 27 percent of them "criminal" aliens, mostly from Mexico and Central America.

83. Department of Homeland Security, Office of the Inspector General, "ICE's Compliance with Detention Limits for Aliens with a Final Order of Removal from the United States, February 2007, 7, http://www.dhs.gov/xoig/assets/mgmtrpts/OIG_07–28_Feb07.pdf. It is interesting to note that this was a pattern seen throughout habeas history. The government's choice to release those confined rather than defend their detention in the face of a habeas petition saves it "great expense." Paul D. Halliday, *Habeas Corpus: From England to Empire* (Cambridge, MA: Belknap Press of Harvard University Press, 2010), 115–16 (describing British Admiralty's "routine surrender of sailors" rather than returning to court with those sailors who alleged through habeas that they were unlawfully impressed in the second half of the eighteenth century).

84. Office of the Inspector General, "The September 11 Detainees," 96; Department of Homeland Security, Office of the Inspector General, "ICE's Compliance with Detention Limits," 36; United States Department of Justice, Office of the Inspector General, "Office of the Inspector General Semiannual Report to Congress," October 31, 2008, 9–10, http://www.usdoj.gov/oig/semiannual/0811/final.pdf.

85. Dow, *American Gulag*, 20. See also Office of the Inspector General, "The

September 11 Detainees," 102 (stating, "The FBI attorney also told the OIG that in December 2001 she briefed FBI General Counsel Larry Parkinson that detainees were filing *habeas corpus* petitions to protest their confinement and that she thought there was very little upon which to defend the case for continuing to detain the aliens.").

86. REAL ID Act of 2005, May 11, 2005, Public Law 109-13, § 106, 119 Stat. 302, codified at 8 U.S.C. § 1252; Lenni Benson, "Making Paper Dolls: How Restrictions on Judicial Review and the Administrative Process Increase Immigration Cases in the Federal Courts," *New York Law School Law Review* 51 (2006–2007): 39, 57.

87. Lenni B. Benson, "You Can't Get There from Here: Managing Judicial Review of Immigration Cases," *University of Chicago Legal Forum* 2007 (2007): 412; Department of Homeland Security, Office of Immigration Statistics, "Immigration Enforcement Actions: 2008," December 2009, http://www.dhs.gov/xlibrary/assets/statistics/publications/enforcement_ar_08.pdf.

88. See, for example, *Aguilar v. U.S. Immigration and Customs Enforcement Div. of Dept. of Homeland Sec.*, 510 F.3d 1 (1st Cir. 2007); *Ruiz-Martinez v. Mukasey*, 516 F.3d 102 (2d Cir. 2008); *Ramadan v. Keisler*, 504 F.3d 973 (9th Cir. 2007); *Iasu v. Smith*, 511 F.3d 881 (9th Cir. 2007); *Flores-Torres v. Mukasey*, 548 F.3d 708 (9th Cir. 2008). See also *Omar v. Geren*, 689 F.Supp.2d 1, (D.D.C. 2009) (collecting cases).

89. *Hernandez-Carrera v. Carlson*, 547 F.3d 1237 (10th Cir. 2008).

90. See William H. Rehnquist, *All the Laws but One: Civil Liberties in Wartime* (New York: Alfred A. Knopf, 1998), 73–74; Amanda L. Tyler, "Suspension as an Emergency Power, *Yale Law Journal* 118 (2009): 600, 637–63.

91. Act of July 6, 1798, R. S. § 4067, 1 Stat. 577, as amended, 40 Stat. 531, codified at 50 U.S.C. § 21; see also *Ludecke*, 335 U.S. 160, 176–77 (1948) (Black, J., dissenting) (discussing history of the act).

92. See Gerald L. Neuman and Charles F. Hobson, "John Marshall and the Enemy Alien: A Case Missing from the Canon," *Green Bag* 9 (2005): 43–45; *Ex parte D'Olivera*, 7 F. Cas. 853 (C.C.D. Mass. 1813).

93. Habeas Corpus Act of 1863, March 3, 1863, ch. 81, 12 Stat. 755.

94. *Ex parte Merryman*, 17 F. Cas. 144 (C.C.D. Md. 1861); Stephen I. Vladeck, "The Field Theory: Martial Law, the Suspension Power, and the Insurrection Act," *Temple Law Review* 80 (2007): 391, 397–408.

95. Mark E. Neely, Jr., "The Lincoln Administration and Arbitrary Arrests: A Reconsideration," *Journal of the Abraham Lincoln Association 1983*, http://www.historycooperative.org/journals/jala/5/neely.html.

96. Charles Fairman, "The Law of Martial Rule and the National Emergency," *Harvard Law Review* 55 (1942): 1284, n. 126 (quoting William H. Herndon, *Lincoln* [1884], 19).

97. Rehnquist, *All the Laws but One*, 49–50, 60, 82–88.

98. *Ex parte Milligan*, 71 U.S. 2, 116–18, 121, 130 (1866). Stated the Court several years later, in *Dow v. Johnson*, 100 U.S. 158, 164 (1879):

> That war, though not between independent nations, but between different portions of the same nation, was accompanied by the general incidents of an international war. It was waged between people occupying different territories, separated from each other by well-defined lines. . . . The people of the loyal States on the one hand, and the people of the Confederate States on the other, thus became enemies to each other, and were liable to be dealt with as such without reference to their individual opinions or dispositions.

99. Curtis A. Bradley, "The Story of *Ex Parte Milligan:* Military Trials, Enemy Combatants, and Congressional Authorization," in *Presidential Power Stories*, ed. Christopher H. Schroeder and Curtis A. Bradley (New York: Foundation Press, 2008).

100. *Ex parte McCardle*, 74 U.S. 506 (1868). The *McCardle* case is also discussed in chapter 3.

101. Ku Klux Klan Act of April 20, 1871, ch. 22, § 4, 17 Stat. 13. The act was invoked by President Grant in quelling a rebellion in South Carolina. "President, Proclamation of Oct. 17, 1871," in James Daniel Richardson, ed., 7 *Compilation of the Messages and Papers of the Presidents* (1899), 136–38. A federal district judge also refused habeas relief to the conspirators convicted and sentenced by a military tribunal for their role in Lincoln's assassination, concluding that the charges were appropriately resolved outside of the civilian courts. *Ex parte Mudd*, 17 F. Cas. 954 (S.D. Fla. 1868).

102. During World War I, at least one German enemy combatant sought review of his military detention through the writ, but the federal government opted to detain subversives during World War I using immigration law and criminal prosecutions under the Espionage Act instead of military detention. See *United States ex rel Wessels v. McDonald*, 265 F. 754 (E.D.N.Y. 1920); Rehnquist, *All the Laws but One*, 183. See also Jennifer Elsea, Congressional Research Report for Congress, "Terrorism and the Law of War: Trying Terrorists as War Criminals before Military Commissions" (December 11, 2001): 22–23, http://www.fpc .state.gov/documents/organization/7951.pdf (court martial trials for nonmilitary personnel accused of espionage, sabotage, or other conduct, the attorney general submitted would be unconstitutional).

103. See Peter Irons, *Justice at War, the Story of the Japanese American Internment Cases* (Berkeley, CA: University of California Press, 1983): vii, 102.

104. *Ex parte Endo,* 323 U.S. 283 (1944).

105. See Rehnquist, *All the Laws but One,* 192, 202; Irons, *Justice at War,* 341–46.

106. *Hirabayashi v. United States,* 320 U.S. 81 (1943); *Korematsu v. United States,* 323 U.S. 214 (1944). Legislation signed by President Ronald Reagan formally apologized to the victims of the injustice, Act of Aug. 10, 1988, Public Law 100-383, § 2, 102 Stat. 903–04, and described the internment as motivated by "racial prejudice, wartime hysteria, and a failure of political leadership."

107. Rehnquist, *All the Laws but One:* 217, discussing *Duncan v. Kahanamoku,* 327 U.S. 304 (1946).

108. Ibid., 221.

109. *Ex parte Quirin,* 317 U.S. 1 (1942).

110. *Johnson v. Eisentrager,* 339 U.S. 763, 765, 776–78 (1950). By contrast, the Court continued to review U.S. service members' habeas attacks on convictions by court martial, although it limited the scope of that review in light of review procedures created by Congress in the Uniform Code of Military Justice. See *Burns v. Wilson,* 346 U.S. 137 (1953) (habeas relief unavailable for claim given fair consideration by military courts). See also Richard H. Fallon, Jr., and Daniel J. Meltzer, "Habeas Corpus Jursidiction, Substantive Rights, and the War on Terror," *Harvard Law Review* 120 (2007): 2029, 2100–2101.

111. Act to Prohibit the Establishment of Detention Camps, September 25, 1971, Public Law 92-128, 85 Stat. 347, § 2.

112. Matthew C. Waxman, "Detention as Targeting: Standards of Certainty and Detention of Suspected Terrorists," *Columbia Law Review* 108 (2008): 1382–83; Robert Chesney and Jack Goldsmith, "Terrorism and the Convergence of Criminal and Military Detention Models," *Stanford Law Review* 60 (2008): 1079; Benjamin Wittes, *Law and the Long War: The Future of Justice in the Age of Terror* (New York: Penguin Press, 2008), 48–51.

113. See *Bismullah v. Gates,* 501 F.3d 178, 181–82 (D.C. Cir. 2007), *vacated by* 128 S. Ct. 2960 (2008), *reinstated by* Order, No. 06–1197 (D.C. Cir. Aug. 22, 2008), *petition dismissed for lack of jurisdiction,* 551 F.3d 1068 (D.C. Cir. 2009).

114. *Hamdi v. Rumsfeld,* 542 U.S. 507, 535–36 (2004).

115. *Rasul v. Bush,* 542 U.S. 466, 481 (2004).

116. See *In re Guantanamo Detainee Cases,* 355 F.Supp.2d 443, 464 (D.D.C. 2005).

117. Detainee Treatment Act of 2005, December 30, 2005, Public Law 109-148, title X, 119 Stat. 2680.

118. *Hamdan v. Rumsfeld,* 548 U.S. 557, 575–78, 613–34 (2006).

119. Military Commissions Act of 2006, October 17, 2006, Public Law 109-366, 120 Stat. 2600, codified in part at 28 U.S.C. § 2241.

120. *Boumediene,* 128 S. Ct. at 2247, 2277.

121. The Court agreed to review this issue in its 2009–2010 term, then in a

brief per curiam opinion declined to reach the merits and remanded the case to the court of appeals in light of the changed circumstances of the detainees, each of whom had been offered resettlement in another country and all but five of whom had accepted. *Kiyemba v. Obama*, 130 S. Ct. 1235 (2010).

122. For example, Daniel J. Meltzer, "Habeas Corpus, Suspension, and Guantánamo: The Boumediene Decision," *Supreme Court Review* 2008 (2008): 1; Benjamin Wittes, Robert Chesney, and Rabea Benhalim, "The Emerging Law of Detention: The Guantanamo Habeas Cases as Lawmaking," Brookings Institute, January 22, 2010 (collecting and analyzing detainee habeas decisions addressing a range of issues), available at http://ssrn.com/abstract=1540601; Michael John Garcia, Congressional Research Service, "*Boumediene v. Bush*: Guantanamo Detainees' Right to Habeas Corpus," September 2008 (noting open issues after *Boumediene*), http://www.fas.org/sgp/crs/natsec/RL34536.pdf. *al-Maqaleh v. Gates*, 605 F.3d 804 (D.C. Cir. 2010) (overturning district court decision that found foreign nationals held at the Bagram Theater Internment Facility at Bagram Airfield in Afghanistan may seek habeas relief); Baher Azmy, "Executive Detention, *Boumediene*, and the New Common Law of Habeas," *Iowa Law Review* 95 (2010): 445.

123. See *al-Marri v. Spagone*, 129 S. Ct. 1545 (2009) (vacating as moot *al-Marri v. Pucciarelli*, 534 F.3d 213 [4th Cir. 2008], vacating and replacing *al-Marri v. Wright*, 487 F.3d 160 [4th Cir. 2007]). See also Jennifer K. Elsea, Michael John Garcia, and Kenneth R. Thomas, Congressional Research Service Report RL 33180, "Enemy Combatant Detainees: Habeas Corpus Challenges in Federal Court" (April 7, 2009), 15–19 (describing *al-Marri* litigation), http://assets.open crs.com/rpts/RL33180_20090407.pdf.

124. Jordan Weissmann, "Trials on Hold as Gitmo Swamps Court: Chief Judge Says Most Civil Cases Will Be Delayed," *Legal Times*, March 23, 2009, 1, 8. Most of the judges in the District of Columbia agreed to consolidate the cases before former Chief Judge Thomas F. Hogan, who later issued a case management order. For a comprehensive analysis of the procedural rulings in these habeas cases, as well as rulings concerning the scope of the government's detention authority, see Wittes et al., "The Emerging Law of Detention."

125. Orders granting and denying the writ are collected at http://ccrjustice .org/files/2010-07-13%20Habeas%20SCORECARD%20Website%20Version .pdf. For examples, see Del Quentin Wilber, "Judge Orders Young Guantanamo Detainee's Release," *Washington Post*, July 30, 2009, http://www.washingtonpost .com/wp-dyn/content/article/2009/07/30/AR2009073000155.html; *Fouad Mahmoud al-Rabiah, et al., v. United States*, No. 02–828, Classified Memorandum Opinion (D.D.C. September 17, 2009), https://ecf.dcd.uscourts.gov/cgi-bin/show _public_doc?2002cv0828–645 (finding petitioner had traveled to Afghanistan for charitable purposes, that "none of the alleged eyewitnesses have provided credible allegations" against him, that his confessions were "entirely incredible,"

and that the government had failed to provide the Court with sufficiently credible and reliable evidence to establish a basis for his detention).

126. *In re Petitioners Seeking Habeas Corpus Relief in Relation to Prior Detentions at Guantanamo Bay*, 700 F.Supp.2d 119 (D.D.C. 2010).

127. "Josh White and William Branigin, Hamdan to be Sent to Yemen," *Washington Post*, November 25, 2008: A01, http://www.washingtonpost.com/wp-dyn/content/article/2008/11/24/AR2008112403159.html.

128. "U.S. Sending a Convict Back to Yemen," *New York Times*, November 25, 2008.

129. http://projects.nytimes.com/guantanamo; http://projects.washingtonpost.com/guantanamo; Charlie Savage, "Guantanamo Detainee Pleads Guilty in Terror Case," *New York Times*, July 7, 2010, http://www.nytimes.com/2010/07/08/us/08gitmo.html.

130. See Matthew Waxman, "Detention As Targeting: Standards of Certainty and Detention of Suspected Terrorists," *Columbia Law Review* 108 (2008): 1365–66; Wittes, *Law and the Long War*, 162–78; Jack L. Goldsmith and Neal Katyal, "The Terrorists' Court," *New York Times*, July 11, 2007, A19; Glenn Sulmasy, *The National Security Court System* (New York: Oxford, 2009); Stephen I. Vladeck, "The Case against National Security Courts," *Willamette Law Review* 45 (2009): 505, 523–25 (criticizing proposals for national security courts). In a speech of May 21, 2009, President Obama promised to "construct a legitimate legal framework" to justify the detention of dangerous terrorism suspects who could not be tried or released. See http://www.nytimes.com/2009/05/22/us/politics/22obama.html?_r=1&hpw. Compare David Cole, "Out of the Shadows: Preventive Detention, Suspected Terrorists, and War," *California Law Review* 97 (2009): 693, 750 (discussing "a carefully circumscribed preventive-detention authority outside the criminal justice system for those engaged in an ongoing military conflict.").

131. See also Janet Cooper Alexander, "Jurisdiction-Stripping in a Time of Terror," *California Law Review* 95 (2007): 1193, 1198 (terming habeas a "reassuring backstop that assures that . . . there will, in the end, be judicial review through habeas if the constitutional question involves deprivation of life or liberty").

Chapter Three

1. Alexander Hamilton, "Federalist, Number 83," in *The Federalist Papers*, ed. Clinton Rossiter (New York: Penguin Putnam, 1999).

2. *Annual Report of the Director of the Administrative Office of the United States Court*, Table 6, Civil Cases Commenced in the U.S. District Courts during the Fiscal Years 1942 and 1943, by Basis of Jurisdiction and Nature of Suit. Annual statistics from more recent years are available in the report "Judicial Busi-

ness of the U.S. Courts," Table C-2, on the Web site of the Administrative Office of the Courts, www.uscourts.gov. Nationwide, the proportion of civil cases represented by state prisoner habeas cases has dropped during the past decade, from one in 12 to one in 16.

3. Nancy J. King, Fred L. Cheesman II, and Brian J. Ostrom, *Final Technical Report: Habeas Litigation in U.S. District Courts* (2007), hereafter King et al., "Habeas Study," http://www.ncjrs.gov/pdffiles1/nij/grants/219559.pdf. The study was funded by Vanderbilt University Law School and the National Institute of Justice.

4. Act of February 5, 1867, ch. 28, § 1, 14 Stat. 385–86. See chapter 1 for a summary of the conventional, albeit contested, view of the scope of habeas review of state criminal judgments prior to the 1867 act. See also *Felker v. Turpin*, 518 U.S. 651, 663 (1996) ("It was not until 1867 that Congress made the writ generally available in 'all cases where any person may be restrained of his or her liberty in violation of the constitution, or of any treaty or law of the United States.' . . . And it was not until well into this century that this Court interpreted that provision to allow a final judgment of conviction in a state court to be collaterally attacked on habeas."); *Ex parte Yerger*, 75 U.S. 85 (1869) ("As limited by the act of 1789, [habeas] did not extend to cases of imprisonment after conviction, under sentences of competent tribunals.").

5. See generally John E. Nowak, "Federalism and the Civil War Amendments," *Ohio Northern University Law Review* 23 (1997): 1209.

6. James Madison, "Federalist, Number 51," in, *The Federalist Papers*. See also *U.S. Term Limits, Inc. v. Thornton*, 514 U.S. 779, 838 (1997) (Kennedy, J., concurring) ("The Framers split the atom of sovereignty. It was the genius of their idea that our citizens would have two political capacities, one state and one federal, each protected from incursion by the other.").

In an important new book, Alison LaCroix argues that American federalism was not invented at the Constitutional Convention in Philadelphia, nor did it grow directly out of the colonial experience with divided government. Rather, federalism was a political ideology that developed gradually over the second half of the eighteenth century. The core of the federal ideology was "a belief that multiple independent levels of government could legitimately exist within a single polity, and that such an arrangement was not a defect to be lamented but a virtue to be celebrated." This ideology "rapidly became identified with the [emerging American] Republic itself," ultimately reaching its theoretical apogee at the Convention. See Alison L. LaCroix, *The Ideological Origins of American Federalism* (Cambridge, MA & London: Harvard University Press, 2010), 6.

7. James Madison, "Federalist, Number 45," in Rossiter, *The Federalist Papers*.

8. Significant expansions of federal power have occurred at the time of the Civil War (to address the violation of rights of citizens by their own states),

during the New Deal (to address the economic crisis known as the Great Depression), and during the civil rights era (to address both private and public discrimination).

9. The so-called Reagan Revolution of the 1980s would be one such period.

10. See, for example, *United States v. Lopez*, 514 U.S. 549 (1995), the first Supreme Court decision since the New Deal to find a federal statute unconstitutional because it exceeded the federal government's powers under the Commerce Clause.

11. The supremacy of federal law is guaranteed by the Supremacy Clause in the Constitution. U.S. Const., art. VI, para. 2. ("This Constitution . . . shall be the supreme Law of the Land; and the Judges in every State shall be bound thereby, any Thing in the Constitution or Laws of any State to the Contrary notwithstanding.").

12. Act of March 27, 1868, ch. 34, § 2, 15 Stat. 44. The statute was interpreted to have effectively withdrawn the Court's jurisdiction over habeas appeals in *Ex parte McCardle*, 74 U.S. 506 (1868).

13. See *Ex parte Yerger*, 75 U.S. 85.

14. Act of March 3, 1885, ch. 353, 23 Stat. 437.

15. See H.R. Rep., No. 730, 48th Cong., 1st Sess. (1884). See also Randy Hertz and James S. Liebman, *Federal Habeas Corpus Practice and Procedure* (Newark, NJ: Matthew Bender, 2005), 55–56.

16. *Ex parte Royall*, 117 U.S. 241 (1886).

17. The Court in 1879 had held that a habeas court was no longer restricted to the record underlying the conviction but could consider new claims based on facts outside the record. *Ex parte Siebold*, 100 U.S. 375 (1879). For example, in 1895, Eugene Debs—a Socialist presidential candidate who was prosecuted under the Espionage Act for criticizing the government—was barred from challenging his contempt commitment in habeas. The writ was denied because the Court found that Debs's claim that he hadn't violated an injunction was a ground not subject to review once the trial court had jurisdiction to issue the injunction and make a factual finding of contempt. *In re Debs*, 158 U.S. 564 (1895); William H. Rehnquist, *All the Laws but One: Civil Liberties in Wartime* (New York: Alfred A. Knopf, 1998), 179–80. Five years earlier the Court had similarly upheld a refusal to grant habeas relief to Samuel Davis, who had been sentenced by a territorial court in Utah for conspiring to deny falsely that he was a Mormon and that he supported polygamy. The Court concluded that because the trial court that convicted Davis "had jurisdiction, we can go no further. We cannot look into any alleged errors in its rulings, on the trial of the defendant. The writ of *habeas corpus* cannot be turned into a writ of error to review the action of that court. Nor can we inquire whether the evidence established the fact alleged. . . ." *Davis v. Beason*, 133 U.S. 333, 341 (1890). On the subsequent development of direct re-

view of federal criminal judgments beginning in the 1890s, see Hertz and Leibman, *Federal Habeas Corpus Practice and Procedure*, 60–61.

18. *Frank v. Mangum*, 237 U.S. 309 (1915).

19. Ibid., 315–16. Frank claimed that he learned only after the verdict had been returned and the sentence had been handed down that his attorneys, without consulting him, had waived his presence for the return of the verdict. The judge had requested Frank's absence after he had secretly warned Frank's attorneys that Frank and even his attorneys might be in danger of violence if he was present when the verdict was returned. Frank's case had a tragic ending. Georgia's governor commuted Frank's death sentence after the Court's rejection of his claim, but Frank was kidnapped from prison and lynched.

20. Ibid., 330–31 (emphasis added). The Court stated,

> The effect [of the 1867 act] is to substitute for the bare legal review that seems to have been the limit of judicial authority under the common-law practice, and under the act of 31 Car. II. chap. 2, a more searching investigation, in which the applicant is put upon his oath to set forth the truth of the matter respecting the causes of his detention, and the court, upon determining the actual facts, is to "dispose of the party as law and justice require."

See also Eric M. Freedman, *Habeas Corpus: Rethinking the Great Writ of Liberty* (New York: New York University Press, 2003), 91 (noting that the power of a habeas court to conduct an independent investigation of the facts claimed to render a state conviction unconstitutional was firmly established by *Frank*). Despite the dicta quoted above, the Court declined to disturb the state court's determination that the defendant's allegations were unfounded, stating, "the mere assertion by the prisoner that the facts of the matter are other than the state court upon full investigation determined them to be will not be deemed sufficient to raise an issue respecting the correctness of that determination; especially not, where the very evidence upon which the determination was rested is withheld by him who attacks the finding." 237 U.S. at 336.

21. *Moore v. Dempsey*, 261 U.S. 86, 92 (1923) (Holmes, J., for the Court).

22. *Johnson v. Zerbst*, 304 U.S. 458, 468–69 (1938), stating that if it was true that the petitioner, as he had alleged, "was unable to obtain a lawyer; was ignorant of the proceedings to obtain new trial or appeal and the time limits governing both; and . . . did not possess the requisite skill or knowledge properly to conduct an appeal," then "it necessarily follows that no legal procedural remedy is available to grant relief for a violation of constitutional rights, unless the courts protect petitioner's rights by habeas corpus." Although *Zerbst* involved habeas review of a federal judgment, it cited as authority the quote from Justice Oliver Wendell Holmes's opinion in *Moore*, a state prisoner case.

23. The expansion of the definition of which claims were "jurisdictional" and therefore cognizable under the habeas statute began in 1874 in cases in which the Court used habeas to review federal sentences. By 1890, the Court had held that a court's jurisdiction to impose a sentence in a federal criminal case was lacking in several circumstances: when the federal statute on which the prosecution was predicated was unconstitutional, when a prisoner had been convicted without indictment by a federal grand jury, and when the prisoner had already been prosecuted for the same offense. *Ex parte Lange*, 85 U.S. 163 (1874); *Ex parte Siebold*, 100 U.S. at 375; *Ex parte Wilson*, 114 U.S. 417 (1885); *In re Nielsen*, 131 U.S. 176, 190–91 (1888) (holding, in a prosecution for adultery in the territory of Utah, that prior conviction of the petitioner of the crime of unlawful cohabitation was a bar to his subsequent prosecution for the crime of adultery and that the court was without authority to impose judgment and should have granted the writ); *In re Snow*, 120 U.S. 274 (1887) (granting the writ to a petitioner who was charged three separate times for the same bigamy offense). The last was a problem that the Court addressed more than once in cases from the Utah territory, where the federal government was crusading against bigamy and adultery. These extensions of the concept of "jurisdiction" had already taken place in state courts construing the reach of their own habeas corpus statutes in reviewing state convictions. See Dallin H. Oaks, "Habeas Corpus in the States—1776–1865," *University of Chicago Law Review* 32 (1964–1965): 243, 263. The Court also held that jurisdiction once possessed was lost when a defendant was tried without a petit jury or was prosecuted on an indictment other than the one signed by the grand jury. *Ex parte Bain*, 121 U.S. 1 (1887); *Callan v. Wilson*, 127 U.S. 540 (1888).

24. Alexander Hamilton, "Federalist, Number 17," in Rossiter, *The Federalist Papers* ("There is one transcendant [*sic*] advantage belonging to the province of the State governments, which alone suffices to place the matter in a clear and satisfactory light,—I mean the ordinary administration of criminal and civil justice.").

25. *Frank*, 237 U.S. at 335.

26. *Moore*, 261 U.S. at 91, stating if

> the whole proceeding is a mask—that counsel, jury and judge were swept to the fatal end by an irresistible wave of public passion, and that the State Courts failed to correct the wrong, neither perfection in the machinery for correction nor the possibility that the trial court and counsel saw no other way of avoiding an immediate outbreak of the mob can prevent this Court from securing to the petitioners their constitutional rights.

The Court in *Moore* remanded the case to the district court to conduct an evidentiary hearing. Professor Michael O'Neill's summary of the *Moore* proceedings encapsulates the reasons for the Court's concern:

In *Moore*, a number of African-Americans peacefully assembled in their church were attacked by a group of armed white men. In the disturbance that followed, one of the whites was killed.

Shortly after the African-American petitioners were arrested on murder charges, a white mob marched on the jail bent on seizing the petitioners and lynching them. The mob was thwarted by federal troops and turned away only after being promised that those found guilty would be executed. The petitioners were ultimately brought to trial in what can only charitably be called a sham proceeding. Blacks were systematically excluded from the grand and petit juries, and the court-appointed defense counsel had never consulted with the defendants before trial . . . [and did not] seek to put on a defense. None of the defendants was called to the stand, nor were any defense witnesses called. In all, the so-called trial lasted approximately three-quarters of an hour and in fewer than five minutes the jury returned a guilty verdict on the first degree murder charges. . . .

[T]he Arkansas Supreme Court summarily upheld the convictions.

Michael O'Neill, "On Reforming the Federal Writ of Habeas Corpus," *Seton Hall Law Review* 26 (1996): 1493, 1519.

27. *Mooney v. Holohan*, 294 U.S. 103 (1935).

28. *Waley v. Johnston*, 316 U.S. 101, 104–105 (1942). See also *Zerbst*, 304 U.S. at 468, stating that the 1867 act authorized review of the denial of counsel where counsel was constitutionally guaranteed and that jurisdiction at the beginning of a trial "may be lost 'in the course of the proceedings' due to failure to complete the court—as the Sixth Amendment requires—by providing counsel for an accused who is unable to obtain counsel." Both *Zerbst* and *Waley* involved challenges by federal prisoners, but *Waley* was soon cited in a case considering a petition filed by a state prisoner. There, the Court noted that in *Waley*, it had observed that "the writ is an appropriate remedy in the federal courts in 'those exceptional cases where the conviction has been in disregard of the constitutional rights of the accused, and where the writ is the only effective means of preserving his rights,' at least where 'the facts relied on are dehors the record and their effect on the judgment was not open to consideration and review on appeal.'" *House v. Mayo*, 324 U.S. 42, 46 (1945), overruled on other grounds, *Hohn v. United States*, 524 U.S. 236 (1945).

29. John J. Parker, "Limiting the Abuse of Habeas Corpus," 8 *Federal Rules Decisions* 171, 174 (1949); *Annual Report of the Director of the Administrative Office of the United States Courts* (Washington, DC: Government Print-

ing Office, 1950): 111–13 (terming the increase in petitions from state prisoners "spectacular").

30. William H. Speck, "Statistics on Federal Habeas Corpus," *Ohio State Law Journal* 10 (1949): 341. See also sources cited in note 2.

31. See *Brown v. Mississippi*, 297 U.S. 278 (1936) (tortured confession); *Ashcraft v. Tennessee*, 322 U.S. 143 (1944) (thirty-six-hour interrogation without rest or sleep); *Leyra v. Denno*, 347 U.S. 556 (1954) (confession after police psychiatrist tricked exhausted defendant); *Rochin v. California*, 342 U.S. 165 (1952) (forced extraction of evidence by stomach pumping); *Rogers v. Richmond*, 365 U.S. 534 (1961) (confession coerced by threats against suspect's ailing wife); *Lynumn v. Illinois*, 371 U.S. 528 (1963) (confession after threat to defendant that she would lose custody of her children); *Townsend v. Sain*, 372 U.S. 293 (1963) (truth serum used on suspect suffering withdrawal, decided the same day as *Gideon*); *Blackburn v. Alabama*, 361 U.S. 199 (1960) (confession of mentally ill defendant); *Klopfer v. State of North Carolina*, 386 U.S. 213 (1967) (denial of speedy trial); *Sheppard v. Maxwell*, 384 U.S. 333 (1966) (failure to protect defendant from prejudice and disruptive influences in courtroom).

32. *Gideon v. Wainwright*, 372 U.S. 335 (1963).

33. *Mapp v. Ohio*, 367 U.S. 643 (1961).

34. *Miranda v. Arizona*, 384 U.S. 436 (1966).

35. Those decisions included *Brown v. Board of Education of Topeka*, 347 U.S. 483 (1954).

36. This resistance, in turn, led to tension between the state and federal courts over the exercise of federal habeas jurisdiction. See Paul D. Carrington, Daniel J. Meador, and Maurice Rosenberg, *Justice on Appeal* (St. Paul, MN: West Publishing Co., 1976), 114–15 (habeas procedures "are needlessly irritating to state appellate judges"); John W. Winkle III, "Judges before Congress: Reform Politics and Individual Freedom," *Polity* 22 (1990): 443 (describing 1958 federal bill to curtail habeas review, defeated due to concern about state court resistance to federal law); *Schneckloth v. Bustamonte*, 412 U.S. 218, 263 (1973) (Powell, J., concurring) ("The present expansive scope of federal habeas review has prompted no small friction between state and federal judiciaries.").

37. Joseph L. Hoffmann and Nancy J. King, "Rethinking the Federal Role in State Criminal Justice," *New York University Law Review* 89 (2009): 101, 117–21.

38. *Brown v. Allen*, 344 U.S. 443 (1953).

39. *Townsend v. Sain*, 372 U.S. 293 (1963).

40. *Sanders v. United States*, 373 U.S. 1 (1963).

41. *Fay v. Noia*, 372 U.S. 391 (1963).

42. See William J. Brennan, Jr., "Federal Habeas Corpus and State Prisoners: An Exercise in Federalism," *Utah Law Review* 7 (1961): 423.

43. *Fay*, 372 U.S. at 399–402.

44. Ibid., 441.

45. This power was always more theoretical than real; reversal rates in federal habeas, except in capital cases, probably never reached double digits, even during the heyday of the Warren Court. David L. Shapiro, "Federal Habeas Corpus: A Study in Massachusetts," *Harvard Law Review* 87 (1973): 321, 334 (reporting that of 255 petitions filed in one district between 1970 and 1972, the grant rate was less than 2 percent); Curtis R. Reitz, "Federal Habeas Corpus: Postconviction Remedy for State Prisoners," *University of Pennsylvania Law Review* 108 (1960): 461, 478–79 (reporting that of six thousand petitions filed between 1949 and 1959, between twenty-six and ninety-eight received relief of some sort, a grant rate of less than 2 percent); Paul Robinson, *An Empirical Study of Federal Habeas Corpus Review of State Court Judgments* (Washington, DC: U.S. Justice Department 1979) (reporting 3.2 percent granted); Victor E. Flango, *Habeas Corpus in State and Federal Courts* (Williamsburg: National Center for State Courts 1994), 64 (reporting grant rates of 15 percent for state petitioners filing first petitions in state court, 2 percent for state petitioners filing second petitions in state court, and 1 percent for state petitioners filing first or second petitions in federal court); Richard Faust, Tina J. Rubenstein, and Larry L. Yackle, "The Great Writ in Action: Empirical Light on the Federal Corpus Debate," *New York University Review of Law and Social Change* 18 (1990–91): 649; Roger A. Hanson and Henry W. K. Daley, *Federal Habeas Corpus Review Challenging State Court Criminal Convictions* (National Center for State Courts, September 1995, NCJ-155504) (reporting 1 percent granted) http://www.ojp.usdoj.gov/bjs/pub/pdf/fhcrcscc.pdf.

46. See T. Alexander Aleinikoff and Robert M. Cover, "Dialectical Federalism: Habeas Corpus and the Court," *Yale Law Journal* 86 (1977): 1035.

47. See Joseph L. Hoffmann, "Narrowing Habeas Corpus," in *The Rehnquist Legacy*, ed. Craig Bradley (New York: Cambridge University Press 2005), 156. Rehnquist also clerked for Justice Robert Jackson during the year that *Brown v. Allen* was argued before the Supreme Court, and he wrote several memos for Justice Jackson critiquing the expansion of habeas corpus that was proposed, and ultimately accomplished, in that case.

For an argument that Justice Brennan's expansive view of habeas, and not Justice Rehnquist's restrictive one, was truer to the original spirit of the 1867 act, see Eric M. Freedman, *Habeas Corpus: Rethinking the Great Writ of Liberty* (New York: New York University Press, 2003).

48. *Wainwright v. Sykes*, 433 U.S. 72 (1977).

49. Ibid., 81.

50. Ibid., 81–82.

51. See *Davis v. United States*, 411 U.S. 233 (1973); *Francis v. Henderson*, 425 U.S. 536 (1976).

52. *Sykes*, 433 U.S. at 88, 90.

53. Ibid., 91.

54. See *Reed v. Ross*, 468 U.S. 1 (1984).

55. See *Amadeo v. Zant*, 486 U.S. 214 (1988).

56. See *Murray v. Carrier*, 477 U.S. 478 (1986).

57. See *United States v. Frady*, 456 U.S. 152 (1982).

58. See *Carrier*, 477 U.S. at 478, 495, 499, 505, 515.

59. The Court delivered the final blow in *Coleman v. Thompson*, 501 U.S. 722 (1991), holding that the *Sykes* cause-and-prejudice standard applied even to the exact kind of failure that had occurred in *Fay v. Noia*.

60. *Sykes*, 433 U.S. at 78–79. Yet another key issue Rehnquist identified had been settled in the first habeas case to reach the Supreme Court after its appellate jurisdiction was restored in 1885: petitioners generally must exhaust available state remedies before pursuing habeas relief. *Ex parte Royall*, 117 U.S. 241 (1886). The modern version of the habeas exhaustion doctrine was declared by the Court in *Rose v. Lundy*, 455 U.S. 509 (1982) (holding that habeas petitions containing both exhausted and unexhausted claims must be dismissed), and *Rhines v. Weber*, 544 U.S. 269 (2005) (holding that district courts have limited discretion to preserve habeas jurisdiction by staying petitions pending the exhaustion of previously unexhausted claims).

61. *Stone v. Powell*, 428 U.S. 465 (1976).

62. The Court has refused to extend the reasoning of *Stone v. Powell* to claims of racial discrimination in jury selection, *Rose v. Mitchell*, 443 U.S. 545 (1979); claims of ineffective assistance of counsel in failing to litigate a Fourth Amendment claim, *Kimmelman v. Morrison*, 477 U.S. 365 (1986); and claims raising *Miranda* violations, *Withrow v. Williams*, 507 U.S. 680 (1993).

A proposal to codify the *Stone* approach for all constitutional claims was rejected as Congress was debating habeas reform in the mid-1990s. See Michael O'Neill, "On Reforming the Federal Writ of Habeas Corpus," *Seton Hall Law Review* 26 (1996): 1493, 1530–31 (describing and defending amendment offered by Senator Jon Kyl).

63. *Teague v. Lane*, 489 U.S. 288 (1989).

64. *The Antiterrorism and Effective Death Penalty Act of 1996*, Public Law 104-132, *U.S. Statutes at Large* 110 (1996): 1214. For a description of the legislative developments leading up to the 1996 Act, see Larry W. Yackle, "The Habeas Hagioscope," *Southern California Law Review* 66 (1993): 2331. For a defense of the need for reform at the time, arguing that restrictions on habeas review were constitutional and justified given the marginal benefit and high cost of federal habeas review of state criminal cases, see O'Neill, "On Reforming the Federal Writ of Habeas Corpus."

65. See 28 U.S.C. § 2254(d).

66. See *Renico v. Lett*, 130 S. Ct. 1855, 1862 (2010) (observing that AEDPA itself never uses the term "deference" but stating, "our cases have done so over

and over again to describe the effect of the threshold restrictions in 28 U.S.C. § 2254(d) on granting federal habeas relief to state prisoners.").

67. See sources collected in note 45.

68. See *Dickerson v. United States*, 530 U.S. 428 (2000).

69. Justice Brennan was instrumental in bringing about this development, having encouraged state courts in 1977 to interpret their own state constitutions more broadly than the federal counterpart, thereby providing more protection to criminal defendants. See William J. Brennan, Jr., "State Constitutions and the Protection of Individual Rights," *Harvard Law Review* 90 (1977): 489.

70. Joseph L. Hoffmann and William J. Stuntz, "Habeas after the Revolution," *Supreme Court Review* 1993 (1994): 65.

Chapter Four

1. *Teague v. Lane*, 489 U.S. 288 (1989).

2. For example, the Court would not impose additional constraints on filing successive petitions for another fifteen years. See *Kuhlmann v. Wilson*, 477 U.S. 436 (1986), and *McCleskey v. Zant*, 499 U.S. 467 (1991).

3. *Griffin v. Illinois*, 351 U.S. 12 (1956); Lester B. Orfield, *Criminal Appeals in America* (Boston: Little, Brown & Co. 1939), 127–53, 283; Note, "State Post-Conviction Remedies," *Columbia Law Review* 61 (1961): 703. For one state's example, see Kenneth Syken, "Operation of Appellate Procedure in Pennsylvania Criminal Cases," *University of Pennsylvania Law Review* 100 (1952): 868.

4. For example, Walter Schafer, "Federalism and State Criminal Procedure," *Harvard Law Review* 70 (1956): 21–22 (arguing that the great variation in filing rates between districts is caused by prison practices, with some prisons interfering with or censoring prison mail to minimize federal filings and others encouraging petition writing and filing as good therapy).

5. *Douglas v. California*, 372 U.S. 353 (1963).

6. *Bounds v. Smith*, 430 U.S. 817 (1977).

7. Paul D. Carrington, Daniel J. Meador, and Maurice Rosenberg, *Justice on Appeal* (St. Paul, MN: West Publishing Co. 1976), 97 (noting the "widespread lack of availability of review of trial court decisions fixing sentences" in the late 1960s).

8. President's Commission on Law Enforcement and Administration of Justice, *The Challenge of Crime in a Free Society* (Washington, DC: Government Printing Office, 1967), 139–40. See also *ABA Project on Minimum Standards for Criminal Justice, Standards Relating to Post-Conviction Remedies*, Curtis R. Reitz, Reporter (January 1967), 2 (noting that "[m]any state systems of post-conviction review are still grossly inadequate to meet today's needs"). Among other problems, the report cited unrealistic filing deadlines, rigid pleading re-

quirements, and limitations on the scope of review. For similar comments by the Justices of the United States Supreme Court, see *Case v. Nebraska*, 381 U.S. 336, 338 (1965) (Clark, J., concurring) (noting that "the great variations in the scope and availability of such remedies result in their being entirely inadequate"); ibid., 345–46 (Brennan, J., concurring) ("If adequate state procedures, presently all too scarce, were generally adopted, much would be done to remove the irritant of participation by the federal district courts in state criminal procedure."). In *Case*, the state conceded that there was no remedy in the state courts for petitioner's constitutional claim and that the state's habeas remedy was limited to assessing whether the convicting court had jurisdiction and the power to impose the sentence. See also Daniel Meador, "Accommodating State Criminal Procedure and Federal Postconviction Review," *American Bar Association Journal* 50 (1964): 928, 929–30 (noting states in which constitutional errors could not be litigated after trial because the only remedy was common law habeas corpus review limited to attacking the jurisdiction of the convicting court).

9. See *Gideon v. Wainwright*, 372 U.S. 335 (1963) (right to counsel at trial); *Douglas v. California*, 372 U.S. 353 (1963) (right to counsel on direct appeal).

10. See Martin O. Osthus, *Intermediate Appellate Courts* (Chicago: American Judicature Society 1976); Joy A. Chapper and Roger A. Hanson, *Intermediate Appellate Courts: Improving Case Processing, Final Report* (Williamsburg, VA: National Center for State Courts, 1990), xi (noting that between 1957 and the 1980s, the number of permanent intermediate appellate courts grew from thirteen to 37).

11. See, for example, Roger A. Hanson and Joy Chapper, "What Does Sentencing Reform Do to Criminal Appeals?" *Judicature* 72 (June-July 1988): 50.

12. Carrington et al., *Justice on Appeal*, 58–59.

13. Ibid., 5, 58–60. See also Federal Judicial Center, "Report of the Study Group on the Case Load of the Supreme Court," 2–3, reprinted in 54 F.R.D 573 (1973) (reporting huge increase in petitions for certiorari from state criminal appeals and state postconviction proceedings between 1951 and 1970).

14. For a comprehensive list of each state's revised statute and the year it was adopted, see Donald E. Wilkes, Jr., 1 *State Postconviction Remedies and Relief Handbook with Forms* (St. Paul, MN: West Publishing Co., 2007), 40–45. See also Federal Judicial Center, "Report of the Study Group on the Case Load of the Supreme Court," 1 (noting, in 1967, that "during the past few years" postconviction review "has become an established part of the criminal process" as "a byproduct of the changes in criteria governing criminal prosecutions wrought by the Supreme Court . . ."); Thomas M. Place, "Deferring Ineffectiveness Claims to Collateral Review: Ensuring Equal Access and a Right to Appointed Counsel," *Kentucky Law Journal* 98 (2009–2010): 301, 313–16 (surveying development of state postconviction remedies); Yakov Avichai, "Collateral Attacks on Convictions (I): The Probability and Intensity of Filing," *American Bar Founda-*

tion Research Journal, 1977 (1977): 319. For example, West Virginia courts first granted postconviction relief for the violation of a constitutional right in 1963. See "The Widening Scope of State Habeas Corpus," *West Virginia Law Review* 67 (1964–65): 237.

15. See Hanson and Chapper, "What Does Sentencing Reform Do to Criminal Appeals?" 50 (noting high rates of relief in some state courts). There is scant research into relief rates for prisoners in state postconviction cases. One 2003 study of three counties in Pennsylvania found that of cases that were not voluntarily withdrawn, relief rates for the three counties were 2, 10, and 16 percent. The most common relief ordered was reinstatement of the right to file an appeal. Donald J. Harris, Kim Nieves, and Thomas M. Place, "Dispatch and Delay: Post Conviction Relief Act Litigation in Non-Capital Cases," *Duquesne Law Review* 41 (2003): 467.

We do not claim here or in the next chapter that state direct appeal and postconviction review is working so well that no other strategy for enforcing federal law is needed. (Indeed, we propose in the next chapter that Congress take a rather radical step in a different direction to address deficiencies in the provision of indigent defense.) Rather, we are arguing that the institutional shift that has taken place in state criminal justice since the 1960s—the provision of the opportunity for judicial review of constitutional claims—has eliminated one of the primary justifications for broad federal habeas review of all constitutional claims from state-convicted prisoners.

16. *Ex parte Royall*, 117 U.S. 241 (1886); *Jones v. Cunningham*, 371 U.S. 236 (1963); *Hensley v. Municipal Court*, 411 U.S. 345 (1973).

17. Avichai, "Collateral Attacks on Conviction," 334, 347, 349–50.

18. Professor Jordan Steiker has argued that the adoption of extensive state postconviction proceedings combined with the exhaustion requirement has introduced delay, which in turn has increased the costs of granting relief. Jordan Steiker, "Restructuring Post-Conviction Review of Federal Constitutional Claims Raised by State Prisoners: Confronting the New Face of Excessive Proceduralism," *University of Chicago Legal Forum* 1998 (1998): 315. Our point is different, not that delay raises the costs of relief, but that delay for most prisoners actually cuts off access to relief entirely.

19. Sean Rosenmerkel, Matthew Durose, and Donald Farole, "Felony Sentences in State Courts, 2006" (Bureau of Justice Statistics, Bulletin No. NCJ 226846, December 2009), http://bjs.ojp.usdoj.gov/content/pub/pdf/fssc06st.pdf (estimating that 41 percent of convicted felons in state court were sentenced to prison, and 28 percent to jail and that 31 percent were not incarcerated).

20. In 2006, the latest figures available, the mean sentence for state felons sentenced to prison was 59 months, ibid., but the average time served until first release was considerably less, only 28 months. Thomas P. Bonczar, *National Corrections Reporting Program: Time Served in State Prison, by Offense, Release*

Type, Sex, and Race, May 25, 2010, available at http://bjs.ojp.usdoj.gov/index
.cfm?ty=pbdetail&iid=2045. Time served in state prison before first release has
increased since 1990, when it averaged 22 months. See Timothy A. Hughes, Do-
ris James Wilson, and Allen J. Beck, "Trends in State Parole, 1990–2000" (Bureau of Justice Statistics, Bulletin No. NCJ 184735, Sept. 2001), http://www.ojp
.usdoj.gov/bjs/pub/pdf/tsp00.pdf.

21. Plea-convicted defendants can and do attack their convictions and sentences on a number of constitutional grounds, including ineffective assistance of
counsel during the plea or sentencing process, a breach of the plea agreement, or
an illegal sentence or sentencing procedure. But trial offers even more opportunity for error. Additionally, trial-convicted defendants generally receive stiffer
sentences than defendants who plead guilty, both because defendants who admit guilt receive credit for accepting responsibility for their crimes and because
trial rates are higher for serious offenses. Nationwide, about one of every three
state defendants convicted of noncapital murder and about one in ten of those
convicted of robbery, sexual assault, and aggravated assault went to trial. Rosenmerkel et al., *Felony Sentences in State Courts—2006*, Table 4.1. Also, unlike
some who enter plea agreements, defendants convicted at trial generally do not
waive their rights to appellate or postconviction review of their convictions or
sentences.

22. *Santobello v. New York*, 404 U.S. 257 (1971); *Brady v. United States*, 397
U.S. 742 (1970). Even as the number of felony dispositions in state courts more
than doubled between 1976 and 2002, the percentage of felony cases resolved
by trial dropped from 9 to 3 percent. See G. Thomas Munsterman and Shauna
Strickland, "Jury News," *Court Manager* 19 (2004): 53, http://www.ncsconline
.org/Juries/JuryNews/JuryNewsCM19-2.pdf. Statistics on felony trial rates nationwide in state courts are collected at www.ncsconline.org/D_Research/csp/
TrialTrends/FelonyDispositions.xls. In California, the state with the largest
prison population in the nation, 72 percent of felony convictions in 1970 were
by guilty plea; by 1972 the proportion was 82 percent, and by 1985 it was over
90 percent. See Gordon Van Kessell, "Adversary Excesses in the American
Criminal Trial," *Notre Dame Law Review* 67 (1992): 403, 467–68. In 2006, approximately 94 percent of state sentenced felons had pleaded guilty. Rosenmerkel et al., *Felony Sentences in State Courts—2006*, Table 4.1.

Other possible explanations for the precipitous drop in the rate at which state
prisoners filed habeas petitions after 1970 include a decline in the number of
prisoners who had counsel on state postconviction (who therefore would have
had access to a lawyer-prepared statement of postconviction claims), a number
that may actually have been greater before 1970 than it was after 1974, when the
Court rejected a right to counsel in state postconviction proceedings. See American Bar Association, *Standards Relating to Post Conviction Remedies* (1967), 65
(noting that in some jurisdictions no counsel is appointed and that others make

appointment mandatory). It is also possible that over time there has been grow-ing prisoner awareness of the futility of filing.

23. See Rosenmerkel et al., *Felony Sentences in State Courts—2006*, Tables 4.1, 4.2, 4.3.

24. Nancy J. King, Fred L. Cheesman II, and Brian J. Ostrom, *Final Techni-cal Report: Habeas Litigation in U.S. District Courts* (2007), 54, hereafter King et al., "Habeas Study," http://www.ncjrs.gov/pdffiles1/nij/grants/219559.pdf.

25. The number of petitions are tracked each year in the Annual Reports of the Administrative Office of the Courts, Judicial Business of the U.S. Courts, Tables B1-A and C2, available at www.uscourts.gov.

26. Most of the remaining four hundred cases alleged a constitutional flaw in a postcommitment decision such as a prison disciplinary hearing resulting in the revocation of good time or a decision to deny or revoke parole release. These cases are discussed in chapter 9.

27. See King et al., "Habeas Study," 47. This does not include dismissals of mixed petitions or voluntary dismissals by the petitioner that may have been in order to exhaust. More than one in five petitioners who had not pursued state postconviction review had their petitions dismissed for failure to exhaust; among those who had sought state postconviction relief, only 5 percent were dismissed for this reason. These figures do not appear in the report and were generated by additional analysis of the data.

28. Ibid., 57.

29. Ibid., 22 (reporting average filing periods for timely petitions (5.6 years) and cases with all claims dismissed as unexhausted (4.0 years), for all cases in-cluding challenges to administrative decisions). Additional analysis of the data, omitting challenges to administrative decisions, shows that the average time be-tween sentence and filing date was 5.11 years. It is possible for a petitioner to file his habeas case prior to exhausting state remedies and obtain a stay to re-turn to state court and exhaust claims. This was not common in noncapital cases: only 57 of the 2,384 cases were stayed for exhaustion. Of these, 33 had informa-tion about the date of conviction of sentence, and as one might expect, those 33 habeas cases were filed sooner after conviction than other cases, on average 3.7 years after conviction or sentence. Looking only at the usual case where no stay for exhaustion was obtained, the average filing period for cases challenging conviction or sentence and filed on time was 5.2 years.

30. Rosenmerkel et al., *Felony Sentences in State Courts—2006*, Table 1.4 (re-porting that in 2006, 0.8 percent of felons receiving prison sentences were sen-tenced to life).

31. King et al., "Habeas Study," 54.

32. Ibid., 20. Additional analysis of the data excluding cases raising challenges to administrative decisions showed that 30 percent were serving life sentences.

33. Ibid. Additional analysis of the data showed that about three in every four

of those who challenged a noncapital murder conviction or sentence had been convicted at trial.

34. American Bar Association, "Judicial Administration Division," in *Standards Relating to Appellate Courts* (1994), vol. 3, § 3.52 (completing 75 percent of intermediate appellate cases within 290 days of filing and 90 percent of state supreme court cases within 290 days, combined with the preparation of the trial record and periods allowed for filing).

35. Roger A. Hanson, *Time on Appeal* (Williamsburg, VA: National Center for State Courts, 1996) (reporting that of thirty-five states studied, only five met American Bar Association [ABA] standards of 290 days, with nine courts taking at least 580 days).

36. Richard B. Hoffman and Barry Mahoney, "Managing Caseflow in State Intermediate Appellate Courts: What Mechanisms, Practices, and Procedures Can Work to Reduce Delay?" *Indiana Law Review* 35 (2002): 467 (concluding in study of six appellate courts that only one met ABA standards). A survey using 2005 data found that the average processing time for just the intermediate appeal stage of criminal appeals in seven states ranged between about ten and twenty-six months. Hillary Taylor, "Appellate Delay as Reversible Error," *Willamette Law Review* 44 (2008): 761, 789 (citing W. Warren H. Binford et al., "Seeing Best Practices among Intermediate Appellate Courts: A Nascent Journey," *Journal of Appellate Practice and Process* 9 [2008]: 37). See also National Center for State Courts, *State Court Statistics*, http://www.ncsconline.org/d_research/csp/CSP_Main_Page.html (reporting criminal appellate caseload growth and listing mandatory appellate caseload per judge). State appellate caseloads increased 32 percent between 1987 and 2004, while judgeships grew by 25 percent in intermediate appellate courts and remained stable in courts of last resort. Lynn Langton and Thomas H. Cohen, "State Court Organization, 1987–2004," *Bureau of Justice Statistics*, Special Report, NCJ 217996 (October 2007), http://bjs.ojp.usdoj.gov/content/pub/pdf/sco8704.pdf .

37. The study of postconviction challenges by noncapital defendants in Pennsylvania courts of common pleas in 2003, for example, found that most of the Pennsylvania postconviction cases took nearly a year and that one in four took more than eighteen months. The study concluded that "it is not unusual to find [postconviction] cases that have been pending for two, three, or even four years." About 80 percent of these cases are then appealed. Donald J. Harris, Kim Nieves, and Thomas M. Place, "Dispatch and Delay: Post Conviction Relief Act Litigation in Non-Capital Cases," *Duquesne Law Review* 41 (2003): 467. Some Pennsylvania judges reportedly granted an evidentiary hearing in "all timely first petitions"; other judges reported granting them in "half the cases or less." Fewer than 0.5 percent of federal habeas cases receive an evidentiary hearing. King et al., "Habeas Study," 36.

38. See Nancy J. King, "Regulating Settlement: What Is Left of the Rule

of Law in the Criminal Process?," *DePaul Law Review* 56 (2007): 389. Not all of these waivers will be enforced in every jurisdiction. See Alan Ellis and Todd Bussert, "Stemming the Tide of Postconviction Waivers," *Criminal Justice* 28 (Spring 2010): 30 (reporting that ethics bodies in five of the six jurisdictions that have considered the question have issued opinions excluding ineffective assistance of counsel claims from the scope of permissible postconviction waivers).

39. *Tyler v. Cain*, 533 U.S. 656 (2001).

40. *Wainwright v. Sykes*, 433 U.S. 72 (1977).

41. *Ford v. Georgia*, 498 U.S. 311 (1991). The Supreme Court continues to clarify what this means. See *Beard v. Kindler*, 130 S. Ct. 612 (2009).

42. *Edwards v. Carpenter*, 529 U.S. 446 (2000); *Sawyer v. Whitley*, 505 U.S. 333 (1992); *Dretke v. Haley*, 541 U.S. 386 (2004). The role of innocence in habeas review is discussed in more detail in chapters 5 and 8.

43. *Teague v. Lane*, 489 U.S. 288 (1989); 28 U.S.C. § 2254(d).

44. The 2007 study estimated whether at least one claim was addressed on the merits in two different ways, each relying on separate variables that after coding had differing degrees of missing values. The most reliable estimate is bounded by the two separate estimates: no merits reached in at least 42 percent and as many as 58 percent of noncapital cases. See King et al., "Habeas Study," 45, 56.

45. Of noncapital cases, those with defaulted claims took up to 17 percent longer than those with no defaulted claims, controlling for other factors. Ibid., 74, 84–85.

46. Ibid., 28. Although ineffective assistance of counsel was raised in half of all noncapital cases, the default defense was expressly rejected by the court in only thirty-six cases. The three most common reasons for rejecting the defense were judicial economy, the inadequacy of the state rule, and the absence of default (the defendant did raise the issue or was not required to). Ibid., 48.

47. Ibid., 36.

48. Ibid., 43.

49. King et al., "Habeas Study," 52. This figure represents the number of randomly sampled cases filed in 2003 and 2004 in the study sample that had terminated (other than transfer) as of October 2006, when the study's coding was closed and analysis begun. The study reports that the docket sheets of the 198 cases that had not yet terminated in October 2006 and were still pending were rechecked in June 2007. Only sixty-nine of the 198 had terminated, and of those, only one had ended in a grant. Recalculating the grant rate using this information, it rises only slightly from 0.35 percent (seven of 1,986) to (0.39 percent).

50. Over three and a half million felony cases are filed each year in state courts, approximately one for every one hundred adults. An estimated four times that many misdemeanor cases are filed in state court each year. See National Center for State Courts, *2007 State Court Statistics*.

51. Anup Malani, "Habeas Settlements," *Virginia Law Review* 92 (2006): 1, 8–9, 19.

52. It is conceivable that a negotiated reduction in sentence might be considered by a state to be a reasonable trade for saved litigation costs, even though success is nearly certain, but most prisoners challenging their sentences also challenge their convictions.

53. These figures do not appear in the report and were generated by additional analysis of the data.

54. See Report of the Judicial Conference of the United States, Annual Report of the Director of the Administrative Office of the United States Courts (September 1950), 142–43, Table C2 (reporting 560 federal question habeas cases out of 54,622 civil cases); Report of the Judicial Conference of the United States, Annual Report of the Director of the Administrative Office of the United States Courts (September 1964), 218–19, Table C2 (reporting 3,531 out of 66,930).

55. These figures are available on the Web page of the Administrative Office of the United States Courts, http://www.uscourts.gov/Statistics/Judicial Business/JudicialBusiness.aspx?doc=/uscourts/Statistics/JudicialBusiness/2009/ appendices/C03Sep09.pdf . Heavy habeas caseloads are reported in the Western District of Michigan, the Southern District of Indiana, the Northern District of Florida, and the Northern District of Texas, for example.

56. *Brown v. Allen*, 344 U.S. 443, 537 (1953) (Jackson, J., concurring in the result). As Professor Larry Yackle has observed, this famous line was coined when William Rehnquist was clerking for Justice Jackson. Larry W. Yackle, "The Habeas Hagioscope," *Southern California Law Review 66* (1993): 2331.

57. Judicially imposed restrictions are discussed in chapter 3 and include *Ross v. Moffitt*, 417 U.S. 600 (1974), and *Murray v. Giarratano*, 492 U.S. 1 (1989), where the Court held that the defendant had no constitutional right to counsel; *Wainwright v. Sykes*, 433 U.S. 72 (1977), and *Coleman v. Thompson*, 477 U.S. 478 (1986), where the Court banned the review of almost all claims a petitioner or his lawyer failed to raise on time in state court; *Teague v. Lane*, 489 U.S. 288 (1989), where the Court mandated the dismissal of almost any claim based on a rule that the Court itself had not recognized before the state made its decision; *Brecht v. Abrahamson*, 507 U.S. 619 (1993), permitting federal courts to deny relief for a proven constitutional violation even when there is a reasonable doubt that it may have influenced the decision to convict or sentence; and *Stone v. Powell*, 428 U.S. 465 (1976), barring federal habeas review of Fourth Amendment claims. For critics, see, for example, Yackle, "The Habeas Hagioscope," 2423–29; Steven Semeraro, "Enforcing Fourth Amendment Rights through Federal Habeas Corpus," *Rutgers Law Review* 58 (2006): 983, calling for overruling of *Stone*.

58. See, for example, Bryan Stevenson, "Confronting Mass Imprisonment and Restoring Fairness to Collateral Review of Criminal Cases," *Harvard. Civil*

Rights–Civil Liberties Law Review 41 (2006): 339, 360; Kenneth Williams, "The Antiterrorism and Effective Death Penalty Act: What's Wrong with It and How to Fix It," *Connecticut Law Review* 33 (2001): 919; John H. Blume, "AEDPA: The 'Hype' and the 'Bite,'" *Cornell Law Review* 91 (2006): 259; Jordan Steiker, "Restructuring Post-Conviction Review of Federal Constitutional Claims Raised by State Prisoners: Confronting the New Face of Excessive Proceduralism," *University Chicago Legal Forum* 1998 (1998): 315.

59. See, for example, Donald A. Dripps, "Ineffective Litigation of Ineffective Assistance Claims: Some Uncomfortable Reflections on *Massaro v. United States*," *Brandeis Law Journal* 42 (2004): 793, 801–802; Stevenson, "Confronting Mass Imprisonment," 359.

Chapter Five

1. William J. Brennan, Jr., "Federal Habeas Corpus and State Prisoners: An Exercise in Federalism," *Utah Law Review* 7 (1961): 423, 439–40.

2. Indeed, in some states, federal constitutional rules are applied even more broadly by state courts than they are by federal courts. See, e.g., *Danforth v. Minnesota*, 552 U.S. 264 (2008) (state courts may remedy violations of "new rules" even though federal habeas courts may not). Constitutional criminal procedure did not become a separate course in law school until the mid-1960s. Since then, lawyers learned that "modern" criminal procedure, as the first textbook in the field termed it in 1965, was no longer a matter of individual state law but was increasingly national in scope, defined by federal constitutional rules that bound both federal and state courts. See Yale Kamisar, "A Look Back on a Half Century of Teaching, Writing, and Speaking about Criminal Law and Criminal Procedure," *Ohio State Journal of Criminal Law* 2 (2004): 69.

3. One frequent critique is the lack of counsel in state postconviction proceedings. See sources cited in chapter 4, in note 59. See also Eric M. Freedman, "*Giarratano* Is a Scarecrow: The Right to Counsel in State Capital Postconviction Proceedings," *Cornell Law Review* 91 (2006): 1079.

4. See the sources collected in note 45, chapter 3.

5. Again, both Justice Brennan and Professor Bator recognized that the Court's expansive federal habeas review in state cases was, ideally, a temporary stopgap. Bator observed, "There must soon come a time in this field when it will be felt that the great battles have been won, that we should return from molar to molecular motion. . . . [W]e should be wary about constructing a remedial system premised on unceasing and revolutionary change." Paul M. Bator, "Finality in Criminal Law and Federal Habeas Corpus for State Prisoners," *Harvard Law Review* 76 (1963): 524.

6. *In re McDonald*, 489 U.S. 180, 184 (1989).

7. Bator, "Finality in Criminal Law," 441, 521–27 (terming this a "bedrock proposition").

8. For more on this point, see Joseph L. Hoffmann and Nancy J. King, "Rethinking the Federal Role in State Criminal Justice," *New York University Law Review* 84 (2009): 791, 836–37, 842. See also chapter 4 at notes 14–15.

9. The "due diligence" language refers to diligence by the petitioner, not his lawyer. In addition, the proposal would limit habeas review only for state criminal cases and would not affect habeas review of petitions challenging detention by state authorities pursuant to other kinds of state court judgment.

10. See *Teague v. Lane*, 489 U.S. 288 (1989).

11. These cases are discussed in chapters 7 and 8.

12. Such sentencing factors are those that are required in order to render the defendant legally eligible for a more severe sentence. See *Booker v. United States*, 542 U.S. 220 (2005); *Blakely v. Washington*, 542 U.S. 296, 313 (2004) ("every defendant has the *right* to insist that the prosecutor prove to a jury all facts legally essential to the punishment"); *Ring v. Arizona*, 536 U.S. 584, 602 (2002) ("If a State makes an increase in a defendant's authorized punishment contingent on the finding of a fact, that fact—no matter how the State labels it—must be found by a jury beyond a reasonable doubt."); *Apprendi v. New Jersey*, 530 U.S. 466 (2000). The *Apprendi* doctrine has spawned a lengthy series of Supreme Court decisions, as well as a massive amount of litigation in the lower federal and state courts. In order that such *Apprendi* claims not swamp the habeas courts, we would limit the jurisdiction of the habeas courts to reviewing only those claims of factual innocence that relate to sentencing factors that have been identified by the Supreme Court as within the *Apprendi* doctrine and are therefore functionally equivalent to elements of a crime.

13. See Brandon Garrett, "Judging Innocence," *Columbia Law Review* 108 (2008): 55.

14. See, for example, *McCleskey v. Zant*, 499 U.S. 467 (1991); *Smith v. Murray*, 477 U.S. 527 (1986); *Murray v. Carrier*, 477 U.S. 478 (1986); *Kuhlmann v. Wilson*, 477 U.S. 436 (1986).

15. *Kuhlmann*, 477 U.S. at 455 n. 17.

16. *Murray*, 477 U.S. at 496.

17. *House v. Bell*, 547 U.S. 518 (2006). For a full account of the *House* litigation, see Joseph L. Hoffmann, "*House v. Bell* and the Death of Innocence," in John H. Blume and Jordan M. Steiker, *Death Penalty Stories* (St. Paul, MN: West Publishing Co., 2009).

18. In addition, state prisoners who can demonstrate that they were convicted at trial despite legally insufficient evidence of their guilt have long been entitled to relief, but the 2007 study found that even though this claim is raised in nearly one in five petitions, it, like other claims, rarely succeeds.

19. This aspect of our proposal is similar to one made four decades ago by

Judge Henry J. Friendly, in his article "Is Innocence Irrelevant? Collateral Attack on Criminal Judgments," *University of Chicago Law Review* 38 (1970): 142. This category would also include a showing of "innocence" with respect to the facts legally necessary to impose the petitioner's sentence, if those facts have been held to be the functional equivalent of elements of an enhanced crime. See *Apprendi*, 530 U.S. 466, and note 12. Note that, by definition, all petitioners who qualify for habeas review under the first part of our proposal would also satisfy the current Supreme Court standard for the miscarriage-of-justice exception. Therefore, although such persons will still need to exhaust their state remedies, they will no longer be subject to the restrictions imposed by the "state procedural default" doctrine and other habeas procedural bars.

20. *Herrera v. Collins*, 506 U.S. 390 (1993).

21. *Herrera*, 506 U.S. at 417.

22. Ibid.

23. Ibid., 415.

24. The two most recent Supreme Court innocence cases are *House v. Bell*, 547 U.S. 518 (2006) (holding that petitioner was entitled to litigate his ineffective-assistance claim in habeas, despite his earlier procedural default, under the "fundamental miscarriage of justice" exception), and *District Attorney's Office for the Third Judicial District v. Osborne*, 129 S. Ct. 2308 (2009) (holding that, given the procedural circumstances of the particular case and relevant Alaska state law, petitioner had no federal constitutional right to seek or obtain post-trial DNA testing of evidence that might establish his innocence). In both *House* and *Osborne*, the Court reiterated its *Herrera* stance, emphasizing that it still remains an open question whether bare-innocence claims implicate anything in the Constitution.

In May 2010, the Court granted certiorari in yet another case, this one involving Texas death row inmate Hank Skinner, which might provide an opportunity to address the bare-innocence issue. *Skinner v. Switzer*, 130 S. Ct. 3323 (2010). The certiorari grant, however, appeared to be limited to a subsidiary procedural issue—namely, whether a request for post-trial DNA testing (whether or not federally cognizable) must be filed in habeas corpus or by means of a Section 1983 civil rights lawsuit.

25. Perhaps the closest the Supreme Court has yet come to recognizing such a constitutional right was the cursory August 2009 order (accompanied by a concurring opinion of three Justices and a dissenting opinion of two Justices) transferring to a federal district court "for hearing and determination" the habeas petition of Georgia death row inmate Troy Anthony Davis. Davis had filed his habeas petition directly in the Court, seeking issuance of an "original writ" under Section 2241 on the grounds of factual innocence. Davis was the first such original writ habeas petitioner to obtain any kind of positive decision from the Court in more than five decades.

In the *Davis* order, the Court commanded that "[t]he District Court should receive testimony and make findings of fact as to whether evidence that could not have been obtained at the time of trial clearly establishes petitioner's innocence." The three-justice concurrence added

> Even if the court finds that §2254(d)(1) applies in full, it is arguably unconstitutional to the extent it bars relief for a death row inmate who has established his innocence. Alternatively, the court may find in such a case that the statute's text is satisfied, because decisions of this Court clearly support the proposition that it "would be an atrocious violation of our Constitution and the principles upon which it is based" to execute an innocent person.

Justice Scalia, joined by Justice Thomas, objected: "If this Court thinks it possible that capital convictions obtained in full compliance with law can never be final, but are always subject to being set aside by federal courts for the reason of 'actual innocence,' it should set this case on our own docket so that we can (if necessary) resolve that question." See *In re Troy Anthony Davis*, 130 S. Ct. 1 (2009).

On remand, the district court held an evidentiary hearing, then ruled that: (1) "the execution of those who can make a truly persuasive demonstration of innocence" would violate the Eighth Amendment; (2) such a claim requires a showing by "clear and convincing evidence" that no reasonable juror would have voted to convict; and (3) Davis's new evidence "casts some additional, minimal doubt on his conviction, [but] is largely smoke and mirrors," and thus Davis "is not innocent." In re Davis, 2010 WL 3385081 (S. D. Ga. August 24, 2010) (denying petition). Presumably the case will return to the Supreme Court, presenting another opportunity to decide whether bare-innocence claims are cognizable. See also chapter 8, at note 27.

26. But compare Jordan Steiker, "Innocence and Federal Habeas," *UCLA Law Review* 41 (1993): 303, 380, where Professor Steiker argues that "[e]ven if post-conviction review of new evidence of innocence is not constitutionally required, the Court should authorize habeas review of bare-innocence claims consistent with its federal common-law approach to the habeas statute." Congressional authority, if it indeed does exist, would likely have to be found in Section 5 of the Fourteenth Amendment, which empowers Congress to enact "appropriate" federal legislation to enforce the remainder of the amendment's provisions— including the Due Process Clause.

27. The standard we have suggested mirrors the standard already used by the Supreme Court to decide whether a habeas petitioner qualifies for the "fundamental miscarriage of justice" exception to various habeas restrictions. The Court has also indicated, in *House v. Bell*, that whatever standard it might adopt

for bare-innocence claims would be at least as stringent as the standard for the "fundamental miscarriage of justice" exception. Thus, any habeas petitioner who qualifies for relief under the yet to be determined standard for bare-innocence claims would also, by definition, meet the standard of "clear and convincing" new evidence of factual innocence as contained in the first part of our proposal. Such a petitioner would therefore qualify for habeas review and relief under our proposal.

28. See George C. Thomas III, *The Supreme Court on Trial: How the American Justice System Sacrifices Innocent Defendants* (Ann Arbor, MI: University of Michigan Press, 2008), 219–22; Christine C. Mumma, "The North Carolina Actual Innocence Commission: Uncommon Perspectives Joined by a Common Cause," *Drake Law Review* 52 (2004): 647; Brandon L. Garrett, "Claiming Innocence," *Minnesota Law Review* 92 (2008): 1629, 1714.

29. In the recent *Osborne* decision, the Supreme Court declined to find that the limits on postconviction access to DNA testing under Alaska state law violated federal constitutional law. *Osborne*, 129 S. Ct. 2308, 2320–23. Access statutes are collected in the concurring opinion in *Osborne*. Ibid., 2326.

30. We freely acknowledge that, even if the Court (as we suggest) were to recognize bare-innocence claims as constitutional in nature, and thus cognizable in habeas, difficult questions would remain. For example, should such claims be limited to the special situation of capital cases, or should all incarcerated prisoners be allowed to file such claims? As we will discuss later in chapter 7, the Court has long indicated that "death is different," in terms of the Eighth Amendment's constitutional requirements. A decision based on the Eighth Amendment (as opposed to the Due Process Clause) might allow the Court to limit the impact to capital cases only. But see *Graham v. Florida*, 130 S. Ct. 2011 (2010) (extending a prior Eighth Amendment ruling, that the death penalty cannot be imposed against juvenile murderers, to also cover juveniles sentenced to life imprisonment without possibility of parole). In chapters 7 and 8, we explain why we believe that in terms of habeas law and policy death is indeed "different," and we present a proposal for habeas review of capital cases that differs significantly from what we outline in the current chapter.

Perhaps even more vexing is the traditional requirement that a petitioner's evidence of innocence must be "newly discovered." One might reasonably ask why it should matter if the evidence was or was not newly discovered, as that legal term of art is commonly understood, if the evidence establishes that the petitioner is likely innocent and thus wrongly convicted and sentenced. On the one hand, it would seem that the criminal law should not be a mere sporting contest in which a defendant might end up spending the rest of his life in prison, or even be executed, because of a strategic blunder that resulted in compelling evidence of his innocence never being presented at trial. On the other hand, if the evidence need not be newly discovered, might defendants (or their lawyers) decide to roll the dice at trial, hoping that the prosecution's case will fail on its own accord, and knowing that, if found guilty, the defendant will get a second bite at the apple?

This issue arose in the *Osborne* case, and it lurks in the Texas capital case of Hank Skinner, in which the Supreme Court recently granted certiorari. *Skinner v. Switzer*, 130 S. Ct. 3323 (2010). Skinner's trial lawyer never requested DNA testing of certain physical evidence from the murder scene, because he was not sure what the results would be and therefore did not want to take the risk of a positive DNA match. The prosecution likewise declined to test the same evidence before trial. Skinner was convicted and sentenced to death. Now Skinner wants to have the evidence tested for his DNA, presumably because he has little or nothing left to lose. Brandy Grissom, "U.S. Supreme Court Will Hear Hank Skinner Case," *Texas Tribune* (May 25, 2010), http://www.texastribune .org/texas-dept-criminal-justice/hank-skinner/us-supreme-court-will-hear-hank-skinner-case/.

31. 428 U.S. 465 (1976). Because our proposal preserves review for state petitioners who raise certain retroactively applicable claims, claims of innocence, and claims in capital cases, it would not go as far one offered by Senator Jon Kyl in the 104th Congress. That proposal stated, "Notwithstanding any other provision of law, an application for a writ of habeas corpus in behalf of a person in custody pursuant to a judgment or order of a State court shall not be entertained by a court of the United States unless the remedies in the courts of the State are inadequate or ineffective to test the legality of the person's detention." For a description and defense of Senator Kyl's proposal, arguing that it is consistent with the Suspension Clause, see Michael O'Neill, "On Reforming the Federal Writ of Habeas Corpus," *Seton Hall Law Review* 26 (1996) 1493, 1529–31.

32. King et al., "Habeas Study," 26.

33. This is somewhat similar to the "no full and fair opportunity" escape valve that the Court created in *Stone v. Powell*, 428 U.S. 465 (1976).

34. Hoffmann and King, "Rethinking the Federal Role."

35. *Strickland v. Washington*, 466 U.S. 668 (1984).

36. For a comprehensive treatment of this problem, see Eve Brensike Primus, "Structural Reform in Criminal Defense: Relocating Ineffective Assistance of Counsel Claims," *Cornell Law Rev*iew 92 (2007): 679, 693–94, 706–10.

37. Hoffmann and King, "Rethinking the Federal Role," 823–28.

38. See Primus, "Structural Reform in Criminal Defense," 679 (arguing that litigation of ineffective assistance claims must be shifted to direct appeal stage).

39. Because this book is about habeas corpus and not about ongoing deficiencies in defense representation, we are reluctant to make the proposed new federal initiative to reform state indigent defense representation an explicit part of our habeas proposal. On the merits, however, we have argued that such a new federal initiative is sorely needed. And we would wholeheartedly support efforts

to connect the two as part of a potentially necessary political maneuver designed to secure passage of both proposals in Congress. Hoffmann and King, "Rethinking the Federal Role."

40. Daniel J. Meltzer, "Habeas Corpus Jurisdiction: The Limits of Models," *Southern California Law Review* 66 (1993): 2507, 2526–27.

41. U.S. Const. art. I, § 9, cl. 2.

42. See Jordan Steiker, "Incorporating the Suspension Clause: Is There a Constitutional Right to Federal Habeas Corpus for State Prisoners?" *Michigan Law Review* 92 (1994): 862, 868.

43. For example, the Court has held that significant procedural restrictions, such as the limits of the Antiterrorism and Effective Death Penalty Act of 1996 (AEDPA) on successive petitions, can be imposed without violating the Suspension Clause. *Felker v. Turpin*, 518 U.S. 651, 664 (1996) (upholding AEDPA's restrictions on successive petitions). The Court itself curtailed federal habeas review in *Stone v. Powell*, barring federal habeas review of Fourth Amendment claims where petitioner had "opportunity for full and fair litigation" of claim in state court. *Stone*, 428 U.S. at 494. Justice Brennan's lead dissent argued, without mentioning the Suspension Clause, that the restriction should have been left to Congress, *Stone*, 428 U.S. at 506 (Brennan J., dissenting), implying that the Suspension Clause would not preclude significant congressional reductions in the substantive scope of habeas.

44. *Boumediene v. Bush*, 128 S. Ct. 2229, 2266 (2008). The Court explained that when a person is detained by executive order without conviction, "The habeas court must have sufficient authority to conduct a meaningful review of both the cause for detention and the Executive's power to detain." Ibid., 2269.

45. Ibid., 2241, 2274–76.

46. Ibid., 2267–71 (asserting that "the necessary scope of habeas review in part depends upon the rigor of any earlier proceedings" and developing examples).

47. Ibid., 2270.

48. Ibid., 2273.

49. We believe that current levels of state judicial review are adequate to provide an overall litigation context in which our proposed restrictions of habeas, together with the few remaining avenues for federal judicial review left open, would pass muster under the Suspension Clause. Although it is difficult to anticipate exactly how the Supreme Court might apply the Clause in such a hypothetical situation, we note that the many significant habeas restrictions that have been applied for more than a dozen years to state criminal cases under AEDPA, have never been successfully challenged under the Suspension Clause. Moreover, we believe that the Suspension Clause analysis in *Boumediene* makes it even less likely that a Suspension Clause challenge to our proposal would be sustained in the litigation context of current state judicial review. With respect to our proposal, the Clause will essentially remain dormant until the Supreme Court needs

to invoke it in response to a future crisis of federalism prompted by the intransigent behavior of a state.

50. Brennan, "An Exercise in Federalism," 439–41.

51. This episode is discussed in James E. Starrs, "The Post-Conviction Hearing Act—1949–1960 and Beyond," *DePaul Law Review* 10 (1960–61): 397, 398. The Court's decision was *Marino v. Ragen*, 332 U.S. 561 (1947). After twenty-two years in prison attempting to navigate the "Illinois procedural labyrinth," Marino, convicted when he was only eighteen years old and unable to speak English, was finally able to establish in state court that he had never pleaded guilty as the record stated but had been sentenced to life imprisonment with only the arresting officer as interpreter and no counsel. Yet the state refused to release him. Not until after the Court received his petition for federal habeas relief and had asked the state for a response did Illinois confess error. *Marino*, 332 U.S. at 564–65 (Rutledge, J., concurring). As Justice Wiley Rutledge explained, "The trouble with Illinois is not that it offers no procedure. It is that it offers too many, and makes them so intricate and ineffective that in practical effect they amount to none."

52. *Felker v. Turpin*, 518 U.S. 651 (1996).

53. *Wainwright v. Sykes*, 433 U.S. 72, 81 (1977) (noting, citing numerous examples, the Court's "historic willingness to overturn or modify its earlier views of the scope of the writ, even where the statutory language authorizing judicial action has remained unchanged . . .").

Chapter Six

1. *Johnson v. Zerbst*, 304 U.S. 458 (1938).

2. *Gideon v. Wainwright*, 372 U.S. 335 (1963).

3. The total number of petitions filed (other than deportation) rose from 318 in fiscal year 1940–41 to 506 in 1947–48, an increase of nearly 60 percent. William H. Speck, "Statistics on Federal Habeas Corpus," *Ohio State Law Journal* 10 (1949): 341. This outpaced the rise in federal prosecutions that had come with stepped-up enforcement of federal criminal law during World War II. See, for example, *Report of the Judicial Conference of the United States, Annual Report of the Director of the Administrative Office of the United States Courts* (1948), 100–101 (noting an increase in prosecutions during the war years, which preceded a decline).

4. Alexander Holtzoff, "Collateral Review of Convictions in Federal Courts," *Boston University Law Review* 25 (1945): 42; *United States v. Hayman*, 342 U.S. 205, 212–13 (1952) (noting that petitions were "[o]ften . . . wholly lacking in merit when compared with the records of the sentencing court . . .").

5. See *Hayman*, 342 U.S. at 214, n. 18; Speck, "Statistics on Federal Habeas Corpus," 350.

6. *Walker v. Johnston*, 312 U.S. 275, 285–86 (1941).

7. *Annual Report of the Director of the Administrative Office of the United States Courts* (September 1943), 12 (also noting that this situation "is inferior to that prevailing in most of the states"). See also Holtzoff, "Collateral Review of Convictions," 52 (explaining that litigants "desiring their trial reported had to make private arrangements with reporters and to compensate them" with the result being that "a large proportion of criminal trials in the Federal courts are not reported"). Although a 1944 act provided for the appointment of official salaried reporters for every district and required the reporting of criminal trials and pleas, as of 1945 many districts continued to lack reporters. See *Report of the Judicial Conference of Senior Circuit Judges, September Session 1945, Annual Report of the Director of the Administrative Office of the United States Courts* (Washington, DC: Government Printing Office, 1945), 29–30 (stating that "during the coming court year all of the district courts will be provided with official reporters"); Act Authorizing the Appointment of Court Reporters, January 20, 1944, ch. 3, Public Law 222, 58 Stat. 5–7, codified at 28 U.S.C. § 753.

8. *Walker*, 312 U.S. 275, 280, 287. See also Holtzoff, "Collateral Review of Convictions," 53 ("It is not infrequent to take the deposition of the trial judge and read it into the evidence.").

9. The report of the Committee appointed by the Chief Justice to study "the entire subject of procedure on applications for habeas corpus in the federal courts" was delivered in 1943, and was then circulated for comment to the entire federal judiciary. See *Report of the Judicial Conference of Senior Circuit Judges September 1947, Annual Report of the Director of the Administrative Office of the United States Courts* (Washington, DC: Government Printing Office, 1947): 17.

10. Louis E. Goodman, "Use and Abuse of the Writ of Habeas Corpus," *Federal Rules Decisions* 7 (1947): 313, 314. See also Rex A. Collings, Jr., "Habeas Corpus for Convicts—Constitutional Right or Legislative Grace?" *California Law Review* 40 (1952): 335, 354, stating that the writ served as "a bid for temporary freedom—a boat ride from Alcatraz to San Francisco—a meal out—a look at the free world."

11. Speck, "Statistics on Federal Habeas Corpus," 358–59; *Report of the Judicial Conference of the United States September 1949, Annual Report of the Director of the Administrative Office of the United States Courts* (Washington, DC: Government Printing Office, 1949): 89. In only one of these cases was any relief granted: a modified sentence. Of the 102 prisoners seeking relief, twenty-nine had counsel and twenty-five received hearings, in twelve of which the prisoner was present. See also Note, "Section 2255 of the Judicial Code: The Threatened

Demise of Habeas Corpus," *Yale Law Journal* 59 (1950): 1183, 1189, n. 30 (explaining that "The Washington district usually disposes of petitions on a show cause hearing, while Georgia always issues the writ to bring the prisoner into court.").

12. *The Report of the Judicial Conference of the United States September 1950, Annual Report of the Director of the Administrative Office of the United States Courts* (Washington, DC: Government Printing Office, 1950): 111–13 (noting that the effect of the new statute in reducing habeas petitions "has not been great").

13. See Note, "Section 2255 of the Judicial Code," 1183; *Hayman v. United States*, 187 F.2d 456 (9th Cir. 1950) (holding that Section 2255 violated the Suspension Clause), *rev'd on other grounds, United States v. Hayman*, 342 U.S. 205 (1952).

14. See *Sanders v. United States*, 373 U.S. 1, 20 (1963). Earlier, in *United States v. Hayman*, 342 U.S. 205 (1952), the Supreme Court avoided a ruling on whether denying a Section 2255 application without the prisoner's physical presence—as the statute clearly contemplated—would violate the Constitution. It held instead that federal district judges possessed the power to order the government to bring an applicant who was imprisoned in another district to a hearing in the district of conviction and should do so whenever there "are substantial issues of fact as to events in which the prisoner participated." It also pointed out that, because habeas review under Section 2241 remained available as a last resort, it was unnecessary to "reach constitutional questions." *Hayman*, 342 U.S. at 222–23. In 1962, the Court again sidestepped the constitutionality of the statute, finding instead that the trial judge had violated Section 2255 when he denied a claim without a hearing and considered only government affidavits. The Court held that the statute required a hearing to examine the prisoner's factual allegations, at least when those allegations were "detailed and specific," "not . . . incredible," "related primarily to purported occurrences outside the courtroom," and could not be conclusively determined by the judge through consultation of the record or "his own personal knowledge or recollection." *Machibroda v. United States*, 368 U.S. 487, 494–96 (1962). The Court in *Machibroda* remanded the case in order to determine whether dispensing with presence was appropriate.

15. *Kaufman v. United States*, 394 U.S. 217, 226 (1969).

16. *Sanders v. United* States, 373 U.S. 1 (1963); *McClesky v. Zant*, 499 U.S. 467, 484 (1991) ("We concluded in *Sanders* . . . that the language in § 2255 'cannot be taken literally,' and construed it to be the 'material equivalent' of the abuse standard [for state prisoners] in § 2244.").

17. *Blackledge v. Allison*, 431 U.S. 63, 74 n. 4 (1977). The flood of challenges to guilty pleas by federal prisoners in habeas and under Section 2255 led the judiciary to propose and Congress to adopt in 1966 an amendment to Rule 11 of the Federal Rules of Criminal Procedure requiring the judge to confirm a litany of waivers.

18. *Jones v. Cunningham*, 371 U.S. 236 (1963).

19. *United States v. Frady*, 456 U.S. 152 (1982); *Davis v. United States*, 411 U.S. 233 (1973). The Court has continued to interpret procedural default rules for each remedy as equivalent. See *Bousley v. United States*, 523 U.S. 614, 623 (1998) (applying to Section 2255 case the procedural default rule from the state case, *Engle v. Isaac*, 456 U.S. 107 (1982), that the futility of raising a claim is no excuse for failing to raise it on time). The Court also adopted a more restrictive "harmless error" standard of review for state prisoner claims, a standard that bars relief for a constitutional error unless the court first finds that that error likely had a substantial influence on the outcome, after first establishing the test in cases reviewing federal convictions. *Brecht v. Abrahamson*, 507 U.S. 619 (1993). See also John H. Blume and Stephen P. Garvey, "Harmless Error in Federal Habeas Corpus after *Brecht v. Abrahamson*," *William and Mary Law Review* 35 (1993): 163.

20. The Court itself has never squarely held that search and seizure claims are equally unavailable under Section 2255. With one exception, courts have assumed for thirty years that the Court's 1976 decision in *Stone v. Powell*, 428 U.S. 465, also modified its 1969 decision in *Kaufman*, 394 U.S. 217, which had held that Section 2255 applicants could raise the same search and seizure claims on collateral review that Section 2254 petitioners were permitted to raise. The exception is the Eighth Circuit, which departed from other circuits that have found that *Stone* governs Section 2255 claims, holding instead that *Stone* did not bar consideration of the constitutionality of a warrant under Section 2255 because the supervisory power of federal appellate courts over district courts is broader than its authority to review state court decisions under Section 2254). *Baranski v. United States*, 515 F.3d 857 (8th Cir. 2008).

21. See, for example, *United States v. Sanchez-Cervantes*, 282 F.3d 664 (9th Cir. 2002).

22. Congress did preserve, with some modifications, one difference that the Court had established in the 1960s. Specifically, a state prisoner can ask the federal habeas court to review a claim denied on its merits in the state courts, while federal prisoners are generally barred from asking a federal judge to review a claim once it has been denied by another federal court on appeal. See 28 U.S.C. § 2254(d); *Davis v. United States*, 417 U.S. 333, 342 (1974) (noting exception allowing reconsideration for intervening change in law).

23. Indeed, the fact that available statistics suggest that Section 2255 applications are granted at a somewhat higher rate than state prisoner claims under Section 2254—notwithstanding that the quality of defense counsel in federal criminal cases generally is conceded to exceed that in state criminal cases— may well reflect this more significant role. Available statistics suggest that up to 5.3 percent of applications under Section 2255 were granted, while petitions under Section 2254 are granted in only one-third of 1 percent of cases filed.

Compare Scalia, U.S. Department of Justice Bureau of Justice Statistics, *Prisoner Petitions in the Federal Courts, 1980–96* (1997), http://www.ojp.usdoj .gov/bjs/pub/pdf/ppfc96.pdf, noting that in 1995, of Section 2255 applications disposed of following judgments by the district courts, 13 percent were decided in favor of the inmate, a "grant rate" of 5.3 percent, with the statistics reviewed in chapter 5.

24. The Court has not yet found any procedural right, other than the one recognized in *Gideon*, to be sufficiently fundamental to deserve this extraordinary status.

25. These cases are discussed in chapters 7 and 8.

26. For example, *United States v. Morgan*, 230 F.3d 1067, 1070 (8th Cir. 2000) (noting, in dicta, that a claim that a statute is facially unconstitutional falls within the exception for claims that a defendant who pleads guilty may raise for the first time on collateral review).

27. *Davis*, 417 U.S. 333, 346–47 (holding that Section 2255 review is available to prisoner who claimed that a decision subsequent to his conviction established that his induction order was invalid under the Selective Service Act and that he could not be lawfully convicted for failure to comply with that order, noting, "If this contention is well taken, then Davis' conviction and punishment are for an act that the law does not make criminal. There can be no room for doubt that such a circumstance 'inherently results in a complete miscarriage of justice' and 'present[s] exceptional circumstances' that justify collateral relief under § 2255."); *Prince v. United States*, 352 U.S. 322 (1957) (Section 2255 case, interpreting bank robbery act to limit sentence in certain situations to twenty years, remanding for resentencing).

28. *United States v. Santos*, 128 S. Ct. 2020 (2008). See also *United States v. Santos*, 342 F.Supp.2d 781 (N.D. Ind. 2004) (explaining why Section 2255 relief is appropriate for new, narrowing constructions of criminal statutes), affirmed *United States v. Santos*, 461 F.3d 886 (7th Cir. 2006), affirmed, 128 S. Ct. 2020 (2008). The Court of Appeals decision affirming the district court's decision in *Santos* had addressed only the meaning of the underlying criminal statute. It declined to question the district court's decision that Section 2255 provides relief if the proper meaning of the statute was narrower than the interpretation that supported the conviction, noting that the "government here presents no argument to the contrary." 461 F.3d at 891.

29. See *Magnuson v. United States*, 861 F.2d 166, 169 (7th Cir. 1988) (applying Supreme Court's decision in *McNally v. United States*, 483 U.S. 350 (1987), which held that the mail fraud statute does not punish schemes to defraud the public of an intangible right to honest government, finding, "Because the indictment, the evidence and the court's instructions to the jury permitted conviction under the mail fraud statute for [the theory rejected in *McNally*] the district court was cor-

rect in vacating the sentences of the defendants and ordering their release from custody."); *Ingber v. Enzor*, 841 F.2d 450, 454–55 (2d Cir. 1988) (granting Section 2255 relief to prisoner convicted under a construction of statute later rejected by the Supreme Court, noting that *McNally* overruled "years of circuit precedent" and reversed a "steady expansion" of the statute that had "continued for more than a decade, unaddressed by the Supreme Court."); *United States. v. Shelton*, 848 F.2d 1485, 1490 (10th Cir. 1988) (noting that the Court's decision in *McNally* had been described as "a total surprise" and "a 'wholly unexpected explication of the law of mail fraud'" and was "a departure from the law of every court of appeals"); *United States v. Davies*, 394 F.3d 182 (3d Cir. 2005) (granting relief when defendant demonstrated that he was innocent under Court's construction of arson statute); *United States v. Ryan*, 227 F.3d 1058 (8th Cir. 2000) (same). Similar applications will be generated by the Court's 2010 decision rejecting a broad interpretation of the mail fraud statute that lower courts had been applying for years. *Skilling v. United States*, 130 S. Ct. 2896 (2010).

30. See *Report of Firearms Policy Team, Sentencing for the Possession or Use of Firearms during a Crime* (January 2000), 5, http://www.ussc.gov/publicat/firearms.PDF.

31. See Scalia, *Prisoner Petitions* (attributing the increase in petitions to vacate the sentence to *Bailey v. United States*, 516 U.S. 137 (1995), which "limited the applicability of 18 U.S.C. § 924(e) to those cases where the defendant actually used the weapon while committing the offense rather than merely possessing it . . ."). See also *Bousely*, 523 U.S. at 620–21 (stating "decisions of this Court holding that a substantive federal criminal statute does not reach certain conduct, like decisions placing conduct 'beyond the power of the criminal lawmaking authority to proscribe,' . . . necessarily carry a significant risk that a defendant stands convicted of 'an act that the law does not make criminal.' . . . Accordingly, it would be inconsistent with the doctrinal underpinnings of habeas review to preclude petitioner from relying on our decision in *Bailey* in support of his claim that his guilty plea was constitutionally invalid.").

The *Bailey* decision, which was unanimous, was later overturned by a Congressional amendment to the relevant statute. The amended statute now prohibits the mere possession of a firearm in connection with a drug crime.

32. Arguably, federal defendants require access to Section 2255 review for another type of claim—violations of rights of procedure guaranteed by federal statute rather than by the Constitution. The Court has recognized that Section 2255 could provide judicial review of procedural protections established by federal statute as well as by the Constitution. But its description of the type of statutory violation cognizable in Section 2255 is so extreme that in Justice Scalia's words it has proved to be, essentially, a "null set." See *Reed v. Farley*, 512 U.S. 339, 357 (1994) (Scalia, J., concurring) ("The class of procedural rights that are

not guaranteed by the Constitution . . . but that nonetheless are inherently necessary to avoid 'a complete miscarriage of justice,' or numbered among 'the rudimentary demands of fair procedure,' is no doubt a small one, if it is indeed not a null set."). See also *Hill v. United States*, 368 U.S. 424, 428 (1962) (holding that relief under Section 2255 is available for a nonconstitutional error only if it is "a fundamental defect which inherently results in a complete miscarriage of justice" and "present[s] 'exceptional circumstances where the need for the remedy afforded by the writ of habeas corpus is apparent'"). In addition, claims that statutory procedures have been violated are generally available on appeal and, if expanded subsequent to a prisoner's appeal, are even less likely to be applied retroactively than constitutional rules of procedure.

33. *United States v. Tucker*, 404 U.S. 443 (1972); *Johnson v. United States*, 544 U.S. 295 (2005).

34. See *Massaro v. United States*, 538 U.S. 500 (2003); *United States v. Cronic*, 466 U.S. 648 (1984); *Rodriguez v. United States*, 395 U.S. 327 (1969). Other non-record claims include misconduct by prosecutors: *United States v. Bagley*, 473 U.S. 667 (1985); *United States v. Henry*, 447 U.S. 264 (1980); claims of coerced or invalid pleas: *Fontaine v. United States*, 411 U.S. 213 (1973); *Brady v. United States*, 397 U.S. 742 (1970); *Machibroda*, 368 U.S. 487; *Sanders*, 373 U.S. 1; and claims based on events following sentencing. See *United States v. Behrens*, 375 U.S. 162 (1963). The text that follows this note is drawn from *United States v. Smith*, 2008 WL 906526 (S.D. Miss. March 31, 2008).

35. There are some differences in limitations on successive attempts to obtain relief under Sections 2254 and 2255. The state prisoner but not the federal prisoner must show clear and convincing evidence of innocence of the offense even when seeking relief under a new retroactively applicable rule of procedure, but since no rules of procedure have been applied retroactively since *Gideon*, and would not be unless fundamental to underlying accuracy, this statutory difference is inconsequential for prisoners serving noncapital sentences. The statutes arguably give federal prisoners a slightly larger window of opportunity to file successive applications than state prisoners. A federal prisoner's clear and convincing evidence that no reasonable fact finder would have convicted him need only be "newly discovered," while a state prisoner's clear and convincing evidence must not have been discoverable previously through the exercise of due diligence and must establish that "but for the constitutional violation" no reasonable fact finder would have convicted him. Even if the difference between "newly discovered" and "undiscoverable earlier" proves insignificant, the "but for" language suggests that new claims unrelated to the fact finder's decision (for example, jury discrimination claims) could conceivably be considered in successive applications under Section 2255 but not in successive petitions under Section 2254. To the extent Congress has already managed to preserve for federal

prisoners a fuller opportunity for collateral review in federal court than it has retained for state prisoners, we approve.

36. Successive petitions were allowed to raise a new claim so long as it was not an abuse of the writ. See note 16.

37. For example, in *United States v. Prevatte*, 300 F.3d 792, 800 (7th Cir. 2002), the court explained,

> Mr. Prevatte has not had an opportunity to obtain judicial correction of a potential fundamental defect in his conviction; [the Supreme Court's decision narrowly construing the arson statute] was handed down after he had filed his initial § 2255 motion. Furthermore, as demonstrated above, [that] decision is "a change that eludes the permission in section 2255 for successive motions," . . . because, like *Bailey*, it involves statutory, not constitutional, interpretation.

See also *Reyes-Requena v. United States*, 243 F.3d 893 (5th Cir. 2001); *In re Dorsainvil*, 119 F.3d 245 (3d Cir. 1997); *In re Smith*, 285 F.3d 6, 7 (D.C. Cir. 2002) (stating that "There is no question that Smith's § 924(c) conviction is no longer valid," after *Bailey*, and concluding that although Section 2255 review is not available, Smith should file a petition under Section 2241).

38. The text of the Antiterrorism and Effective Death Penalty Act of 1996 presently bars review of a claim raised in a second application that the prisoner is innocent of his *sentence*, even if, for example, after his first application under Section 2255, a prior conviction used to enhance his sentence was vacated. See, for example, *Unthank v. Jett*, 549 F.3d 534 (7th Cir. 2008). If the sentence the prisoner received was greater than the maximum he could have received under the law without the prior conviction, however, he has essentially been convicted of a greater offense he did not commit and should have access to judicial review.

Chapter Seven

1. The 1982 execution in California of Robert Alton Harris was an extreme but noteworthy example of last-minute frenzy in capital habeas litigation. A few days before Harris's scheduled execution, a federal district judge issued a ten-day temporary restraining order to allow for consideration of the constitutionality of the gas chamber. A panel of the Ninth Circuit then decided, by a 2-1 vote, to issue a "writ of mandate" overturning the restraining order and allowing the execution to proceed. Over the next two days, other judges and panels of the Ninth Circuit issued four more stays of execution; the U.S. Supreme Court vacated each one. At last, the Court added the following extraordinary sentence

to its order: "No further stays of Robert Alton Harris' execution shall be entered by the federal courts except upon order of this Court." *Vasquez v. Harris*, 503 U.S. 1000 (1992). Harris was executed on April 21, 1992. For more on the Harris execution, see Henry Weinstein, "Appeals Judge Responds to Wilson's Criticism of 'Macabre Legal Circus'—Courts: Jurist says governor should look at 'highly extraordinary' order by two federal judges that allowed Harris' execution to proceed," *Los Angeles Times*, April 24, 1992, http://articles.latimes.com/1992-04-24/news/mn-1093_1_court-judges?pg=1; Evan Caminker and Erwin Chemerinsky, "The Lawless Execution of Robert Alton Harris, *Yale Law Journal* 102 (1992): 225.

2. *The Antiterrorism and Effective Death Penalty Act of 1996*, Public Law 104-132, *U.S. Statutes at Large* 110 (1996): 1214.

3. See Alex Kozinski and Sean Gallagher, "Death: The Ultimate Run-on Sentence," *Case Western Law Review* 46 (1995): 1 (documenting processing time in capital cases in California, concluding that thirty defendants have been on death row more than twenty-five years, 119 more than twenty years, 240 more than fifteen years, 408 more than ten years, and 575 more than five years).

4. See, for example, California Commission for the Fair Administration of Justice, Report and Recommendations on the Administration of the Death Penalty in California, 10 (June 30, 2008), http://www.ccfaj.org/rr-dp-official.html (estimating cost to California of death penalty at $137 million a year); Kozinski and Gallagher, "Death: The Ultimate Run-on Sentence" (estimating in 1995 the cost to California of the death penalty at $90 million a year and the cost of housing a prisoner on death row as $90,000 more per year than the cost of housing a prisoner in the general prison population, for a total of $60 million more per year spent on death row than on general prison population); Ed Barnes, "Just or Not, Cost of Death Penalty Is a Killer for State Budgets, *FOXNews.com*, March 27, 2010, http://www.foxnews.com/us/2010/03/27/just-cost-death-penalty-killer-state-budgets/ (reporting studies from several states).

5. See, for example, *Strickland v. Washington*, 466 U.S. 668 (1984) (ineffective assistance of counsel); *Brady v. Maryland*, 373 U.S. 83 (1963) (prosecutorial disclosure); *Miller-El v. Dretke*, 544 U.S. 660 (2005) (race discrimination in jury selection).

6. See Corrinna Barrett Lain, "Deciding Death," *Duke Law Journal* (2007): 1, 13–16 (noting that six states abolished the death penalty and that in 1970 public support for capital punishment dipped to 49 percent and detailing other indications that the nation was moving toward abolishing the death penalty on its own).

7. See Joseph L. Hoffmann, "On the Perils of Line-Drawing: Juveniles and the Death Penalty," *Hastings Law Journal* 40 (1989): 229, 245–47 (discussing 1957 abolition of capital punishment in Great Britain).

8. *Furman v. Georgia*, 408 U.S. 238 (1972).

9. *Gregg v. Georgia*, 428 U.S. 153 (1976); *Proffitt v. Florida*, 428 U.S. 242 (1976); *Jurek v. Texas*, 428 U.S. 262 (1976).

10. Today, all states are required, as a matter of federal constitutional law, to give juries a prominent role in capital sentencing; the Supreme Court has held that, under the Sixth Amendment's right to jury trial as well as the Due Process Clause, all facts that are legally required to impose the death sentence must be found by a jury beyond a reasonable doubt, at either the guilt or the sentencing phase of the capital trial. *Ring v. Arizona*, 536 U.S. 584 (2002). Most states now choose to place the entire decision about whether or not to impose the death penalty into the collective hands of the jury.

11. *Lockett v. Ohio*, 438 U.S. 586 (1978) (plurality opinion).

12. *Godfrey v. Georgia*, 446 U.S. 420 (1980).

13. See Margaret Jane Radin, "Cruel Punishment and Respect for Persons: Super Due Process for Death," *Southern California Law Review* 53 (1980): 1143.

14. Efforts to establish a constitutional procedure for imposition of the death penalty in conformity with the decisions of the Supreme Court began in earnest in the early 1980s. See *Report of the Judicial Conference of the United States*, September 1985, at 81. These efforts culminated in the Violent Crime Control and Law Enforcement Act of 1994, September 13, 1994, Title VI, §§ 60001–26, Public Law 103-322, 108 Stat. 1796, which provided new procedures for capital cases and thereby revived the constitutionality of dozens of moribund federal death penalty statutes.

15. Justice Antonin Scalia is an exception, having written in a recent capital case, "Like other human institutions, courts and juries are not perfect. One cannot have a system of criminal punishment without accepting the possibility that someone will be punished mistakenly. That is a truism, not a revelation. But with regard to the punishment of death in the current American system, that possibility has been reduced to an insignificant minimum." *Kansas v. Marsh*, 548 U.S. 163, 199 (2006) (Scalia, J., concurring).

Justice Harry Blackmun, just before retiring from the Court, expressed essentially the same view, that perfection cannot be achieved in the context of capital punishment. But this led him to a very different conclusion. In a now-famous quote, Blackmun declared, "From this day forward, I no longer shall tinker with the machinery of death." *Callins v. Collins*, 510 U.S.1141, 1145 (Blackmun, J., dissenting from denial of certiorari).

16. Although a majority of the Court believes that the Eighth Amendment's "cruel and unusual punishments" clause contains a "proportionality" component, Justices Scalia and Thomas do not agree. See *Harmelin v. Michigan*, 501 U.S. 957 (1991); *Graham v. Florida*, 130 S. Ct. 2011, 2043–58 (2010) (Thomas, J., dissenting).

17. The Court also has held that the states are not constitutionally required to conduct their own case-by-case proportionality analysis, at least as long as other

safeguards exist to help ensure rational capital sentencing outcomes. *Pulley v. Harris*, 465 U.S. 37 (1984).

18. See *Roper v. Simmons*, 543 U.S. 551 (2005) (juveniles); *Atkins v. Virginia*, 536 U.S 304 (2002) (mentally retarded); *Tison v. Arizona*, 481 U.S. 137 (1987) (felony murder); *Coker v. Georgia*, 433 U.S. 584 (1977) (rape).

19. *Ewing v. California*, 538 U.S. 11 (2003).

20. *Harmelin*, 501 U.S. 957.

21. *Ewing*, 538 U.S. at 31.

22. At the time of the *Atkins* decision, sixteen states had recently abolished the use of the death penalty against the mentally retarded, although twenty other states still allowed for its use; at the time of the *Simmons* decision, five states had recently abolished the use of the death penalty against juveniles, but twenty others still allowed it. See *Simmons*, 543 U.S. at 564–67.

23. *Graham v. Florida*, 130 S. Ct. 2011 (2010).

24. The last previous example was *Solem v. Helm*, 467 U.S. 277 (1983), which technically remains good law but was essentially gutted by the subsequent deferential decisions in *Harmelin* and *Ewing*.

25. In the early years of the development of the Court's modern Eighth Amendment jurisprudence, habeas retroactivity was not governed by a clear rule but instead by a more discretionary approach that allowed the Court to take into account, in each case, not only fairness to defendants but also the potential impact of retroactive application on the administration of criminal justice by the states. See *Linkletter v. Walker*, 381 U.S. 618 (1965).

26. See *Teague v. Lane*, 489 U.S. 288, 311 (1989) (recognizing exception to general rule of nonretroactive application for new constitutional rules that place "certain kinds of primary, private individual conduct beyond the power of the criminal law-making authority to proscribe."). This has been interpreted to include new rules making certain individuals legally ineligible to receive the death penalty.

27. See William J. Stuntz, "The Uneasy Relationship between Criminal Procedure and Criminal Justice," *Yale Law Journal* 107 (1997): 1, 43 ("All this procedural Eighth Amendment law has generated a large number of claims, especially on appeal and habeas corpus, and the claims have been surprisingly successful— for a time, capital murder defendants enjoyed a more than fifty percent success rate in federal habeas corpus litigation."); Donald P. Lay, "The Writ of Habeas Corpus: A Complex Procedure for a Simple Process," *Minnesota Law Review* 77 (1993): 1015, 1044, n. 166 (noting 50–75 percent grant rate for capital habeas petitions). See also James S. Liebman, Jeffrey Fagan, Valerie West, and Jonathan Lloyd, "Capital Attrition: Error Rates in Capital Cases, 1973–1995," *Texas Law Review* 78 (2000): 1839.

28. See Joseph L. Hoffmann, "Is Innocence Sufficient? An Essay on the U.S.

Supreme Court's Continuing Problems with Federal Habeas Corpus and the Death Penalty," *Indiana Law Journal* 68 (1993): 817.

29. *Wainwright v. Sykes*, 433 U.S. 72 (1977).

30. *Fay v. Noia*, 372 U.S. 391 (1963).

31. Rule 9(b) of the Rules Governing Habeas Corpus Proceedings, promulgated in 1976, provides, "A second or successive petition may be dismissed if the judge finds that it fails to allege new or different grounds for relief and the prior determination was on the merits or, if new and different grounds are alleged, the judge finds that the failure of the petitioner to assert those grounds in a prior petition constituted an abuse of the writ." See *McCleskey v. Zant*, 499 U.S. 467 (1991).

32. *Teague v. Lane*, 489 U.S. 288 (1989).

33. See Hoffmann, "Is Innocence Sufficient?," 827 ("[I] n developing these limits on habeas, the Court has been sensitive to the need for an exception that permits case-by-case federal review of the merits of an individual petitioner's conviction or sentence.").

34. Jordan Steiker, "Restructuring Post-Conviction Review of Federal Constitutional Claims Raised by State Prisoners: Confronting the New Face of Excessive Proceduralism," *University of Chicago Legal Forum* 1998 (1998): 315.

35. See Joseph L. Hoffmann, "Substance and Procedure in Capital Cases: Why Federal Habeas Courts Should Review the Merits of Every Death Sentence," *Texas Law Review* 78 (2000): 1774 (the Supreme Court's modern capital habeas jurisprudence "has helped to ensure that capital habeas litigation almost always focuses solely on the procedures by which the defendant was convicted and sentenced rather than on the crucial substantive questions of whether the defendant is in fact guilty and, even if guilty, whether he deserves a death sentence").

36. The first federal execution in the modern era of capital punishment was that of Timothy McVeigh, who planted the bomb that destroyed the Murrah Federal Building in Oklahoma City in 1995.

37. See note 2.

38. Attorney General Holder has proposed withdrawing the regulations proposed in 2008. See *Certification Process for State Capital Counsel Systems: Removal of Final Rule*, 75 Fed. Reg. 29,217 (May 25, 2010). For commentary on the amendments and subsequent regulations, see Betsy Dee Sanders, "The Antiterrorism and Effective Death Penalty Act ('AEDPA'): Understanding the Failures of State Opt-in Mechanisms," *Iowa Law Review* 92 (2007): 1969; Casey Cole Kannenberg, "Wading through the Morass of Modern Federal Habeas Review of State Capital Prisoners' Claims," *Quinnipiac Law Review* 28 (2009): 107.

39. Anti-Drug Abuse Act of 1988, 21 U.S.C.§ 848(e) et seq.

40. See note 14.

Chapter Eight

1. See Joseph L. Hoffmann and William J. Stuntz, "Habeas after the Revolution," *Supreme Court Review* 1993 (1994): 65, 122. Carol S. Steiker and Jordan M. Steiker, "Opening a Window or Building a Wall? The Effect of Eight Amendment Death Penalty Law and Advocacy on Criminal Justice More Broadly," *University of Pennsylvania Journal of Constitutional Law* 11 (2008): 155, 200–204.

2. See Betsy Dee Sanders, "The Antiterrorism and Effective Death Penalty Act ('AEDPA'): Understanding the Failures of State Opt-in Mechanisms," *Iowa Law Review* 92 (2007): 1969.

3. *Lockhart v. McCree*, 476 U.S. 162 (1986).

4. *McCleskey v. Kemp*, 481 U.S. 279 (1987).

5. *Baze v. Rees*, 128 S. Ct. 1520 (2008).

6. For an example of such a prediction, see Richard Lacayo, Anne Constable, and Daniel S. Levy, "Law: Clearing a Path to the Chair," *Time*, May 4, 1987, http://www.time.com/time/magazine/article/0,9171,964240-1,00.html (asserting that *McCleskey* decision "may prove to be [the] final major challenge" to the death penalty).

7. In 2006, about 1,132,290 adults were convicted of felony crimes in state and federal courts. Sean Rosenmerkel, Matthew Durose, and Donald Farole, "Felony Sentences in State Courts, 2006," Bureau of Justice Statistics, Bulletin No. NCJ 226846, December 2009, http://bjs.ojp.usdoj.gov/content/pub/pdf/fssc06st.pdf. The number of persons sentenced to death each year in the United States, during the modern era of capital punishment, has dropped from a high of approximately three hundred per year in the 1990s to 111 in 2008. See Tracy L. Snell, *Capital Punishment, 2008—Statistical Tables* (December 2009, NCJ 228662). In 2009, 248 capital habeas petitions were filed in federal district courts.

8. See American Law Institute (ALI), *Model Penal Code*, Section 210.6 (Proposed Official Draft 1962); Gerard E. Lynch, "Revising the Model Penal Code: Keeping It Real," *Ohio State Journal of Criminal Law* 1 (2003): 219, 232–33 (discussing *Model Penal Code* [MPC] death penalty provision).

On October 23, 2009, the ALI council voted overwhelmingly to accept a resolution withdrawing the MPC's death penalty provision. The resolution adopted at the annual meeting, and accepted by the council, reads as follows: "[F]or reasons stated in Part V of the Council's report to the membership, the Institute withdraws Section 210.6 of the Model Penal Code in light of the current intractable institutional and structural obstacles to ensuring a minimally adequate system for administering capital punishment."

9. See chapter 7, note 15.

10. *Walton v. Arizona*, 497 U.S. 639, 656 (1990) (Scalia, J., concurring in part and concurring in the judgment).

11. *Roper v. Simmons*, 543 U.S. 551 (2005).

12. *Roper*, 543 U.S. at 578. See also *Graham v. Florida*, 130 S. Ct. 2011 (2010).

13. *Atkins v. Virginia*, 536 U.S 304 (2002).

14. See John H. Blume, Sheri Lynn Johnson, and Christopher Seeds, "An Empirical Look at *Atkins v. Virginia* and Its Application in Capital Cases," *Tennessee Law Review* 76 (2009): 625, 628 (reporting that at least 234 of the more than three thousand death row inmates nationwide have filed claims under *Atkins*, with "nearly 40%" proving retardation, a relief rate that varies dramatically between states).

15. The Gallup polling on this topic, for example, shows support for the death penalty peaking at 80 percent in 1994 and dropping over the next fifteen years to 65 percent in October 2009. Between June 1991 and May 2003, the percentage of respondents listing "persons may be wrongly convicted" as a reason for not supporting capital punishment jumped from 11 to 25 percent. http://www.gallup.com/poll/1606/Death-Penalty.aspx.

16. See Joseph L. Hoffmann, "On the Perils of Line-Drawing: Juveniles and the Death Penalty," *Hastings Law Journal* 40 (1989): 229, 245–47.

17. An academic debate has raged for years about whether any innocent defendant has been executed in the modern era of capital punishment. See, for example, Hugo Adam Bedau and Michael L. Radelet, "Miscarriages of Justice in Potentially Capital Cases," *Stanford Law Review* 40 (1987): 21; Stephen J. Markman and Paul G. Cassell, "Protecting the Innocent: A Response to the Bedau-Radelet Study," *Stanford Law Review* 41 (1988): 121; Hugo Adam Bedau and Michael L. Radelet, "The Myth of Infallibility: A Reply to Markman and Cassell," *Stanford Law Review* 41 (1988): 161. The debate also surfaced in the opinions of Justice Scalia and Justice Stevens in *Kansas v. Marsh*, 548 U.S. 163 (2006). But there is still no clear consensus about the existence, or nonexistence, of such a case. The latest controversy surrounds a 2004 execution in Texas. See Alan Turner, "State panel revives review of arson inquiry: New members look into claims of shoddy work in death penalty case," *Houston Chronicle*, April 24, 2010 (reporting on case of Cameron Todd Willingham), http://www.chron.com/disp/story.mpl/metropolitan/6973628.html; David Grann, "Trial by Fire: Did Texas execute an innocent man?" *New Yorker*, September 7, 2009, http://www.newyorker.com/ reporting/2009/09/07/090907fa_fact_grann. Additional investigations are reported in Steve Mills and Maurice Possley, "'I didn't do it. But I know who did,'" *Chicago Tribune*, June 25, 2006, http://www.chicagotribune.com/services/newspaper/eedition/chi-tx-1-story,0,7844122.story (case of Carlos de Luna); Lise Olsen, "The Cantu Case: Death and Doubt," *Houston Chronicle*, July 24, 2006, http://www.chron.com/disp/story.mpl/front/ 3472872.html.

18. See Samuel R. Gross, "The Risks of Death: Why Erroneous Convictions Are Common in Capital Cases," *Buffalo Law Review* 44 (1996): 469.

19. See Keith A. Findley and Michael S. Scott, "The Multiple Dimensions of Tunnel Vision in Criminal Cases," *Wisconsin Law Review* 2006 (2006): 291.

20. For a full account of the *House* case, see Joseph L. Hoffmann, "*House v. Bell* and the Death of Innocence," in *Death Penalty Stories*, edited by John H. Blume and Jordan Steiker (New York: Foundation Press, 2009).

21. This claim was based on *Strickland v. Washington*, 466 U.S. 668 (1984).

22. This claim was based on *Brady v. Maryland*, 373 U.S. 83 (1963).

23. *House v. Bell*, 547 U.S. 518, 554 (2006).

24. See Jamie Satterfield, "House's Case Dismissed: Former Death Row Inmate Legally Set Free 24 Years Later," *Knoxville News-Sentinel*, May 13, 2009, http://www.knoxnews.com/news/2009/may/13/houses-case-dismissed/.

25. George Will, "A Must-Read Horror Book," *Jewish World Review*, April 6, 2000, available at http://www.jewishworldreview.com/cols/will040600.asp.

26. "Justice O'Connor Doubts Fairness of Death Penalty," *Los Angeles Times*, July 3, 2001, http://articles.latimes.com/2001/jul/03/news/mn-18121.

27. See *In re Troy Anthony Davis*, 130 S. Ct. 1 (2009). See also note 25, chapter 5. For a summary of the "innocence revolution" and its impact on the justices' statements about the death penalty, see Steiker and Steiker, 168–77.

28. See, for example, Samuel R. Gross, "Update: American Public Opinion on the Death Penalty—It's Getting Personal," *Cornell Law Review* 83 (1998): 1448; ABC News/Washington Post Poll: The Death Penalty Revisited, "Public Ambivalence Fuels Support for a Halt in U.S. Executions," May 2, 2001, http://www.icrsurvey.com/Study.aspx?f=ABC_deathpen050201.html ("Support for executions drops to 46 percent when life without parole is offered as an alternative.").

29. This phrase first appeared in *Woodson v. North Carolina*, 428 U.S. 280 (1976), and has since been repeated at least twenty times in other Court cases.

30. For example, Rachel E. Barkow, "The Court of Life and Death: The Two Tracks of Constitutional Sentencing Law and the Case for Uniformity," *Michigan Law Review* 107 (2009): 1145 (criticizing the Court's bifurcated approach to regulating sentencing).

31. *Graham v. Florida*, 130 S. Ct. 2011 (2010).

32. Nancy J. King, Fred L. Cheesman II, and Brian J. Ostrom, *Final Technical Report: Habeas Litigation in U.S. District Courts* (2007), 63, hereafter King et al., "Habeas Study," available at http://www.ncjrs.gov/pdffiles1/nij/grants/219559.pdf. The study was funded by Vanderbilt University Law School and the National Institute of Justice.

33. See Jeffrey Fagan, James S. Liebman, Valerie West, Andrew Gelman, Alexander Kiss, and Garth Davies, "Getting to Death: Fairness and Efficiency in the Processing and Conclusion of Death Penalty Cases after *Furman*," Final

Technical Report, Department of Justice Document No. 203935, Award Number 2000-IJ-CX-0035 (February 2004).

34. King et al., "Habeas Study," 89.

35. Ibid. Claims of ineffective assistance during the guilt phase were not associated with a greater likelihood of relief.

36. See *Roper v. Simmons*, 543 U.S. 551 (2005) (invalidating death penalty for juveniles); *Atkins v. Virginia*, 536 U.S. 304 (2002) (invalidating death penalty for mentally retarded); *Rompilla v. Beard*, 545 U.S. 374 (2005) (finding "ineffective assistance of counsel" during capital sentencing); *Wiggins v. Smith*, 539 U.S. 510 (2003) (same result); *Porter v. McCollum*, 130 S. Ct. 447 (2010) (same result).

37. Of the additional seven grants, there was another *Atkins* grant, an additional grant based on ineffective assistance during the sentencing phase, and two grants based on faulty jury instructions during sentencing.

38. King et al., "Habeas Study," 89.

39. See the discussion in chapter 5 of the "stand-alone" innocence claim in *Herrera v. Collins*, 506 U.S. 390 (1993).

40. King et al., "Habeas Study," 38–45; Jon B. Gould, "Justice Delayed or Justice Denied, a Contemporary Review of Capital Habeas Corpus," *Justice System Journal* 29 (2008): 273.

41. King et al., "Habeas Study," 86.

42. Ibid., 36. The pending cases were reexamined in mid-May 2009.

43. Ibid., 30–33 (reporting findings on the length of stays ordered so petitioners could litigate their claims in state court).

44. See *Rhines v. Weber*, 544 U.S. 269 (2005). The Court explained,

> stay and abeyance is only appropriate when the district court determines there was good cause for the petitioner's failure to exhaust his claims first in state court. Moreover, even if a petitioner had good cause for that failure, the district court would abuse its discretion if it were to grant him a stay when his unexhausted claims are plainly meritless. . . . [D]istrict courts should place reasonable time limits on a petitioner's trip to state court and back. . . . And if a petitioner engages in abusive litigation tactics or intentional delay, the district court should not grant him a stay at all.

45. These stays were coded but not reported in the study.

46. King et al., "Habeas Study," 84.

47. King et al., "Habeas Study," 84–85.

48. See John P. Jeffries and William J. Stuntz, "Ineffective Assistance and Procedural Default in Federal Habeas Corpus," *University of Chicago Law Review* 57 (1990): 679, 684–85 and n. 25; Donald P. Lay, "The Writ of Habeas Cor-

pus: A Complex Procedure for a Simple Process," *Minnesota Law Review* 77 (1993): 1015, 1031–40.

49. King et al., "Habeas Study," 84.

Chapter Nine

1. Much of the analysis in this chapter first appeared in an article by Nancy J. King and Suzanna Sherry, "Habeas Corpus and State Sentencing Reform: A Story of Unintended Consequences," *Duke Law Journal* 58 (2008): 1. That article, however, took the existing statutory structure of habeas and state sentencing policy as a given and therefore proposed relatively modest changes designed to facilitate more effective handling of sentence-administration claims by the federal courts. In this chapter, we do not make the same underlying assumptions and conclude with a very different proposal for solving the problem of sentence-administration claims in habeas.

2. Nancy J. King, Fred L. Cheesman II, and Brian J. Ostrom, *Final Technical Report: Habeas Litigation in U.S. District Courts* (2007), 26, hereafter King et al., "Habeas Study," http://www.ncjrs.gov/pdffiles1/nij/grants/219559.pdf. The study was funded by Vanderbilt University Law School and the National Institute of Justice.

3. Ibid.

4. Ibid., 30.

5. Ibid., 52.

6. See, for example, Note, "The Rebirth of *Morrissey*, Toward a Coherent Theory of Due Process for Prisoners and Parolees," *Hastings Law Journal* 57 (2006): 1213, 1214–15; Comment, "The Parole System," *University of Pennsylvania Law Review* 120 (1971): 282, 286 (collecting cases holding parolee had no right to a hearing before revocation because release was considered an act of grace). Cf. *Board of Regents v. Roth*, 408 U.S. 564, 577 (1972) ("To have a property interest in a benefit, a person clearly must have more than an abstract need or desire for it. He must have more than a unilateral expectation of it. He must, instead, have a legitimate claim of entitlement to it.").

7. See, for example, *Goldberg v. Kelly*, 397 U.S. 254 (1970) (holding that denial of welfare benefits required adequate prior notice and an opportunity for an evidentiary hearing).

8. For a classic statement of the argument for recognizing such "new property," see Charles A. Reich, "The New Property," *Yale Law Journal* 73 (1964): 733.

9. *Morrissey v. Brewer*, 408 U.S. 471 (1972).

10. *Superintendent, Massachusetts Correctional Institution v. Hill*, 472 U.S. 445, 455 (1985).

11. *Wolff v. McDonnell*, 418 U.S. 539 (1974).

12. Neb. Rev. Stat. § 83–1,114 (1) (1976).

13. *Greenholtz v. Inmates of Neb. Penal & Corr. Complex*, 442 U.S. 1 (1979).

14. *Greenholtz*, 442 U.S. at 12. See also *Teague v. Quarterman*, 482 F.3d 769, 774 (5th Cir. 2007) (contrasting discretionary parole with mandatory release); *Sandin v. Conner*, 515 U.S. 472, 487 (1995) (finding that no due process protections were required for the disciplinary hearing at issue, distinguishing *Wolff*, and noting that the case was not one in which the "State's action w[ould] inevitably affect the duration of his sentence").

15. *Preiser v. Rodriguez*, 411 U.S. 475 (1973).

16. *Preiser*, 411 U.S. at 490–92.

17. See *Wolff*, 418 U.S. at 554–55.

18. See *Heck v. Humphrey*, 512 U.S. 477 (1994) (challenges to state criminal conviction); *Edwards v. Balisok*, 520 U.S. 641 (1997) (challenges to state prison administrative decision). This development is examined extensively in King and Sherry, "Habeas Corpus and State Sentencing Reform." The issue is also before the Supreme Court this term in *Skinner v. Switzer*. See note 24 in chapter 5.

19. See Lawrence A. Greenfeld, "Prison Sentences and Time Served for Violence," Bureau of Justice Statistics, Bulletin No. NCJ 153858 (April 1995): 1, http://www.ojp.usdoj.gov/bjs/pub/pdf/psatsfv.pdf ("In 1977, 72% of those released from State prisons had served an indeterminate sentence, and a parole board decided their release.").

20. See Francis A. Allen, *The Decline of the Rehabilitative Ideal* (New Haven: Yale University Press, 1981).

21. See Kevin R. Reitz, *Reporter's Introduction, Model Penal Code: Sentencing, Discussion Draft No. 2* (April 8, 2009): 2, 9–13, 30 (making the case for eliminating discretionary parole release and collecting authority, noting that "American parole boards have proven to be . . . the most disappointing of administrative agencies"; questioning the evidence that discretionary release facilitates rehabilitation; and arguing that parole boards are too susceptible to political influence and "a natural institutional drift toward severity in practice").

22. See, for example, Sara Sun Beale, "Interdisciplinary Perspectives on Restorative Justice: Still Tough on Crime? Prospects for Restorative Justice in the United States," *Utah Law Review* 2003 (2003): 413, 414–18 (detailing growth of retributive justice model during the 1980s and 1990s).

23. Greenfeld, "Prison Sentences and Time Served," 1 (reporting that as of 1995, a majority of state prisoners were serving presumptive sentences, that 90 percent of state inmates could estimate their probable release date, and that from 1977 to 1992, the percentage of those released from state prisons who had served an indeterminate sentence and were released by a parole board dropped from 72 to 40 percent). See also Daniel Medwed, "The Innocent Prisoner's Dilemma," *Iowa Law Review* 93 (2008): 491, 497–504 (tracing history of parole and

noting that between 1990 and 1999, the number of discretionary parole releases declined nearly 20 percent, while the number of mandatory parole releases almost doubled); Christy A. Visher, "Returning Home: Emerging Findings and Policy Lessons about Prisoner Reentry," *Federal Sentencing Reporter* 20 (2007): 93, 98 (reporting that the portion of prisoners released by parole boards dropped from 65 percent in 1976 to 24 percent in 1999). For useful summaries of this shift and the forces that brought it about, see Joan Petersilia, *When Prisoners Come Home: Parole and Prisoner Reentry* (New York: Oxford University Press, 2003): 55–75; Jeremy Travis and Christy Visher, *Prisoner Reentry and Crime in America* (New York: Cambridge University Press, 2005): 55–75.

24. Petersilia, *When Prisoners Come Home*, 65; Reitz, *Model Penal Code*, 3–4 (stating two-thirds of jurisdictions have retained some paroling authority, while one-third have eliminated it entirely).

25. Petersilia, *When Prisoners Come Home*, 65–68; Bureau of Justice Statistics, "Reentry Trends in the U.S., Releases from State Prison," http://www.ojp.usdoj.gov/bjs/reentry/releases.htm. New York adopted mandatory release for some offenders in 1987. For a state-by-state listing of prison populations, see Heather West, "Prison Inmates at Midyear 2009," Bureau of Justice Statistics, NCJ 230113 (June 2010): Table 2, http://www.ojp.usdoj.gov/content/pub/pdf/pim09.pdf.

26. California, the state with the nation's largest prison population, has had an incredibly high rate of returning violators. See Petersilia, *When Prisoners Come Home*, 11 (reporting that 61.5 percent of inmates in California returning to prison are violators). Eighty percent of parolees returned were returned because of criminal offenses never prosecuted separately. Ibid., 73–74.

27. James Stephan, "Prison Rule Violators," Bureau of Justice Statistics, Bulletin No. NCJ 120344 (December 1989).

28. Bureau of Justice Statistics, *Sourcebook of Criminal Justice Statistics 2003*, Table 6.44, http://www.albany.edu/sourcebook/pdf/t644.pdf. Average time served jumped from 22 to 30 months for first releases from state prison between 1990 and 2004, and the percentage of sentence served increased from 38 to 48 percent. Thomas P. Bonczar, *National Corrections Reporting Program*, May 25, 2010, http://bjs.ojp.usdoj.gov/index.cfm?ty=pbdetail&iid=2045.

29. *Sourcebook of Criminal Justice Statistics 2003*, Table 6.29.2006 (nationwide, the number of state prisoners per 100,000 population doubled from 130 in 1980 to 272 in 1990, then jumped again to 445 by 2006). Indeed, in states in which prison construction could not keep up with the explosion in the prison population, increasing reliance on good time for early release has served as a stopgap; see Petersilia, *When Prisoners Come Home*, 62. This added reliance on good time only exacerbates the problem addressed in this chapter.

30. Many states did not adopt truth-in-sentencing initiatives limiting discretionary parole for violent offenders until after Congress provided monetary in-

centives for them to do so in the 1994 Violent Crime Control and Law Enforcement Act. See William J. Sabol et al., "The Influences of Truth-in-Sentencing Reforms on Changes in States' Sentencing Practices and Prison Populations," NIJ 98-CE-VX-0006 (April 2002): 23–29, http://www.ncjrs.gov/pdffiles1/nij/grants/191860.pdf (examining the effects of the Violent Offender Incarceration and Truth-in-Sentencing Incentive Grants Program in the 1994 Crime Act).

31. Cases with time-barred claims were resolved 10 to 12 percent faster than those without time-barred claims, controlling for other factors. King et al., "Habeas Study," 70–73, Tables 17–19.

32. King and Sherry, "Habeas Corpus and State Sentencing Reform," 63–64.

33. 28 U.S.C. § 2244. There is no agreement about if or when this bar even applies in these cases, and those courts that apply the successive-petition provision to sentence-administration claims have also reached different conclusions about how it works. Is a petition seeking relief for an unconstitutional sentence-administration decision successive to a petition challenging the underlying sentence itself? Maybe, say some but not all courts, if the sentence-administration claim was ripe by the time an earlier petition challenging the underlying sentence was filed. Nor do courts agree about whether a petition challenging one disciplinary hearing or parole denial is "successive" to another petition challenging a similar, but separate, sentence-administration decision.

34. In some states, constraints on the ability to order the early release of prisoners who pose little serious threat of violent crime, combined with lack of fiscal or institutional constraints on legislators who vote for longer and longer mandatory sentences, have led to steep prison growth and strained state budgets. See, for example, David Muradyan, "Review of Selected 2007 California Legislation: Government: California's Response to Its Prison Overcrowding Crisis," *McGeorge Law Review* 39 (2008): 482 (discussing causes for prison overcrowding in California). But compare Reitz, *Model Penal Code*, 18–22 (arguing that the correlation between determinate sentencing and prison growth appears only in some states not most).

35. See Beale, "Interdisciplinary Perspectives on Restorative Justice."

36. See generally Petersilia, *When Prisoners Come Home*, 189–91; Christopher Slobogin, *Proving the Unprovable: The Role of Law, Science, and Speculation in Adjudicating Culpability and Dangerousness* (New York: Oxford University Press, 2006); Wayne LaFave, Jerold Israel, Nancy King, and Orin Kerr, 6 *Criminal Procedure* (St. Paul, MN: West Publishing Co., 2007), § 26.1(c), n. 46 (collecting commentary advocating a return to discretionary parole release).

Index